FROM
A BURNING
HOUSE

FROM
A BURNING
HOUSE

THE AIDS PROJECT LOS ANGELES
WRITERS WORKSHOP COLLECTION

EDITED BY

Irene Borger

March '97

FOR AKASHA,
SISTER OVER THE
WATERS.

I CAN SEE YOU.

X

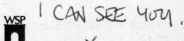

WSP

WASHINGTON SQUARE PRESS
PUBLISHED BY POCKET BOOKS

New York   London   Toronto   Sydney   Tokyo   Singapore

"Warts and All," copyright © 1992 by Joe Hogan, appeared in a somewhat altered version in *Christopher Street* magazine in the September 14th, 1992 issue.

"A Litany for Survival" from *The Black Unicorn* by Audre Lorde. Copyright © 1978 by Audre Lorde. Reprinted by permission of W.W. Norton & Company, Inc.

"The Ninth Duino Elegy" from *The Selected Poetry of Rainer Maria Rilke* Stephen Mitchell, trans. Copyright © 1982 by Stephen Mitchell. Reprinted by permission of Random House Inc.

A WASHINGTON SQUARE PRESS *Original* Publication

A Washington Square Press Publication of
POCKET BOOKS, a division of Simon & Schuster Inc.
1230 Avenue of the Americas, New York, NY 10020

From a burning house : the AIDS Project Los Angeles Writers Workshop
    collection / edited by Irene Borger.
        p.   cm.
      ISBN 0-671-53517-X (pb)
        1. AIDS (Disease)—Patients—California—Los Angeles—Literary
collections. 2. Caregivers—California—Los Angeles—Literary
collections. 3. American literature—California—Los Angeles.
4. American literature—20th century.   I. Borger, Irene Marian.
II. AIDS Project Los Angeles.
PS509.A43F76   1996
810.8′0356—dc20   96-10465
                                                            CIP

First Washington Square Press trade paperback printing June 1996

10 9 8 7 6 5 4 3 2 1

WASHINGTON SQUARE PRESS and colophon are registered
trademarks of Simon & Schuster Inc.

Cover design by Jeanne Lee, cover photo by Scogin Mayo
Text design by Stanley S. Drate/Folio Graphics Co., Inc.

Printed in the U.S.A.

CONTENTS

---

1 ✤ ORIGIN

2 ✤ JOURNEY

3 ❧ RAPTURE

4 ❧ SOMETHING

5 ❧ HOMO PHARMACEUTICUS

6 ❧ ENSEMBLE

7 ❧ VANISHING

FOREWORD
James Loyce Jr.

Executive Director
AIDS Project Los Angeles

AIDS
PROJECT
LOS ANGELES

From a Burning House: The title alone explains where every one of us in the world is standing in this second decade of AIDS, whether or not we are aware of it, or whether we want to admit it. We are inside an epidemic that can barely be controlled and is a long way from being put out.

The staff, clients, and volunteers of AIDS Project Los Angeles have recognized the fire and are working daily, individually and collectively, to control the flames. It is AIDS Project Los Angeles' mission to improve the quality of life for people living with HIV/AIDS and their families, and to reduce the transmission of HIV through prevention education programs.

The Writers Workshop provides an arena to put into words the emotions, confusions, and clearheaded accounts of living with HIV/AIDS for both the infected and affected. Under the direction of Irene Borger, artist-in-residence, the workshop is currently composed of people living with HIV/AIDS, as well as writers and health professionals taking part in the "Teaching the Teachers" workshop. Since 1991, members of APLA's Writers Workshop have given public readings to enthusiastic audiences, as well as received national attention on radio (NPR), television *(MacNeil-Lehrer News Hour),* and in print *(The Advocate, Poets and Writers).* Due to the talents of Irene Borger and every writer involved, AIDS Project Los Angeles has gotten much more out of this Workshop than imagined. I can only hope the writers feel the same.

The Workshop is funded in part by the California Arts Council, the National Endowment for the Arts, the City of Los Angeles Cultural Affairs Department, the John M. Lloyd Foundation, the

Audrey and Sydney Irmas Charitable Foundation, and the Klein Family Foundation.

But the Writers Workshop would not exist without the writers. *From a Burning House* is made up of vitally important voices that need to be heard to heal the writer *and* the reader. Please read these stories and poems as a call to action, as a reminder that the fire is still raging.

I want to thank the Writers Workshop for what follows, and for continuing this invaluable outreach with their words.

INTRODUCTION
Tony Kushner

I am seronegative. Torn between the fear that I'm distancing myself from the defining struggle of my times, and the fear that I'm masquerading as full-blooded participant in something I can finally only observe, I choose disclosure; because this is a book about AIDS by people who know more about it than I know, or hope I'll ever know. I read these writings grateful for the information, the wisdom they contain; grateful for the talent, the labor, and the courage that produced them; and guiltily grateful to have been spared—by nothing but the merest chance—this intimacy with the subject.

Let's begin by stating the obvious: AIDS is about death. The reason that we take AIDS so seriously, the reason that the epidemic politicized the gay male community and mobilized it, and forged the first strong alliance between lesbians and gay men, and forged shaky but occasionally effective alliances between previously unaffiliated communities of the disenfranchised, such as between the queer and the poor, the reason that so much factionalism and disengagement was swept away, is that AIDS is about death; but death of a particularly complexified kind. AIDS is both a destroyer and a creator of community. It is after all not a single entity but a syndrome, with ill-defined boundaries and categories, and as such it spreads, both biologically and politically, dismantling but also forging connections by uniting in pain and in anger people with very different histories and lives, helping to clarify which lives are regarded as dispensable by America's ruling class. Those in the margins, unless united in resistance, die. So AIDS is also about resistance; AIDS is, and I hesitate to write this, about life.

As much as it is fatal, HIV infection and AIDS can be a creative force in the lives of the people afflicted. I make this ordinary statement fully aware of its outrageousness, aware of the inherent, implicit denial. But I've known far too many people who are seropositive or who have full-blown AIDS who have said as much, even as they betrayed a certain—embarrassment? wonder? guilt?—at making a declaration many would regard with skepticism or incredulity.

This is the paradox of AIDS. It is one of the greatest calamities ever to befall the human race, and yet such is our species' penchant for learning, for understanding—such, I believe is our hunger for *progress*—that even calamity is read, deciphered, parsed, and becomes in the process instructive. Understanding must flow from even the hardest of eventualities. As Wallace Stevens wrote: "There is no wing like meaning."

Those who labor from deep within the midnight recesses of the epidemic to bring understanding back to the world, those who labor in the face of their own mortality, cannot avoid seeming heroic to everyone else, to the bystanders. Visible manifestations of any serious illness frighten and alienate. Owing to a shameful lapse of compassion and decency on the part of the unafflicted, people who are identifiable as ill are frequently stigmatized and rendered nonpersons. This has been true of AIDS as of no other illness in modern times. (It's unnecessary here to rehearse the story of AIDS in America to date, largely disgraceful, of the already holocaustal level of suffering and death met by governmental inaction, truculence, and vacillation, by public indifference and much, much worse—by the kind of satanic satisfaction evinced by Buchanan, Helms, and other assorted demons, imps, and revenants, the whole mephitic crowd on the loony-Right, more virulent than any viral strain. But I digress . . .) As time unfolds, the stigmatizers and vilifiers are themselves revealed as villainous. Stigmatization is a stage of martyrdom. Those of us who think about history are certain that the history of these times has already assembled its heroes, and among the assemblage stands the self-reporting, self-analyzing, performing, composing, painting, photographing, writing, fiercely articulate, fiercely activist community of people with AIDS.

(I once told Ron Vawter, the great actor and performer who died of AIDS-related illnesses a year ago, that I considered him heroic. "It's tasteless," he responded, "to call someone a hero to his face.")

Yet nothing can spare us from wincing at the palpable obscenity of declaring holocaust morally instructive, useful, beneficial. If progress is the result of holocaust, then the cost has been too high. If there is an accounting to be made, the losses must be reckoned greater than anything gained. It seems a betrayal of any lesson these terror-filled times might have taught us to believe that any lesson these terror-filled times might have taught us was worth the tuition. My closest friend, Kimberly Flynn, says that sometimes it's in the refusal of the redemptive possibility of suffering that redemptive possibility seems to lie. Or as Bertolt Brecht puts it, the political valence of optimism or pessimism changes with its context. Sometimes pessimism is the path towards hope.

In September 1988 the Museum of Modern Art exhibited photographs, by Nicholas Nixon, of a group of three men and one woman with AIDS. Several of the photographs recorded the physical decline of these people from the onset of serious opportunistic infections until immediately before their hard deaths: ravaged, scarred by lesions, emaciated and exhausted.

After the show had been hanging on MOMA's walls for several weeks, a small group of members of the AIDS Coalition to Unleash Power, ACT UP, decided to "zap" the exhibit by handing out leaflets one evening at the Museum. The protesters argued that the photographs repeated the familiar, offensive mass-media practice of presenting people with AIDS as passive, doomed victims.

At the ACT UP meeting at which the zap was discussed, those who endorsed the action accused Nixon and the Museum of making, out of the terminal stages of AIDS-related illnesses, a kind of pornography, or fetishization, for the secret delectation and gratification of AIDSphobic, homophobic, moralizing audiences. ACT UP members opposed to the zap (and in ACT UP there are fifty sides to nearly every question) pointed out that Nixon had made the series in collaboration with the people who were its subjects. The photographs represented a kind of testament—and also a (partial but critical) biological truth about the epidemic. People do die of the diseases associated with HIV infection, and the deaths are exceptionally difficult.

I find Nixon's photographs unsentimental and deeply moving, brave, disturbing and true. I wasn't in town at the time but I disagreed with the demonstration (apparently many did; it was poorly attended). The discussion begun that night continued for some time after the floor fight and the event itself. Thinking back, it occurs to me that the debate was interesting as a new installment in the history of a dilemma every political movement eventually faces. Is effective resistance, a claiming of power and agency, fed by visions of a better future, or by anger at a monstrous injustice? Isn't hope an essential concomitant to action, and if so, how does any person who is willing to look at the world as it truly is, and who wants to change unacceptable conditions, going to preserve hope in the face of circumstances that, if honestly examined, might easily lead one to despair? In the battle against a formidable adversary, what drives you forward—do you dwell on the fearfulness of the fight ahead, and the bodies left behind, or dream about a possible future in which you have triumphed and are at peace? Although too rigid, these antinomies raise useful questions about the various sources of resistance to evil. Walter Benjamin wrote provocatively that agency and the "spirit of sacrifice . . . [are] nourished by the image of enslaved ancestors rather than that of liberated grandchildren."

The Negative has its powers. The single most immediately identifiable visual sign of a militant response to the AIDS epidemic, and surely one of the most effective works ever of graphic art, is ACT UP's forbidding and galvanic SILENCE-DEATH logo, the power of which derives from its skull-knockingly blunt, bleak, dire admonition. A few years ago the Los Angeles ACT UP chapter offered its revisionist West Coast version of the graphic, ACTION-LIFE, and while that cheerier message still makes its occasional appearances, it has never remotely rivaled the thunderclap appeal of the original. In a nod towards optimism, the SILENCE-DEATH creators inverted the traditionally base-up,

point-down pink triangle; but the black background and the
Weimar-inflected typography overwhelm that gesture. The word
that leapt off the walls of New York when the logo first appeared
on posters, I remember, was DEATH. It was a trumpet-call; busi-
ness-as-usual was over, and a war was on. Score one, I suppose,
for Benjamin.

Where AIDS is concerned the Negative is never in short supply. The face of the epidemic is changing. While its visibility is
being transformed through more effective therapies, its demo-
graphics are shifting—slowly but inexorably—away from its
original "target" populations. The epidemic is spreading fastest
among our urban poor, in African-American and Latino communities. The disease may be spreading more slowly than expected
among women in America—in the rest of the world the disease
is predominantly heterosexual, and by the millennium half the
cases may be female—but among women of color, especially
among African-American women, the incidence of seropositivity
and AIDS is staggeringly high. There are over six thousand
American children with full-blown AIDS under the age of thirteen, and over four thousand adolescents. And while the Conference of Catholic Bishops blushes and balks at distributing
condoms to kids, we learn that 50 percent of all HIV infection
begins between the ages of fifteen to twenty-four. AIDS is now
the leading cause of death of young adult men in sixty-four
American cities. The importance of AIDS education in preventing new infection is frequently transmuted into something that
sounds, in the mouths of health officials and politicians, like a
plan to abandon the search for treatment, health care, and all
those who are already HIV-infected, in favor of a (less costly)
campaign to save those who aren't. As the late Robert Massa
wrote in the *Village Voice,* "from day one of AIDS there has been
a tendency to write off the infected, one that has arguably increased as the epicenter has shifted (is shifting?) from middle-
class gay America to the poor." That AZT and the other drugs
targeting viral replication were approved for patient use in a relatively timely fashion is an achievement of the AIDS activist movement; the doubt cast on the value of those drugs is politically

discouraging, and certainly frightening for the thousands who are currently taking them.

There was a time when the cure seemed withheld from us by nothing more insurmountable than the moral turpitude of our political and religious leaders, and that turpitude, however vast it inarguably is, is something any community with will and anger can tilt at and expect results. Results can still be expected, and more money will expedite discovery of a cure—more money is certainly needed for patient care; but the processes of biochemical research, and the insidious complexities of viral life, suggest that the main prize, a cure, is something historical agency and political resolve alone will not accomplish. Time is a formidable foe.

Several years ago I was hired by *Vanity Fair* to write a text to accompany a series of Annie Liebowitz portraits of people living with AIDS. The series was, as far as I know, never printed in the magazine, and my text was never used. One of the Liebowitz photographs was of the ever-remarkable Tom Stoddard, a founder of Lambda Legal Defense and avatar of lesbian- and gay-related jurisprudence. In the portrait Stoddard is seated in front of a blackboard at NYU, on which he's written these words:

"The arc of the moral universe is long but it bends towards Justice."

Stoddard told me that the quote was originally from a sermon by Theodore Parker, a nineteenth-century abolitionist, but most people know it from the speeches of Martin Luther King Jr. In the famous speech during the march on Washington, Dr. King gives the quotation as an answer to the repeated question-and-response device "How long? Not long." So Stoddard's quote in King's context: "How long? Not long? Because the arc of the moral universe is long but it bends towards Justice." Thus while offering reassurances of the inevitable triumph of the cause of liberation, King is also giving voice to a problem. The ardent desire for change is addressed, and change is declared immanent (How long? Not long),but at the same time the full answer given to the urgent question describes a process in which, however much the moral universe may be bending towards Justice, and however essential that bending may be, its arc is long. There is no promise of immediate, or even proximate, redress. This contradictory construction is repeated elsewhere in the speech, as in "How long? Not long. Because no lie can live forever." Again, that is both reassuring and not, its initial guarantee of the swift arrival of truth made just a little hollow by the proof offered—a lie may not live *forever* but can still live a very, very long time.

I believe this is what King, master of rhetoric, student of history, and moral visionary, intends. He knows how entirely central hope is, and how much hope depends on faith—that the wall against which you batter yourself will yield; and yet anyone as well-acquainted with the wickedness of the world and the cruelties of history as King was knows that change may well be generationally slow in coming. "Patience is a revolutionary virtue," according to Brecht, but patience is an operation of time and in a war against an acquired immune deficiency, for many, time is in short supply.

Though the medical breakthrough when it comes may be sudden as a lightning flash, AIDS remains inescapably about death. It's about the death of home. The environment, the fabric of our lives, the quality of life, love, sex, liberty, justice—innocence and decency—are all under such assault these days, and the body withers. AIDS is part of the present destruction of the social and the physical worlds, whether literally connected through environmental cofactors, or figuratively, as a manifestation of what ails us all. The delineations of AIDS are not clear. Its boundaries do not stop at the biochemical, everything is implicated, everything involved: how we take care of each other and ourselves; the ways we let sick people know they are of value, and the ways we let them know they're a nuisance and a burden; the place we make for illness, or the pronounced lack of such places; the economic structures that are needed to make universal care possible. And education. And housing. And food. And air to breath and water to drink, and a world in which our country exists with justice, peaceably. The treatment and survival of AIDS babies begin with pharmaceuticals and loving care and will lead us, if we ask the hard questions and follow every route of transmission, viral and otherwise, to the most profound and difficult matters about human beings and their societies.

The poet Audre Lorde, who was African-American and lesbian, died three years ago of breast cancer after decades of battling with death, and succeeding at survival so well that the news of her succumbing at long last was a shock—I and I think many others had begun to believe she might be immortal. Among her many accomplishments and contributions it was Lorde, I believe, in her book *The Cancer Journals,* who first formulated the equation that silence is a kind of death. One of Lorde's best poems is called "A Litany for Survival." It is a threnody and a praise-song, written "For those of us who live at the shoreline / standing on the constant edges of decision / crucial and alone . . . / For those of us / who were imprinted with fear / like a faint line in the center of our foreheads / learning to be afraid with our mother's milk . . . / For all of us," the poet writes, "this instant and this triumph / We were never meant to survive."

A long time ago when I first read this poem I thought to myself, when I came to that line, "some triumph." One thing AIDS has taught me is at least one possible way to understand the final line of this poem. We would all like to see death defeated, and all political struggle may be a struggle to defeat death, but death is a fact of life—even if you carry the struggle beyond the grave, as do those AIDS activists like Tim Bailey, who asked that, after his death from AIDS-related illness, his body be tossed onto the White House lawn, you will still not have triumphed entirely over death. You may, however, have transformed it.

"We were never meant to survive." After fifteen years of the AIDS epidemic, I embrace the line's ambiguity. We were never meant to survive—and we may or we may not. We may thwart what was "meant," intended for us, or we may meet what may be our fate. The word "meant" is the key, suggesting that, however improbably, we *may* defeat what has been planned for us (We were never *meant* to survive and yet, somehow, we have); and suggesting, too, that the death that has been planned for us is not without the participation, intention, and aggression of other human beings who would oppress or even murder us—our death is "meant," intended for us *by* someone else.

Our survival, Lorde means, depends on embracing this ambiguity: Even as we claim our identities, we must claim our mortality, our human frailty, our susceptibility to disease and also to oppression—we must claim these in order to transform them, not to accept them, for this claiming is to be a triumph. I remember the Spanish-language subway poster, *AIDS es Mortal,* meaning "AIDS is Fatal"; but to an English speaker it associatively suggests that AIDS is, in another sense, *mortal,* not in the sense of death or frailty only but also of being of the flesh, being *human,* being mortals. And the struggle against AIDS teaches us: Death, if faced, can be transformed; even cruel unjust death can be transformed into a source for the living, of coming into justice and power.

> *. . . when we are loved we are afraid*
> *love will vanish*
> *when we are alone we are afraid*
> *love will never return*
> *and when we speak we are afraid*
> *our words will not be heard*
> *nor welcomed*
> *but when we are silent*
> *we are still afraid.*
>
> *So it is better to speak*
> *remembering*
> *we were never meant to survive.*

—Audre Lorde, "A Litany for Survival"

OPEN SESAME
Irene Borger

A zillion stories could be told about the making of this book, stories inside stories and stories behind stories. But before I reel off a single one, I have to tell you this: nothing in this volume was written in order to be published. While most of the material has been honed and polished, some of it printed in a chapbook, presented at two major museums, and on national radio (one story was blasted to Australia on satellite, another was stacked next to the tissues in a "Slumber Room" at Forest Lawn), every single piece in this volume began as a creative jaunt, an investigation or a confession to the self scrawled in a notebook and read aloud in a room with the door closed.

The room and the door and the Writers Workshop, where all these pieces were hatched, are at AIDS Project Los Angeles, one of the largest grassroots AIDS service agencies in the United States. APLA, as it's known, provides more than five thousand clients with a great range of support, including psychological and legal counseling, dental care, educational seminars, food, and public-policy advocacy. The Workshop is APLA's tiniest program; perhaps one hundred and fifty people have taken part since we began.

How we began still amazes me. I think the Workshop's intense, numinous, highly charged creative energy developed, in part, from the spirit of the Workshop's origin. The notion to initiate it *came to me* in 1989 toward the end of a weeklong silent meditation retreat. "Why not start a writing workshop for people living with AIDS?" a voice in my head said. Why not? I was a journalist and a teacher, one of the millions of people who love to listen to others tell stories—and one of the thousands who has spent the first five minutes of every morning of the last decade scanning the obituary page of the *New York Times*. By 1989, feeling the loss of voice after voice and vision after vision had become an insistent, dull pain.

I had a hunch—that's all that it was—that writing might be useful for people living with the virus. I knew, after all, that *crisis* in Chinese is composed of the characters for danger *and* opportunity. Too, maybe the stories and poems these imagined people would write would touch others. Both hunches have turned out to be so true. Several years ago, when I read Paul Monette's remark that "the most important book to come out of World War II was written by a fourteen-year-old girl," I recognized Anne Frank's urgency and truth-telling as qualities the Workshop writers possess. But how did a voice in my head go on to become the very particular voices in the Workshop and this book?

With the blessing of AIDS Project Los Angeles, a grant from the City of Los Angeles Cultural Affairs Department, and a strong fools-rush-in intuition that it was "going to be oh-kay" (that's what the voice said on the very first day), the Workshop began in October 1990, as a once-a-week, nine-month-long group for "people living with HIV, ARC, and AIDS." The following September, with a grant from the California Arts Council, a state agency, I was leading three weekly groups—two for "people living with HIV and/or AIDS," and one for "caregivers, health professionals, significant others, APLA staff and volunteers— that continued for the next three years. (I'm no longer running a caregivers group. This past fall, I started a new ten-month-long training program called "Teaching the Teachers" for people committed to starting pilot writing workshops in other AIDS service agencies in Los Angeles County.) Except for an occasional guest artist or a site visit from a funder or a onetime taping by the *MacNeil-Lehrer NewsHour* crew, no one drops by or is invited to observe what ensues. Even in Hollywood, while gathered around a table next to a dozen other people, the process of writing is not meant to be performance.

Each group meets once a week, for three hours, to write and read aloud and has from twelve to fourteen members. In case you're thinking that people trudge in and hunker down to draft mournful dirges, consider that they—people who are HIV-positive, or living with AIDS, and those who love, work, or live with people who are living with HIV/AIDS—write about everything from arousal, lime green high heels, plutonium, and the theater to, yes, morphine, warts, and hospices. "Here, in this world of the virus," I wrote in my notebook one day, "what gets spread is infectious laughter."

As you might imagine, change is ever-present in the Workshop. Metaphors for what transpires change, too. At times when people read aloud, it's as if we're all perched around a campfire. At other moments, the room seems like an enormous radio with each writer a different frequency. When the world feels topsy-turvy—too much sickness, too many weeks of rain—I sometimes think of a painting from the Middle Ages with its tiny figures caught up in a big red tidal wave. Then, even if the restaurant across the street is blasting music again, with writing as the vessel the room becomes a refuge for our fabulous ship of fools. Once, when I found myself imagining that as long as everyone was there *writing,* we all were out of harm's way and our room became a shelter from the Blitz. (After witnessing the first death, one member of the first Workshop wrote a piece to the man who died: "You've wrecked my 'magical faith' that being in this class protects people, saves them from the worst.")

Of course, the Workshop is more than a metaphor: it *is* a laboratory for writing. And it's mysterious how the amalgamation of a memory, an exercise, and a day's particular mood act like a Bunsen burner to fuel creation. One Friday we were working with Tess Gallagher's poem "I Stop Writing the Poem," simultaneously discussing the impact of line breaks and looking at ordinary activity carried on amidst crisis. (Doug Bender's piece "Dishes" grew out of this exercise.) One man who was slowly going blind began to read the piece he'd just written. "I'm much too cheap to have my gasoline pumped for me," he started. By his second paragraph, he'd begun writing about having to learn to use a white cane. I will never forget how he and several others plunged into weeping as he attempted to read the line "I have a counselor coming this week to take me out in public." His difficulty in reading was not that he couldn't see the page—he had his magnifying glass with him.

If there is any constancy to living with HIV and AIDS and living or working in the AIDS community, it's the *constant unknowns*. So, in the Workshop, we work with staying on the edge in and through writing, bringing attention to the images, lines, and narratives that pop up full-blown or arise at the corners of the mind. Learning to put one sentence after another may be a good way to learn to put one foot after the next. And one needn't write "about" death or illness, or any *particular* subject in order to do so. It's this surrendering to the page and developing attention that serve as a teacher.

In spite of the fact that Workshop members seem to write about everything, the pieces selected for this book very naturally fell into constellations. The stories in "Origin" address hometowns, initiations, and childhood. The selections in "Journey" are accounts of war and travel that moved the writer further out into the world. "Rapture" contains tales of eros, cities, danger, and scintillation. "Something," the title drawn from the last line of Michael Martin's story "Nothing," moves into the world of HIV and AIDS. The writing in the chapter called "Homo Pharmaceuticus"—a term originated by Robbie Hilyard in his story "Chemical Man"—deals with drugs, treatments, and hospitals. The tales in "Ensemble" are chronicles of love, dying, death, writing, and relationship. The final chapter, "Vanishing," presents narratives that focus on the end of life; it is titled after Ricky Hoyt's work of fiction "The Vanishing," the last story in the book.

Whether in the caregivers and training workshops or in the two groups for people who have tested seropositive, something happens in every single session to make it apparent that this Workshop takes place under "conditions of extremity," a term used by poet Carolyn Forché to describe circumstances endured in times of social and historical crisis. In her important collection, *Against Forgetting: Twentieth Century Poetry of Witness,* Forché included the work of writers who have created literature under the impress of "exile, state censorship, political persecution, house arrest, torture, imprisonment, military occupation, warfare and assassination."[1] Although the fifteen-year duration of the AIDS pandemic has led, in some circles, to the ugly appearance of normalization, it is no less a *crisis* than the years of apartheid in South Africa or the war in Northern Ireland.

Forché has limited her selection of poets to "those for whom the social had been irrevocably invaded by the political in ways that were sanctioned neither by law nor by the fictions of the social contract."[2] One might argue that this is the case for many of the authors included in this book.

The blunt effects of HIV and AIDS are always apparent somewhere in the Workshop room. But while I am aware of the persistent coughs, the stubborn scratching, the fragility of the lover who has stayed up all night, the canes, needles, and cans of nutritional supplement, and the late arrival of the radiation-bald man who had, just two weeks before, walked in with his Lyle Lovett hairdo, these traces of the epidemic are neither the focus of what we're doing in the Workshop nor are they how I think of the writers. Still, I've learned to sit down and breathe when I check my voice mail. "I don't think I'll make it tomorrow, I've got to have a transfusion." "Sorry, I won't see you tonight, one of my clients had an emergency." "Shit, honey, I'm in the hospital, my Hickman's infected." "Diarrhea again, I can't get out of the house." I have not invented these scenarios. I am compelled to write them down. Of course, not all the messages are bleak. Some are euphoric. So and so is (a) leaving for Paris! (b) singing with the chorus! (c) off to direct a play in New York!

Some of the qualities Carolyn Forché finds in her investigation of poetry written in times of crisis—direct address, writing as evidence or testimony, the abundance of fragmented pieces—are also prevalent in Workshop texts. But Forché's collection, *Against Forgetting: Twentieth Century Poetry of Witness,* differs from this one in a significant way. To be included in that volume, the authors had to be "considered important to their national literatures." Few of the people whose work appears in *From a Burning House* are Writers with a capital *W,* that is to say, those who think of, or thought of, themselves—or are or were thought of—as professional writers.

Over the years, one novelist, two magazine editors, a writer/

editor/publisher, several screen and television writers, and a couple of journalists have been members of the Workshop. But most Workshop members have focused their creative and professional attention elsewhere. Still, whether they work, or worked, as dancers, chorus boys, photographers, waiters, public-school teachers, nurses, therapists, garment and TV executives, Army medics, social workers, masseurs, lighting and clothing designers, or as a choreographer, chiropractor, lawyer, hairdresser, business consultant, yoga teacher, animator, Top 40 singer, bookstore clerk, railroad engineer, cosmetics-company owner, casting director, florist, therapist, stockbroker, travel agent, musician, private investigator, or even a clown, inside the writing room, *everyone* who is in, or has been in, the Workshop has had significant things to say and the burning desire to write. (I once heard Grace Paley say that she thought all good stories carried the impulse of a child yelling, "Ma, I gotta tell you something!" Although "Ma" might not be the ideal reader of many of the texts, this urgent drive to communicate has been a sine qua non for all who take part in the Workshop.)

Why do people come to this Workshop? Why—and how—does someone drive straight from the hospital to the Workshop the day after brain surgery instead of home to bed? Or have the urgency to write when exhaustion has shrunken their handwriting to—I am not kidding—the size of rice grains? What impels people to get to a morning session after a year of intolerable depression or a night of uncontrollable sweats? Why do Workshop members sneak out of hospitals to present their work before crowds at our public readings? Why would someone healthy wish to go to a writing workshop in an AIDS-service agency? And why might someone gripped by illness choose to go to a Writers Workshop instead of a support group?

Some participants want to develop craft, are ambitious to complete a memoir, or to put themselves in a place where they are *forced* to work. Some hope to find creative comrades, a community or a lover, or intuit that writing might be healing for them. Here's how a few people responded, on their first day, to the question, What do you want to get out of the Workshop? "To have a tinge of pleasure each session." "An outlet for my anxiety and fear." "To get my confidence back." "To rediscover my own feelings." "To write about my friends, to remember them and our time together." "To take part in the world of the living." "Now that the life is winding down, it's time to let the secrets out." "To put together a collection to touch others." "I need to reach the truth inside faster, to help me create, not just practice." "So that someone knows who I am."

The people who show up and stay, whether for some months or some years, *all* discover a terrain and a voice. No matter where he or she starts, each person who attends with any regularity writes clearer, truer, freer, more specific, funnier, braver stuff; each writer inevitably takes more formal and psychological risks and grows more articulate. Still, not everyone who comes remains. One man called me after his first time at the Workshop to say that much as he liked the format and the people, asymptomatic as he was, he simply wasn't ready to be in a room with others with full-blown AIDS. It terrified him. After his first opportunistic infection and hospitalization, and suddenly going from being "HIV-positive" to being a "person with AIDS," a gay man who loved to write and had been in the Workshop for many months by then railed that he didn't want to be in a group "with fags and PWAs." He returned a month later and stayed in the Workshop for the next year until he became too sick to attend.

People laughed when one longtime participant announced, "I went to another workshop but it didn't work out; they were talking iambic pentameter and I only knew pentamidine." He wasn't referring to the demands of formal poetry versus an insider's knowledge of AIDS, he was saying that he found an alternative equation of *psyche* (spirit) and *techne* (craft) more inspirational. For what goes on in the Workshop is an attention to both *psyche* and *techne:* to form, rhythm, language, image, to those things called "quality" and "art" and to the writing process, its benefits and content. Even as strong emotions surface, the task and the focus, over and over again, is to work with the writing, to turn one's allegiance from raw experience—however difficult, however present in the moment—to the text at hand. This is why the Workshop is a Writers Workshop and not a therapy group.

The format of each group is similar, although in the "Teaching the Teachers" training workshop, I offer a running commentary on listening, feedback, teaching techniques, and literature. We often start the three-hour session with a five-minute warm-up, which we've come to call a "wild write." That could be an automatic writing exercise based on a word or a line, or it might be an open-the-brain-and-senses scan. These pieces are read aloud in a quick go-round, and then, after presenting a short short story, or a couple of poems or a provocative quote perhaps on narrative strategy, or memory (or spreading out one hundred picture postcards with which to work on fiction), we settle into a thirty-to-thirty-five-minute writing period based on an exercise I've conjured. (It's remarkable to see how much can be written in thirty minutes if you focus.) These exercises introduce or continue an area for exploration, and whether soul-baring truth-telling or outrageous lying ("the beginning of fiction," says Jamaica Kincaid), each exercise is never only a formal conceit or meant to be purely therapeutic journal writing.

After writing comes the tea break, and then an hour to an hour and a half of on-the-spot reading aloud with feedback. It's not line-edit response—after all, we're talking about first drafts—but it's more than tea and sympathy. Nevertheless, this putting of images, rhythms, and insights into each other's imaginations is a wild and intimate process. People come to know one another through their visions, memories, and distinctive use of language, rhythm, and syntax. Someone becomes the guy whose mother had eleven children and a tightrope, or is recognized as an associative poet, or as a person with a jones for paragraph-length sentences, adjectives, or travelogues peopled with dark men. I have been sitting in the writing room for more than five years now, and over and over, I get the shivers when people read aloud what they've written. I might well have written "*we* get the shivers," so regularly does this phenomenon occur to everyone who sits around the table and listens.

People who take part in the Workshop are there because they

want to WRITE. Although I am something of a control queen when the conversation veers too far from writing and turns to, say, a comparison of "meds" (medications), I also recognize that people write for different reasons and that this changes from week to week. I am thinking now of a man who took part in the Workshop for several years. He wrote profusely outside of the weekly meetings, enjoyed rewriting, and *loved* sentences. Yet his stamina for criticism abruptly changed when he began caring for a sick ex-lover. I didn't realize the pressure he was under (nor how sick he himself was becoming) and kept returning one piece to him, with comments scribbled in the margins. This proved intolerable for him. He left the group and died six months later. I still feel awful about this. Another man who had written for years and usually requested sturdy feedback told me bluntly, when I suggested he might push a certain piece further, that he was completely satisfied with having written it. In his last year of life, he had begun to find the process of writing more important than the results. The commitment of the people in the Workshop to their writing is more fierce than not, though, and they go to heroic lengths to get things "right." ("Those who labor from deep within the midnight recesses of the epidemic to bring understanding back to the world, those who labor in the face of their own mortality, cannot avoid seeming heroic . . ." writes Tony Kushner in the introduction. This heroic quality is doubly true of those who write about their own lives, the word *hero* meaning someone noted for "feats of courage" or "nobility of purpose" *and* "the principal male [*sic*] character in a novel, poem, or dramatic representation.")

If there were two inscriptions over the door of the room we meet in, they might be the quotes that I read each year when the Workshop reconvenes after a brief summer break. One of the things we work with is the concept of the "inner critic," so useful in polishing writing but lethal in its inception. In the first quote, Martha Graham, speaking to Agnes de Mille, addresses this:

"There is a vitality, a life-force, an energy, a quickening that is translated through you into action and because there is only one of you in all time, this expression is unique. And if you block it, it will never exist through any other medium and be lost. The world will not have it. It is not your business to determine how good it is nor how valuable nor how it compares with other expressions. It is your business to keep it yours clearly and directly, to keep the channel open. You do not even have to believe in yourself or your work. You have to keep open and aware directly to the urges that motivate you. Keep the channel open . . ."[3]

The other quote, also about censorship, comes from a talk given by Adrienne Rich:

"Whatever is unnamed, undepicted in images, whatever is omitted from biography, censored in collections of letters, whatever is misnamed as something else, made difficult-to-come-by, whatever is buried in the memory by the collapse of meaning under an inadequate or lying language—this will become, not merely unspoken, but *unspeakable*."[4]

Work that is written under conditions of extremity may not bear the signs or sounds of *emotion recollected in tranquillity*. Its psycho-aesthetic heritage may be more a case of *signaling through the flames*. On the other hand, because there's an urgency to write, one doesn't generally find poetry or prose that's all dressed up with no place to go. The most powerful work grapples with issues of real concern *and* haunts in terms of language, structure, and image. That's the kind of writing I try to bring in as models and inspiration. (I've listed many of these authors' names in "On Starting a Writers Workshop" to be found in the appendix.)

One narrative strategy not mentioned by Forché is humor. Even in the darkest moments, wit regularly surfaces in Workshop writing. Someday, no doubt, I will write about the on-going experience of being the only woman in a room filled with very smart, very funny, both very healthy *and* very sick gay men. (Ninety-eight percent of the people who have joined the two workshops for people living with HIV/AIDS have been gay men. Both the caregivers and the new "Teaching the Teachers" workshop have included women. One of the reasons I started the training workshop was precisely to reach people not being served: women, homeless people with HIV/AIDS, those in recovery, more people of color, and younger HIV-affected individuals. Ages in the APLA Workshop have ranged from twenty-three to eighty; the majority of people are between thirty and fifty.) There aren't any archetypes I know of to describe the vital experience as a woman working with a roomful of gay men: Snow White and the Seven Dwarfs doesn't apply nor does Wendy and her Lost Boys. Closer in spirit is Bette Midler at the Continental Baths, but that was about performance, and besides, nobody ever shows up at the Workshop in a towel. Where else could you hear such great drag names as Mimi C'est Moi and Anne Aesthetic? Or take a master class in the essential art of deconstructing obituaries? "See the word *witty* in a death notice, and you know he didn't die of frost bite," one man counseled.

At inspired moments, the groups have named themselves— Cock & Quill, The Men with Big Pens, The Warrior Queens— and once even threatened to get jackets. (Has anyone done a dissertation on that old TV show *Queen for a Day* and its impact on AIDS narratives?) Doing an exercise on family trees, one wag said he *had* to include Olivia de Havilland. Even when it came time to think up a subtitle for this book, someone insisted it should be *From a Burning House: Tales of Gay Firefighters*. "No, *From a FLAMING House*," someone else countered.

I've noticed that wit often surfaces when pain is most palpable. It is not that humor removes the sting of anguish or recognition, yet, as if it were coming to the rescue, humor can momentarily banish terror, rage, or numbness in a writer, reader, or listener. Michael Martin's description of impending chemotherapy as "harvested white cells" being cultivated "by Asian farmers toiling away upon flooded rice-paddy-type floors at UCLA" uses wit to de-escalate a frightening experience. Steve Smith's story "The Pact," concerning assisted suicide, and Doug Bender's piece "Tubes," about having a Hickman catheter, similarly employ campy retorts to lighten difficult moments.

Witty writing has broken edgy moments during our meetings. I recall the dead silence in the room as Arthur Shafer read a description of his friend Joseph in his coffin. (It grew to be "Janesville's Own," which you'll find in the seventh chapter.)

When he got to the sentence " 'It's a blessing he's dead,' I said to my friends, 'because this outfit would surely have killed him,' " the group burst out in relieved laughter. It was as if Shafer had made a triple score in Scrabble, the line reverberating first in the church, then in his notebook, then in the social life of the Workshop.

Although the emotional commitment to their writing is unshakable, Workshop members may not write on their own, outside the meetings, except for the weeks before the twice-yearly public readings. Many of the stories in this book have been written in thirty-minute installments in go-back-to-pieces-you-want-to-continue sessions. Still, much of the writing begun in the Workshop hasn't been completed. In his account of going to see a fortune-teller, Alan Erenberg literally stopped midsentence and never went back to finish it. Sometimes the writing itself—having an insight, an imaginative flash, a memory, or expressing a feeling, and reading it aloud—feels sufficient. All of us have said, keep going, crack the code, make it shimmer, for God's sake, tell us the end of that story! But often there isn't the will or the energy to write the next section, to go back and polish something. Many Workshop members work full-time or are caring for partners or are grappling themselves with illness. So notebooks become filled with fragments. (You will find some in this collection.)

Perhaps a piece *wouldn't* have gone on to be as terrific as it promised. Maybe reading fragments and remembering potent unfinished work is like standing before the mesmerizing brokenness of classical statues. But, can't you imagine the vital work that might have grown from these first lines?

"The second date was more civilized."

"There's a balcony here we can almost taste."

"I want to see my hair get gray."

"He forgave me for stains on my shirt, I forgave him for dying."

"They're in some sort of love, again."

"This is Shirley's story, Shirley in the Buccaneer Lounge."

"My cousin Kenneth and I had sex when he was ten and I was twelve and he hasn't looked me in the eye since."

"My fear of heights is gone now."

Gone, gone, so many people and stories and notebooks are gone. About a year ago, I actually began to corral people over to the copy machine after they'd written something strong and unfinished. Not knowing what I was going to do with the pieces, I put them in a folder and wrote "Frags" on the top. I think I simply wanted to conserve them. A friend noticed the folder on my desk and explained that a frag was a hand grenade the size of a baseball that sent out bits of shrapnel when it exploded. I thought of the prairie fire.

The writer's name was Bill; he was an English teacher who called me to say he'd like to join the group. But he didn't show up until nearly a year later, when he telephoned again to say that just that morning he'd written his first poem in an eon. Was there still room for him? He joined us the very next day and composed what I remember now as a tiny masterpiece.

What I recall is this: that he wrote for maybe twenty minutes, then stopped and sat there. After the tea break, he read a spartan piece about witnessing a prairie fire where many animals were killed. The description was riveting. Then there was that silence that comes over the room when someone's written something so true and searing that everyone seems to inhale collectively. Someone broke the silence: "That sounds like an AIDS story."

Bill came to the Workshop two more times. Once he wrote a brief account of a conversation he'd had the day before with his doctor, who said, "There's nothing more I can do." The following week, he just sat there with his eyes closed. Two weeks later he was dead.

I imagine his notebook was discarded. The only trace I have of an event he never wanted forgotten[5] are the words that I scribbled down as he read aloud to the group:

Somewhere he smelled smoke. A prairie fire. . . . porcupine exploded . . . wind whipped fire . . . deer . . . mind-crazed jackrabbit ran into the inferno. Carnage and stench remained.

A few years ago, the *New York Times* made note of a research project that studied writing about traumatic experiences. "Writing about [these] upsetting topics, which many of the subjects had never discussed with anyone, resulted in significant boost in their levels of T cells, which fight infection and virus."[6] Even though we are not in the business of conducting double-blind studies at the Workshop, nor any clinical trials, I could tell you one hundred accounts of cathartic moments, of the laughter that spirals up while people are writing, and of stories never revealed to anyone until they were written in the Workshop. Giving voice to what has been unspoken, doing it in *writing,* and in this process finding out you know so much more than you think is one of the aspects of healing that people in the Workshop often speak about. (One longtime member of the Workshop said, "Every state of being has a place in this room." Another person told me that writing about living with AIDS was like "watching a horror movie through your fingers and finally deciding to look.")

Many of the stories in this book are—or were—talismans for their authors: coded, custom-made instructions on how to live. And die. Many more pieces and fragments that will never be published have functioned in this way. Describing how his grandfather, a miner, would spend ten hours a day underground and then walk home in the dark at twenty below zero, his clothes icy and frozen, was one man's means of teaching himself about survival.

In the Workshop we continue to work on craft, on locating stories that *must* be told, and on what Joan Didion once called "the niceties of inflection." But what does it mean to work on "voice" in a room where, just a few weeks ago, a man with enlarged vocal chords who had suffered a stroke read his piece aloud in the frailest whisper and wept afterward? What does it mean to play and labor with language in a community where memories are overburdened with witnessing, where memory, encoded in that language, is being lost? I could talk about this forever or maybe just say, *it means so much.*

Rilke's words are coming to me now, words from his "The Ninth Duino Elegy," a poem I keep returning to for its lessons on writing and on impermanence:

". . . everything here / apparently needs us, this fleeting world, which in some / strange way / keeps calling to us. Us, the most fleeting of all . . .

"Perhaps we are *here* in order to say: house, / bridge, fountain, gate, pitcher, fruit-tree, window— / at most: column, tower . . .

"*Here* is the time for the *sayable, here* is its homeland. / Speak and bear witness. More than ever / the Things that we might experience are vanishing . . ."[7]

We do a warm-up exercise in which we gather every word that comes into our minds in, say, five or ten minutes, as if we were saving them from destruction. Once I found myself happily jotting down *Abracadabra, Open Sesame, Presto Change-o.* In the Workshop, side by side the most alive people one could ever know, I learn, over and over again, how magic words are.

Yet, sometimes, I find myself wondering what magic words can do when too many people who write them are vanishing.

—Irene Borger
January 1996
Los Angeles

NOTES

1. *Against Forgetting: Twentieth Century Poetry of Witness,* edited and with an introduction by Carolyn Forché (New York: W. W. Norton and Company, 1993), 29.

2. Ibid., 45.

3. Agnes de Mille quotes this conversation in her book *Dance to the Piper* and *Promenade Home: A Two-Part Autobiography* (New York: Da Capo Press, 1979), 335.

4. Adrienne Rich's speech "It Is the Lesbian in Us . . ." may be found in her book *On Lies, Secrets and Silence: Selected Prose 1966–1978* (New York: W. W. Norton and Co., 1979), 199.

5. We worked that day with the notion of forgetting. I recall I read this quote from Milan Kundera's *The Book of Laughter and Forgetting:* "The bloody massacre in Bangladesh quickly covered over the memory of the Russian invasion of Czechoslovakia, the assassination of Allende drowned out the groans of Bangladesh, the war in the Sinai Desert made people forget Allende, the Cambodian massacre made people forget Sinai, and so on and so forth until ultimately everyone lets everything be forgotten."

6.   Dan Goleman, "Researchers Find That Optimism Helps the Body's Defense System," *New York Times,* April 20, 1989, National Edition, B9.

7.   In *The Enlightened Heart: An Anthology of Sacred Poetry,* translated by Stephen Mitchell (New York: Harper and Row Publishers, 1989), 140–43.

THANKS
Irene Borger

It is six o'clock in the morning on Thanksgiving and I am gazing out the window at the top of a canyon ridge some fifteen miles west of the Dorothy Chandler Auditorium, where the Oscars are given, and I'm thinking of how, in our culture, public thanks are often hyperbolic—or cut off. (You've seen it: the winners for Best Achievement in Sound are right in the middle of thanking the crew and their producer/director/mother/first-grade teacher when the music swells and, midsentence, they are pressed off the stage by party-clothed Ken and Barbie types.) I am glad that books are not (yet) engineered this way because this volume—and Workshop—has been made in community and, thus, engenders many thanks.

"If I had not met . . ." the first line of W. S. Merwin's poem "One of the Lives" begins. The idea to start the Workshop came to me in 1989 while I was on a meditation retreat led by Jack Kornfield, and I thank him for his brilliant heart and for the opening of the dharma. I would not have met Jack (nor had the confidence to start the workshop) were it not for my dear friend Deena Metzger, who embodies the words *writer, teacher,* and *healer* better than anyone else I know.

Over and over again, my beloved pals Marvin Heiferman, Deborah Irmas, and Louise Steinman have envisioned, each in his or her own way, what was possible and enriched my understanding of what it means to do this work.

The Writers Workshop, the smallest program at AIDS Project Los Angeles, is harbored by an organization that passionately continues, to mix metaphors, to be at the front lines of the epidemic. Many thanks to Executive Director Jimmy Loyce for his leadership and for his introduction and to Allen Carrier, Paul Serchia, Lorette Herman, former staff member Ricky Hoyt, Colleen Johnson, Kristen Laskaris, Mark Senak, and Jolie Shartin for their loving labors. Appreciations to former board chair David Wexler, who helped me get the ball rolling, and to board members Harold I. Huttas and Steve Tisch and chair Dana Miller, who understand what words can mean in a time of crisis.

I am also grateful for the ongoing support from other members of the APLA staff: Chris Bennett, Arnel Cedeno, Stephan Ceryanek, Phil Curtis, Mike Dugan, Leah Goodwin, Tonya Hendricks, Richard Levin, Lauren Llewellyn, Mike Lucia, Noah Mariano, Jamie Marquez, Mirasol, Bill Misenhimer, Bill Morrison, Robert Sanchez, Rebecca Solomon, Wayne Wagner and Allen Yoakum.

This workshop would not have been possible without the continued benefactions of Audrey, Deborah, and Sydney Irmas and the Audrey and Sydney Irmas Charitable Foundation; Mary Lloyd Estrin and Heidi Mage Lloyd and John M. Lloyd Foundation; Randee Klein and the Klein Family Foundation; Beth Rudin deWoody and The Rudin Foundation. Harold I. Huttas and Alan Lithograph Inc., Christena Schlundt and the Museum of Contemporary Art, have also been special angels. Gifts from the estates of John Bell and William Franklin have provided joyous occasions; numerous friends of John Olson have made contributions in his honor toward the establishment of a Workshop Library. Generous donations have also been made by the friends and family of Philip Justin Smith, by Kathy Riquelme and Dr. Harvey Abrams.

The desecration and dismantling of public arts funding is right in line with the thinking that sought to "bomb Vietnam back to the Stone Age." While this *book* has not been funded by the National Endowment for the Arts, from the very first session the Workshop *has* been supported by public money. I appreciate the funding from the California Arts Council, a state agency, the City of Los Angeles Cultural Affairs Department, *and,* yes, the National Endowment for the Arts, a federal agency, and I am moved by the extraordinary commitment of their staffs. Thank you to Wayne Cook and Carol Shiffman, Roella Hsieh Louie and Jeffrey Herr.

I am also thankful to my Los Angeles family for their love

and our ongoing conversations (and wish I could tell you about *each* of their gifts, but I can hear the music rising): Nancy Bacal, Erica Clark, Suzanne Ecker, Lloyd Hamrol, Joe Hogan, Dan Nussbaum, Katina Shields, Deidre Sklar, Bill Stern, Janet Sternburg, Sylvia Sugar, Sarah Tamor, and the late Hella Hammid. I celebrate poets Cathy A. Colman and Regina O'Melveny for encouragement and longtime creative comradeship.

The menschy Tony Kushner not only took the time out of a fierce schedule to write an introduction to this book but graced the Workshop with his presence when he might have gone to the beach. Artists Remy Charlip and Barbara Kruger generously created original made-for-the-Workshop artworks. (Workshop member Steve Maher, of On white Design, fashioned their images into nifty T-shirts.) My colleagues, writers Dinah Berland, Bernard Cooper, Richard Garcia, Jim Krusoe, Nancy Krusoe, and Peter Levitt, have been inspiring guest artists.

The Workshop's twice-yearly readings at the Museum of Contemporary Art would not take place without the devoted (and overtime) work of our favorite art-world champions: David Bradshaw, Colette Dartnall, Richard Koshalek, Julie Lazar, Alma Ruiz, Dawn Setzer, and Brent Zerger. Julie Galant and Martin Bondell of Fotofolio, Inc.; Jarrett Hedborg, Dominique Daniels, and A. Rudin; the *MacNeil-Lehrer NewsHour*'s Charles Krause, Anne Taylor Fleming, Mike Saltz, and Moira Rankin, and Joyce Ritchie of the National Public Radio program *Soundprint*, have each conjured marvelous gifts. Filmmaker Dennis Chicola dedicated much time to envisioning and shooting portions of a documentary, *You Can Hear Their Voices*. May he raise the funds to complete this work.

For other acts of valor and kindness, I want to thank Bill Alexander, Suzy Becker, Joseph Cady, Kip Cohen, Pamela Cook, Steve Frank, Weba Garretson, Tino Hammid, Kevin Hummer, Charlotte Innes, Sarah Jacobus, Jeanie J. Kim, Geoffrey Landis, Julia Laurie, Steven D. Lavine, Philip Littell, Joan Logghe, Veronica Mard, Pacy Markman, Robin and Meade Martin, Don and Linda Novack, Saul Ostrow, Sandra Peterson, Chuck Pruce, Priscilla Regalado, Peter Reiss, Adrienne Rich, Lynn Rosenfeld,

Christena Schlundt, Judy Schoen, Nancy Silverton, Sharon Siskin, Virginia and Dwayne Smith, Edward Spencer, Larry Stein, Inju Sturgeon, Tess Timoney, Richard Turner, Andrea Vaucher, Leor Warner, Sharon Oard Warner, and Jack Weinstein, as well as the intrepid folks in the Thursday-night "Teaching the Teachers" workshop and the Monday-night group (who arrived at the perfect time.)

One couldn't wish for more supportive colleagues with whom to make a book. Gratitude to my vibrant editor, Amy Einhorn, to forward-thinking Tom Spain, to my divine agent, Muriel Nellis. Also to copy editor Steve Boldt, cover designer Jeanne M. Lee and book designer Stanley S. Drate.

Many people helped track down, type, write biographies for, and, in numerous cases, permit usage of work, and I am grateful to them: Sam Avery, Jan Bellon, Jon Bernstein, Arlen Bishop, Tom Burke, Jose Candelario, Peter Carley, Olga Chrysostomides, Doug Erenberg, Diana Fontes, David Gere, Steve Hanna, Richard Hermann, Candace Howerton, Jim Long, Karen Marcus, Edna Mishkin, Sheri Bellon Peterson, Kathy Riquelme, Jon Sacco, Barry H. Schoenfeld, Virginia Smith, Peter Sykes, and Mark Winsten.

There would be no book without writer David Touster, who played aide-de-camp and majordomo and George to my inevitable Gracie. Computer-savvy whizzes Christian Conti and Susan Hamilton astonished me with their coolheadedness and great gifts of time. Marvin Heiferman, Geoffrey Landis, and Louise Steinman gave me invaluable feedback on my opening essay. Buzz Spector carefully scrutinized the appendix. Jeff Cohen, Christopher Gorman, Joe Hogan, Radha Marcum, Jerry Rosenblum, Jim Rudolph, Arthur Shafer, Steve Smith, and Frank Wang reviewed the copyediting.

Appreciations to Ruth and Lawrence Borger, my parents, for all the tools, electronic and genetic, and Margaret Borger and Kate Borger, my sisters, for love and research. May the babies, Michael and Levon, grow up surrounded by stories—in a world without the virus.

I tend to wince when someone says, "I have no words to say

this," because I think one of our gifts—and tasks—as humans is to *find the language*. Yet now, the sun full up on Thanksgiving morning, I watch myself fall silent as I try to write the final thank-you.

This book is dedicated to the smart, funny, bighearted, courageous, talented, amazing members of the Writers Workshop, those who are here, and those who have, in Philip Justin Smith's words, "gone to Paris." Thank you for teaching me everything I need to know about life and death. And bathhouses.

Carpe diem.

This does not mean "fish of the day."

—Los Angeles, 1995

1

ORIGIN

I remember when Hickman was the star of *Dobie Gillis* . . .

—*Christopher Gorman*

I want to tell the story of a little boy in a fireman's cap. But that's not really how it happened (and yet that's the image that works). The real story is that I was crossing the street when a fire truck drove by and the fireman on the back winked at me. I was eleven years old and set by this on my course for life: trying to find that fireman again. This isn't factually accurate either, but it's a good myth . . .

—*Robbie Hilyard*

LAVABO

Christopher Gorman

In the spring of 1981 an article appeared in the *New York Times* about a mysterious deterioration of the immune system that physicians across the United States were observing in the sexually active homosexual community. I read the chilling article on the Long Island Rail Road in the time it took the train to travel between Syosset and Kew Gardens. The day was unusually warm for spring, and the air-conditioning was not working. Sweat appeared on my upper lip and forehead. It trickled down my neck and soaked my shirt. Between Kew Gardens and Penn Station, I stared blankly out of the dirty train window—past the billboards and factories of Queens (where I was born in 1955) to the familiar skyline of my beloved Manhattan in the too-fast-approaching distance. I tried to forget the article in the *New York Times*, but I could not forget it. Destiny had arrived before I had arrived at my destination.

In the steamy bowels of Penn Station I stuffed the *New York Times* into an already overflowing trash can, then disappeared into the crowd that surged upward to Seventh Avenue.

That evening I mixed drinks and opened bottles of beer at Uncle Charlie's North, a neighborhood gay bar on the Upper East Side. The men sat before me, puffing their Marlboro's and silently sipping their drinks. The party was over. Throughout the long night one would occasionally whisper to another, "Did you read the article?"

A regular patron asked for his usual Scotch and water. "Water from Lourdes—if you've got any." I knew he'd read the article.

Similar articles continued to appear all that summer, in *The Advocate* and *Newsweek, New York,* and *Time.* They discussed it on the *Today* show and *Live at Five* and *Nightline.* We discussed it at Don't Tell Mama and the Ice Palace and the Works. All summer I prayed to be spared this scourge, this punishment, this ultimate shame. I visited churches and lit candles like an old woman praying for her alcoholic son.

One Friday afternoon in July, after applying for a position at Saks Fifth Avenue, I ducked into the comforting darkness of St. Patrick's Cathedral. I pushed past tourists and fanatics, moving purposefully toward the cool sanctuary of the Lady Chapel behind the main altar. I emptied my pockets of loose change and subway tokens and lit four votive candles in front of a familiar statue of the Blessed Mother. Taking my petition to the highest levels of power, I prayed to Mary to intercede on my behalf. "Oh, Mary, conceived without sin, pray for us who have recourse to thee." I prayed, I begged, and I bargained. No more missing mass on Sundays and holy days. No more cruising Bloomingdale's. No more gossiping. No more amyl. My hands were clasped tightly together. My forehead rested on my hands. This was my approximation of Jesus in Gethsemane. After many agonizing minutes I lifted my head. Looking at my hands, I played an old game from childhood. "Here is the church, here is the steeple, open the doors and see all the—"

Oh, my God! What is this? Blood! Blood on my palms, blood on the pew, blood on the marble floor. I wiped my hand on my trousers, then examined them. In the center of each palm was a deep, painless puncture. How did this happen? Where? At the employment office at Saks? I looked up to the Blessed Mother. She stared ahead with a look of no concern. Leaping up out of the bloody pew, I jammed my hands into my pant pockets and fled. Past the crypt where the dead cardinals are interred, past the statues of St. Patrick and St. Theresa of the Roses, running past the confessional with the red light on above, past the bust of Pope John XXIII—emerging at last from the shadows of the cathedral into the blessed sunshine.

Weary office workers moved up and down Fifth Avenue like ants on a picnic blanket. Foolishly, I looked for a familiar face, but recognized no one. I looked once again at my hands. Jesus, Mary, and Joseph! The wounds in my palms had gone straight through my hands. Blood so red it was practically purple oozed from the gaping holes.

"I am in big trouble," I thought as I ran to the subway. "Does this mean I can't go to Fire Island tomorrow?"

In my apartment in Queens, my best friend has helped me bandage my hands. He is a flight attendant for New York Air, first aid is part of their training. We are standing in the tiny bathroom I have painted cranberry red. Around the sink are cotton swabs, bottles of rubbing alcohol and hydrogen peroxide, gauze, iodine, Band-Aids, and a styptic pencil. My mysterious wounds are clean, have stopped bleeding, and are bandaged as perfectly as a airline attendant and a former Boy Scout of America could manage.

Afterward, we settle down on the sofa to watch *The Dukes of Hazzard* together. John Schneider looks particular handsome in this episode, and I decide it would be foolish not to go to Fire Island the next morning.

"You're bleeding," I hear a strange voice say. I am lying on the beach at Fire Island in a red Speedo. "You're *bleeding*." I open my eyes and squint into the sun hanging over the stage-left corner of the Atlantic Ocean. A blindingly handsome young man wearing a bathing suit the size of a ticket stub is staring down at my side, perplexed. Propping myself up on my elbows, I nervously look at my side. Blood is trickling from a tear in the skin directly below my rib cage. "Thank you!" I improvise. "I had my appendix out last week and the stitches were removed yesterday. I'll be fine." The stranger moves on down the beach in the direction of Calvin Klein's house.

I lurch toward the ocean like a broken doll, my legs weak, my head spinning. I hear my Irish grandmother say, "Salt water is good for wounds." She believed that every year on August 15, the Feast of the Assumption, the ocean acquired miraculous powers to heal. On that day every summer she would force her fifteen grandchildren into the waves at Rockaway Beach. This is not August 15, but I am desperate for healing and I plunge into the dangerous surf.

The waves knock me down and a powerful undertow threatens to pull me back to Ireland. In the tumult of sand and sea, I scrub my side, hoping to wash this blood, this nightmare, away. After several minutes, I crawl out of the ocean like a frightened child. Confused, I scan the beach for my grandmother, but she has long since abandoned her room at the shore for the smaller confines of a plot at Calvary.

The blood has stopped flowing from my side and I can see a wound six inches long. I don't even look at my feet; the blood on the sand tells me what I already know. Heaven has answered my prayers of summer: I have received the stigmata, the wounds of the crucified Christ.

I had fervently prayed for this experience as a young boy. Excluded from serving as an altar boy because I attended public school, I imagined that the stigmata would impress Monsignor McCarthy sufficiently to make an exception in my case. Chosen by God for this extreme honor, I would be the best altar boy they ever had at Our Lady Queen of Martyrs Church. I would be interviewed in *The Long Island Catholic* and my family would not have to stand in line at the World's Fair to see the Pietà. I stopped praying for the stigmata when Sean Livingston taught me to masturbate in the eighth grade. After that, I didn't want to be an altar boy anymore.

I stand against a scrub pine in the dunes on Fire Island. I am smoking a cigarette I got from the last guy. My hands and feet are bandaged, my DREAMGIRLS T-shirt hides the wound in my side. The almost full moon finds me like a spotlight. I pass the night in this secret place filled with other men who cannot sleep. Beautiful men who do not yet know they are dying. I couple with them, one after the other, dancing under the stars. We are watched by owls and raccoons and all the saints of heaven. We are lit by the moon. Bodily fluids soak into my bandages and mix with my blood. I am infected with what I fear most. It is finished.

Walking home in the early-morning light, I see a baby deer, a fawn, alone on the boardwalk. "Where is your mother, Bambi?" I whisper. The fawn hobbles away, afraid of me.

I arrive at the house where I am staying and close the gate quietly behind me. I enter the sandy house and move slowly through the dark hallway in the direction of the bathroom. It is time to clean my wounds.

MY AUTOBIOGRAPHY IN FIVE MINUTES

Sioux de Nimes

Born at a racetrack. A bolt of lightning. Labor began. What's this? Almost died. Three months early. Papa wanted me to die I'm sure. Hated me because I wasn't a real girl. Divorced Mum, married whore from wrong side of the tracks. "We're going to Memphis to see the fair," my mother said as we drove on two-lane blacktop between verdant cotton fields. Same shit there. You can feel the oppression in the cheap, consistently stalwart white columns that adorn most of the brick, three-bedroom suburban houses. Bye-bye, cruel plantation. Hated that bitch already. Him and his slaves. Would I get into big trouble for losing my flash cards? Forced to stick my head between his legs as he whipped me with a riding crop? Mrs. Perry hugged me and said it was okay. At nine years old I thought I had very handsome veiny hands and wouldn't a Timex look nice on my wrist. Jacked off a lot. Built rockets. Had first crush of my life on that handsome young astronaut who died of smoke inhalation on the ground in a practice mission at Cape Kennedy. I wanted to hold his beautiful face in my hands, kissing him and rubbing my skinny frame all over his ultrawhite suit. I would probably have sucked his dick. Sent off to military school after blowing bubbles in Coach Thorn's face. Thank God he didn't find the nickel matchbox in my pocket. My roommate at military school had broken every pole-vaulting record in the Southeast Conference. He carried a picture of his dick in his wallet. "No son of mine is going to

NYU." Why not, Papa, the school of the arts is the best. "It's a hotbed of niggers, hippies, and Jews." Burst into tears, left the room, cried all the way back to Memphis. He saw me in a Megan Terry play three months later. I was twenty years old. Simulated anal sex with a man in prison. At least I was on top—you would have thought that meant something. But he sat there expressionless in the front row, red tie, white shirt, gray suit, with his executive friends from the utilities company and their wives. He never liked to go to the theater so much, out of school. Moved to L.A. Thank God for L.A. Kicked around in show business and kept busy. Met Peter—I loved him. He was viciously rude to my friends. Insulted their fat. Ridiculed their intelligence. What did I see in this asshole? they wanted to know. One, he is one of the most talented men I've ever known. Two, he has a handsome face and the physique of a rugby player. Three, he has a big dick and knows how to use it. Tested HIV-positive in Paris where I lived in 1985. That's okay. Came back to the USA. Why worry, surely a cure in five years. And then I did something very strange. Moved to Nevada to work on my dad's ranch. He was dead. Cowboys aren't scared of blood. They rather like to bleed and the more it covers their shirt and their chaps, the more noble. Having a near-death injury is very important in that world. I saw a lot of blood in my year there. Animal and human. I saw people getting themselves bloody with other people's blood. What if it was me who got kicked in the head or gored by an angry mother cow or got my fingers chopped off in a hay swather? I would tell them at that point, don't touch my blood. I would be run out of Nevada. I was anyway. They didn't like me. "Go back to L.A.," the bartender shouted. It was packed and smoky and all the cowboys laughed in their bourbon. I took his advice. These were my concerns—giving to someone else. No sex—no blood spilled. Except at Pacific Oaks every week. There's a real cute black nurse from New Orleans who likes me. She made a big mess of red beans and rice and brought it to the office in Beverly Hills the other day when she drew my blood, a big old pot of red beans just sitting there. Stink. It's gross and not one bit healthy, but I'm telling you, good big old greasy ham hocks. Pork attached to fat attached to bone, simmering and boiling. Strange animal sausages and innards from the depths of some god-awful low beast her mother shipped out Federal Express. Beans in a witch's brew boiling an ugly hard brown red. Absolutely fucking divine. Stinking away in a steel pot so deep and high you can't ever imagine eating it all. She presents this gift of love to me as I wait in the steel gray examination room to have my PIC line cleaned. Healthy, happy white starched doctors clip by the door in too much of a hurry, looking in with forced smiles on their faces. Alleged curiosity and manufactured good cheer. As if to say, "You're in the right place!" They try to instill confidence as they lose their patients, one by one by one. And they are overworked and they do care, but we have all been so numbed by it all and they add to their list of clients and write out scripts of AZT, DDC, DDI, DHPG. All antivirals, all quick fixes. I've used them all. DHPG in my PIC line. Don't wanna go blind, don't wanna go blind.

Laissez bon temps roulet
A Nouvelle Orléans
Baby, *s'il vous plaît*

MAGIC EYE

John D'Amico

Mother's magic eye could look out and find my father no matter where he was. "I can see him getting in his car in the parking lot at his office," she would say at 5:45 P.M. with four sets of eyes staring at her, while pretending to adjust her private telescope. "He's on his way." I never questioned that she could see, not only through the brick walls of our house, but could manage to see Dad in his car, miles from home, no matter where he was. "Just twenty-five minutes and he'll be home," she'd insist.

The wait for Dad and dinner was filled with everyday things: the news from Vietnam would drone on, homework would be finished, or the riots would begin between my brother and me. My sisters, high school girls, were never very patient; they would sometimes get fed up with waiting and begin picking food from the pots on the stove or in the oven.

"I can see him at the corner of Gratiot and Thirteen Mile Road," she'd say at the moment when she thought we'd all lost hope. "Ten minutes." I'd picture Dad waiting at a stoplight, in his white-on-white-on-white Cadillac sedan DeVille, cigarette lit, Frank Sinatra playing on the *click click* eight-track tape player, ringed fingers tapping the steering wheel, happy to be on his way home.

At 7 P.M., more than an hour after Mom had first spotted Dad with her magic eye, we would get to eat. "I know I saw him leave the parking lot at his office," my own version of *Bewitched* would say.

As we all headed toward the dining room and our places at the table, Mom would say, "You kids go ahead, I think I'll wait for your father," and she would sit at her place, next to his, across from mine, plate empty, watching us eat, just like hundreds of other meals she had prepared for him, to which only we showed up to eat.

During dinner Mom's conversational tone never changed. She would quiz us on our day's events and we would oblige her by filling in the gaps that all the silences left open. My brother would pretend to be Marlon Brando from *The Godfather,* complete with paper napkin stuffed in his mouth, or pull his lip down to mock where my sister had once been hit by a baseball, or try to decide which he'd rather have, "a hundred dollars or John's nose full of nickels." Laughter would fill the house.

After dinner I would watch television with my brother, while my sisters fought over who would wash and who would dry. My mother would leave two places at the table in the dark dining room.

"Maybe he had an accident," a sister would hopefully suggest, at a quarter to ten, during a commercial break. That would start my sisters on a whole round of "This always happens" and "How can you stand it?" and "I would never put up with that from my husband." Mom would end those uncomfortable blameful conversations with, "Don't you talk that way about your father. He has always provided you children with everything you have ever needed."

By 11 P.M. the dishes washed, the pots scrubbed, the fights over, the popcorn popped and eaten, with the local news on, the magic eye was put away for another day. I would lie in bed or sometimes at the top of the stairs, in my pajamas, feet up on the wall, half-dreaming, drawing patterns in the shag carpet, waiting for some confirmation that whatever had made the magic eye not work, Dad would get home safely and I could fall asleep.

Sometimes in those pre-sleep moments, as I listened to the news from downstairs, disasters would flood to mind as reasons for his absence. I would think of lightning storms, and the damage they had done to our lilac tree, a time before I could remember. Or maybe the time our car was stolen or the time those guys came to our house and took the television because they said Dad owed them money. I would worry about the people my mother had said were friends of Uncle Tiziano's and that he should stay away from.

I don't ever remember the magic eye working, and I also don't ever remember not believing in it. Eventually, I would fall asleep. Sometimes I would hear Dad come in. He would have a brief conversation with Mom, and she would fix him some bacon and eggs, over easy with toast, and I would say a thank-you prayer to God for bringing him home safely.

In the morning, after my brother and sisters left for school, and Mom was busy downstairs being Mom, I would sit on the edge of the tub and watch Dad shave. Whatever disaster it was that had kept him away was gone, didn't even merit mentioning. Instead, I would listen to him talk about the baseball game or someone else's sales records. Even now, sometimes I take out my magic eye and look for things, but I don't ever find them that way.

ME AND THE KING

John Terry Bell

U h-oh, she's straightening her orange skirt to cover her high-heeled sandals. If I step to the left and peek under my eyebrows, I can just see her without that amber light blinding me. She always does that when it's nearly time. And she's staring at me again wearing that little smile. Why does she do that? Every night standing at the edge of the stage giving me that same little smile. I don't think it's funny at all!

Well, tonight they all have a surprise coming. It's not going to happen, I'm not going to let it. Not tonight!

Uh-oh, here we go, all the kids in our little line like little soldiers dressed in giant gold diapers. "Bearing! Poise!" Mr. Symon, the director, tells us. "Remember, you are *royalty!* Be it!" I'm not sure what he means, but if I keep my shoulders back and my chin up, it seems to make him happy.

The queen in her dark orange shirt coughs lightly. "Silence," the king says weakly from his golden bed on the opposite side of the stage. On cue everyone falls flat on the floor. "Up, up, up," the king says, "we do not grovel any longer. Mrs. Anna has made this so."

I take a deep, silent breath as I always do when I see the king lie back on his laced pillows. It helps.

The prince of Siam begins his last sad speech. If I really listen to him harder, maybe I can forget the king completely. Why are the lights making the stage so hot tonight?

14

Uh-oh, here she comes, the first queen in her dark orange dress stepping onstage into the light. Bow as she goes past, then kneel on the blue pillow with the ugly green elephant. No more smiles, she looks sad, really sad. Well, let her! It won't happen tonight. I'm too old to let it happen. It's never going to happen again ever!

Owww! The sequins on his vest really scratch. Well, let them, let them cut into my neck until I bleed, then I can think about that instead.

There goes the bamboo screen up into the soft, yellow lights above. And Mrs. Anna is there in her shiny blue dress with the white lace. She looks so pretty. I wish she wouldn't have a sad look on her face, too, like she's going to start crying right now, like she knows someone who really *is* going to die.

Uh-oh, the violins. Violins are dangerous. They sound like little puppies crying when they're alone. Bite down, lock your jaw! Now there's the cello, moaning so sadly; goose bumps up my back! Oh, no, don't let it start!

The old Kralahome raises his hands mumbling his weird prayer from ancient Bangkok. He steps to Mrs. Anna looking like he's about to throw up. Crud! A little tear on Mrs. Anna's cheek glints in the pink light.

It's okay for her, everybody understands, she's a grown-up, an actress, and besides, she's a girl, she can cry anytime and no one thinks she's weird.

"Children, dear children," Mrs. Anna says, opening her arms. I look at the other kids as we rise together, faces humbly cast down. During rehearsal we used to giggle during this part; now everyone looks like their favorite goldfish just died. I squeeze my eyes shut hard, make everything blurry, think of a happy tune, count the ripples in the curtain as I cross the stage to the king on his golden bed. Sometimes he looks a lot like my uncle Bob.

Uh-oh, he's staring at me, his face pale from the new makeup. Sometimes he only glances at me, but tonight he's staring. Why does he have to make it so hard! He tries to smile as he reaches out to touch my arm. He stops. That look of pain sweeps across his face. Mrs. Anna rushes to support him as again he sinks slowly back onto the bed. This is murder!

But he's not dying, not really. It's only a play, it's only a play! Say it over and over. It's not real, it's only a play! Don't cry!

Uh-oh, the first queen is stepping forward, taking a breath. I can always tell; her stomach pushes out and the dark orange dress swishes at her feet. The violins swell, the other king's wives step up behind her. This is it! They're going to sing!

"He has a thousand dreams that won't come true . . ."

Don't listen! Don't look at anything!

"You know that he believes in them and that's enough for you . . ."

Bite your lip, dig your fingernails into your palms, make them bleed; glue your eyes to the floor. And don't cry!

"He's something wonderful . . ."

The whole orchestra joins! I'm choking. My throat makes gurgly sounds. I can't breathe, my body's shaking. The king's hand reaches toward Mrs. Anna, stops in midair, then dramatically drops to the edge of the bed. Mrs. Anna leans forward taking it, pressing it to her heart.

I can't take it! The song builds higher, stronger. A great sob forces its way from my throat, tears cascade from my eyes. The other children start to whimper. Great gulping sounds flow out into the sniffling blackness of the audience.

Shivering, sobbing, I drop to my knees beside the king's bed. I feel the vibration of percussion as my tears soak into a corner of his golden blanket. The curtain slowly, slowly falls.

I gasp, drained. My throat is choked, the muscles of my jaw cramp tight. "Nice job," the king says, pushing himself off the bed. The queen passes, smiling again, and pats my head. I wipe my nose on my gold-lamé sleeve, not wanting to look at anyone.

I failed again. Hard as I tried not to let it happen, it happened. It's only a play and I cried for real! I'm still not a real actor like the grown-ups. But I can do it! They'll see, they'll see. Wait till tomorrow night!

THE HUMMING STORY

Alan Erenberg

When I think back over my life, I remember that as a boy it was very hard to be just me. There I was, just ten years old, happily minding my own business, and I immediately knew that my father disapproved of me, of something "queer acting" about me. I knew because of his "humming."

"I'm going to have a signal with you, Alan," my dad once told me. "Whenever you act too much like a girl, I'm going to hum 'Hum hum hum.' "

Now, I never doubted that my father loved me. After all, this signal of his was "a secret, just between us men," he said. I just thought I was stupid, that's all. I thought that the progeny of my mother and father has lost a few chromosomes or something when it got to me.

And damn if I didn't hear that hum when I least expected it. It could have been graduation day from junior high or I could have been playing in the backyard. We could have been on a family vacation in Palm Springs or I could have been in the school auditorium during the Annual Eighth Grade Speech Contest and I would hear "Hum hum hum," and I knew I was doing something "gay."

What was it? Was I clapping my hands like a girl and not like a man? I know I used to do that because my father told me that after I won first prize in the Contest.

"You clap your hands just like a girl," he said. "A man claps his hands by cupping them together and making a strong-sounding clap, but a girl just pats her hands together very softly."

Another time I'd hear "Hum hum hum," and I'd wonder, "What the hell am I doing wrong now?" Maybe I was crossing my legs like a girl and not like a man. I know I did that because my father told me. I was running for class vice president and my dad pointed out that I'd been seated on the stage with my legs crossed like a girl.

"If you're going to cross your legs, cross them like this"—he showed me—"like a man."

"Boy, I just don't know how to do anything right," I said to myself. Even at home, I thought I was too dumb, not able to catch myself acting like a fag.

It was graduation day and my friends and I were taking Polaroid snap-shots. In one group picture I was photographed making a sweeping arm gesture with my hands, and my dad viewed that as being too queer for comfort. He started humming louder than ever. "Hum hum hum, hum hum hum hum." And I finally figured out what he was humming! It was Burt Parks's "Her she comes, Miss America!" But it wasn't funny. I took all of this very seriously!

The next morning at breakfast, my father asked me to excuse myself from the kitchen table and took me into the pantry and closed the door behind us. From his pocket he pulled the previous day's Polaroid picture, of me and my friends, and he began to mimic me, copying my sweeping hand gesture. I was so humiliated. I sank to a new low.

"My son, the fagele," he cried hysterically. "If you can't control your female tendencies, then I will!"

I rarely talked back to my father, and true to form, I remained silent. Funny, it was right before school, too. I never did that well in school. And, come to think of it, I never ran for office again either. And I didn't like being photographed when I was young. I thought I looked like a creep.

So whenever I heard my dad "hum," I would snap to attention and take inventory of every affectation coming from my body.

"Let's see," I would say to myself, "my butt's not sticking out and I'm not swaying my hips. Uh, I can stand and applaud like a man cupping my hands and not just patting them. And I'm not, God forbid, walking like a girl, am I?"

I kept this "humming" story a secret until one day, after a lifetime of therapy, it just popped out of my mouth in my psychiatrist's office. Jim's eyes widened as he sat up to hear the end of the story, and he asked me sarcastically, "Could you see doing that to your sons, Alan?"

With a smile on my face, I shook my head and said, "No, Jim, I couldn't even imagine it."

A PAIR OF FIGURE SKATES

Ezra Litwak

It was winter in Michigan. They froze the playfield and turned it into an ice-skating rink. They had organ music and my dad would sing "and the band played on" and hold my hand. I remember his old Army jacket. He felt like a real man and enjoyed this time he spent with me. It was precious. I don't remember much about my dad in childhood except that he was pretty docile, but when he exploded, it was with an uncontrollable rage. Since I've been sick, that's all changed. He hugs me and kisses and shows his love. I still don't think I know him, but his affection feels so good, like a warm bath.

But back to the ice skates. Our class was going to have a party—this was fifth grade—and after lunch we'd all go skating. When I got home for lunch, I started to panic. First, I got upset about my pants. My mother had bought them. They were blue wool in a houndstooth pattern. I suddenly realized they were all wrong. These weren't the kind of pants the other boys wore. They wore jeans, rough and ready. I felt like a sissy in these pants.

And then the skates, they were black figure skates instead of hockey skates like all the other boys had. I announced I wasn't going to *go*. I was hysterical at how I felt, effeminate, a mama's boy. My parents tried *talking* logic and reason—*their* two favorite things—but it *had* no effect. Mine was a completely emotional response. I ended up hiding on the floor of my closet, threatening to take LSD if they wouldn't leave me alone.

I can't imagine their puzzlement. Their son acts like a hysterical lunatic over a pair of pants and skates.

But I knew why. And I couldn't tell them. I was different from the other boys. I would never be like them, swaggering with their easy macho, flirting with all the girls. I was friends with all the girls but I had no desire to go out with them. It just didn't occur to me. I just knew I was different and it was the wrong kind of different. It was going to cause me trouble as I progressed through school. And it did.

(UNTITLED)

Michael Cedar

I can feel the stranger behind me, his hand reaching for my elbow, as I hurry out of the theater lobby into the brisk San Francisco night air. My father waits outside, under the bright rows of incandescent bulbs that cover the bottom of the marquee. It's 1974, and his hair is still dark, no gray, and the skin is tighter on his face, with no wrinkles but the character lines, and the scar on his nose shines brightly under the stark lights. Behind the reflections in his glasses, I think I see him glance past me and scowl, and I want to run, too terrified to turn around and acknowledge the stranger if he's there, fearing the grip of his hand at any second. I can still smell the pungent stink of urine and smokers' sweat, and I think it's clinging to my ratty coat; and I'm glad that it's cool and windy.

"How was it?" my dad asks. *The Return of Billy Jack* is slated on the marquee above.

"Good," I say, not thinking about the picture at all. I am trying hard to mask my feelings of shame and embarrassment, and I can feel the warmth of blushing on my skin. As we walk up the steep boulevard to the hotel, my legs hurt bad, and my stomach is on fire. Up until now, our visit to San Francisco has been fun and exciting, and Haight-Ashbury Square is bustling with entrepreneurs, wheelers and dealers, bums, and the last remnants of the hippies selling art, drugs, leathers, and watches, and all this amuses my father, but I am lost, still in the theater, with a Coke on my lap, and the stranger in front of me, looking back at me.

"Hey, sailor!" a girl in the back shouts. If anything prompts me to act, that's it. I can't even follow the story on the big screen in front of me, I just keep seeing the stranger, looking at the ten-dollar bill he has placed on his knee, and then, looking back at me. He has a big straight nose, black eyes, and sharp features, and he looks sinister in the dim light of the picture. He is two to three times my age, with light-colored dirty slacks, a wind-breaker, and sneakers. The leg with the ten-dollar bill is crossed over the other in a man's fashion.

I'm only fifteen, but I know what he's doing and I've already entertained similar seedy fantasies, but this is real. I remain paralyzed while he does this, my heart jumping into my chest. When the girl in the back shouts, I realize she's noticed, too, and I must look like a sailor because of the Navy pea-coat I am wearing. This sudden attention shocks me, and I make a decision. I steel myself and stand, and ascend the aisle with shaky legs and adrenaline, my repressive lid jumping up and down with each new puff of steam.

The odor in the men's room is so strong, it makes me queasy. I walk to a urinal, unzip my trousers, and pull it out. The stranger is right behind me, and he does the same, taking the urinal next to mine. I look at him, as he looks at my flaccid penis and then into my eyes, and back again, over and over. I can only look at him, waiting for his move, but he makes none. Finally I say, "Well?" in a shaky voice.

"Well what?" he asks. I don't expect a response like this. I begin to come apart.

"Well, you followed me here . . .," I start to say. Frustration shakes my voice, and he says, "Okay, okay," with a kind of calming. He ushers me into a stall and tells me to stand on the toilet seat. He pulls down my pants and looks at my penis, touching it, before he brings his mouth to it and takes it in. I rest myself on his back, trying to relax, but I can't feel him. I can only feel fear, and confusion, and the splashy-yellow-lit bathroom smells like a wino's liver. I don't know how long this goes on, a half hour or more, when I hear the footsteps of people in the lobby outside. Men suddenly begin coming in, the door squeaking each time, and I have to close the door behind him. He leaves me, and I am left, standing on the toilet, waiting for everyone to leave. Outside the stall, men are having polite conversations, and I can't believe I put myself here. I suddenly feel so alone.

Someone sits down in the stall next to mine, and as people filter out, I can hear the noises he makes. Finally, he is the only one, but I am still afraid to leave, waiting for him to finish. Now I am beyond terror, and I fear being caught the worst of all, while he takes his time. My right leg begins to shake uncontrollably, while the toilet seat I am standing on is not plumb, and it starts to rhythmically hammer the porcelain lip of the toilet bowl. I can sense the awareness of the man in the stall next door, and so I finally fix my trousers and step down onto the floor of the stall and head back to the theater.

The stranger is waiting at one of the concession stands, and I try to avoid him, but he catches up to me in the dark theater and pulls at my sleeve. I ignore him and walk a few rows down, but I am aware of him, sitting behind me, waiting.

I hold it as long as I can, but I realize I'm going to have to take a piss soon. I hurry back to the toilet with its foul odor, and the stranger follows again. This time, he sees my visit is for another reason. He pulls out the ten-dollar bill and holds it out. "I wanted to give you this because you tried," he says. Now, the man who spoke three words and walked out on me speaks with kindness, with directness, like a friend. In my eyes, his sharp features soften and he loses his sinister quality. "No, that's okay," I say. "It's just not for me." He looks at me quizzically, but says nothing. I leave and go back to the theater until it's time to meet my father, and even though it's all over, I still feel scared and ashamed. I feel horrible.

Two days later, we head home over the Golden Gate Bridge. My legs still hurt, and I still have heartburn, and I am afraid that I caught something from the stranger. My parents sense something has been bothering me, but I don't think they have a clue.

My dad sings, "I left my heart in San Francisco," in a shaky-voice imitation, and I laugh, for just a second.

It takes a thousand days to blot out the memory, but when the brush of each day is applied, I finally bury it, so that for years after, I remember my first encounter as another place and time, and it takes more than a tug on the sleeve to make me remember.

CHASTITY

Paul Canning

Tenean Beach 1969 to 1975 was the center of sexual activity for a city of Irish Catholic children and teenagers. It just didn't want to be a family beach. Its sand was brought in from some inferior quarry, its waters lapped the shore with anemic regularity. A band of fourteen-year-olds and their pubescent siblings once organized SOS: Save Our Shores, they demanded, as the feds tested water-pollution levels, a mere scientific gesture to justify the shutdown of that claptrap once and for all.

Dino and Phyllis discovered Tenean Beach together, two planets colliding out of orbit. He was from the Port, a seedy tract of shacks behind the rivulet that flowed past the Seymour Ice Cream factory and the Chris-Craft boatyard. Dino was a water rat who played bass drum in the marching band: half-Italian, lots of acne, and dangerous with sexual possibility. Phyllis was a milky Irish girl with red hair who lived across the street from the rectory compound on Neponset Avenue, the proudest street in the neighborhood. In a parked Impala or Bel Air, they humped with concentration on the blacktop parking lot next to Tenean Beach. Soon Phyllis could no longer become the nun her mother imagined she would be. She stopped carrying the United Nations flag in St. Ann's CYO band competitions and overnight became a fifteen-year-old parent. Dino and Phyllis made a beautiful child, another little Dino, pure and dangerous.

Low tide was best. The stench was downright horrible as wa-

26

ters receded shockingly. Kids sank in mud with dead jellyfish, trying to recover beach glass, smooth fragments of beer and tonic bottles smashed by angry drunks against the rocks.

Tenean Beach was not on any map of Boston. It was a man-made harbor in Dorchester Bay, no longer than two football fields. Still, a fifteen-year-old, breathing heavy after secreting fluids, could gaze out at the lights on the buoys and be trans-fixed, transformed at this land's end. It was the only known neighborhood escape route. You could swim out among the blinking lights and disappear, becoming a fast legend.

The north one hundred yards was a cove formed by the Southeast Expressway and a landfill of gull waste. This was the most private stretch of the grainy shore. Above the cove, a bath-house divided the women from the men inside. A line of showers facing the beach were divided also, but you could cross over as needed outside. I lost my virginity with a girl here at thirteen. She was the smartest girl, I just one studious boy, in Sister Ursul-ina's eighth-grade class. She was adopted. We laughed that whole bright summer between grammar and high schools. We hung with Arlene (who lived in the Port—our gateway to pot and speed) and Jimmy (the boy I lost my virginity to a few years earlier). The smartest girl and I fucked against the chipped yel-low tile of the Tenean Beach bathhouse. It was our only summer between Catholic grammar and Catholic high school. I left for coed Cathedral, she for all-girl Mount Saint Joseph Academy. At fourteen, the smartest girl got pregnant by her next boyfriend, dropped out, gave birth to another girl who would be adopted. Her mother made her give her up.

The story of the smartest girl and her lost baby fell into mem-ory except when I'd see her strange younger sister, also adopted, at the bus barn at Fields Corner Station. She'd give quick bits of information, none true. The smartest girl got a great job or was graduating from a distant high school for gifted students or was out of state somewhere. The smartest girl was a dark girl, the first one to have to shave her short, muscular legs. She had pink nipples at Tenean Beach, under the stiff training bra that she'd outgrown, leaning against the chipped tile wall of the bathhouse.

On the other side of the wall was a men's filthy bathroom where skinny, fat, and muscular boys, or little boys with hairy dads, removed their wet, sandy bathing suits and paraded or hid their genitals—no doors on the stalls, always a dump in the toilet, the floor wet with urine or high-tide seawater. I'd catch a glimpse of all those dicks and asses furtively and get so excited my balls would shrivel. I would hide my genitals and make sure I didn't arouse suspicion in the dark, smelly men's room of Tenean Beach. I'd lurk in a cold shower outside afterward, longing for something.

Sitting in the dirty sand at Tenean Beach we'd play 500 rummy and smoke menthol cigarettes, drink Kool-Aid out of a thermos, throw girls in the water, especially ones we'd be sure were wearing falsies, hoping rubber breasts would pop out of their bikini tops, floating to the surface for the whole crowded beach to howl over. We'd swim out to the Chris-Craft fence and the aging piers. My friend Eddie jumped off the tallest point at low tide and broke his neck. He was short but very athletic for his age, played hockey, drank tall beers. We'd have sex in the shed behind his house on Arbroth Street in our sleeping bags. I'd kiss his bum in the pink bathroom of our Houghton Street house after my mother went to work on summer nights. Eddie's mother died and he got fat and became an electrician.

Jimmy and I would masturbate elaborately with his sister's panty hose, or more simply, underneath the porch. His grandfather caught us once. We pretended we were just smoking cigarettes. After this interlude, Jimmy taught me to hunt pigeons and squirrels with a bow and arrow on the nameless street between his house and the Garvey Trucking Company. We'd throw bricks through the windshields of junked trucks and run away screaming. Our smoking and vandalism was like sex at ages eight, nine, and ten. Jimmy became a fisherman after high school I heard. I searched for him at age twenty but he was out to sea.

Back to the beach. Some boys and girls would jump off the roof of Seymour Ice Cream into a shallow lagoon. The Seymour management put nails on the tar roof to discourage this, but the kids just wore sneakers, adapting like starfish missing a point. I met Paula on my way home from band practice. She went to Girls' Latin, was the fourth of six Polish sisters, most plump and blond. She had thick Pantene hair, broad shoulders, and large breasts that she covered at Tenean Beach with a homemade bathing suit cut from a Simplicity Pattern. Blue and orange, I think. We baby-sat together and fell in love. We bunny-fucked in the cellar TV room of her family's three-decker. She left puddles on the floor. She never got pregnant either. I must have been sterile. We loved Tenean Beach and tans and transistor radios and cards and sandwiches and alliterations like "spikes to spin on." We'd laugh about prim high school teachers and broke up first year of college. She went to all-girl Emmanuel and had a lesbian roommate. I went to theater school and came out grudgingly after a nervous breakdown a few years later. Paula married a wife-beater and evaporated like mist over moonlit Tenean waters. To my knowledge we have no children.

MAIN STREET

Dave Knight

All we did was have sex. I worked in a bar. It was my best semester. *Semester* I say because quarters had just changed to semesters. We had to pay twice a year instead of three times a year.

I didn't make any money at the bar. I drank for free. I guess you can consider that a living. My duty was to walk from table to table to pick up empties. I avoided touching the mouthpieces of bottles where I pictured lips still hanging on to and sucking, stuck to as if frozen. The table hopping, incessant, included some dialogue with patrons, identical looking. They looked for the same things. I said to them, "Hi . . . we're having an after-hours party at forty-nine Ridge Street." That was my house.

I was five foot eight inches back then in cowboy boots, dressed in a navy blue polo shirt with the monogram MAIN STREET PUB on the left chest, tucked into jeans. I wandered, never sure of what I wanted except for the next beer.

It was this contemplation I wandered in under the disco lights, full-fledged regret walking past the bartender John, though overall I was happier than ever. I had spent a summer in Colorado. It was fall at home. I felt reattached to the planet. One of the best moods ever, I even said HI to strangers.

So Bold.

When her flannel shirt touched my back, I turned around and said, "Hi," without even thinking about it. I mean, she was a farm girl, but with cow eyes set beautifully in a roundish-frame face. Big curling-iron hair. Sweet, shy, her whole face smiled when she looked back at me.

I am reminded of this little framed plaque Sue gave me, gold with an opening on the top as if I would hang it up. It was countrylike but store-bought needlepoint. It said, "I smile when I think of you!" When I got it, I thought—well, should I say this—"I cum when I think of you." Sue's plaque, if I got her one, would say, "I knock on your bedroom window at night when I think of you." I opened the window at night when Sue knocked.

It was bad, my room. We decided as a house not to have heat on until dire need and frost inside the windows absolutely necessitated it. I kept cozy with lots of blankets Mom bought me, and Sue. It was warm when we did it. Sometimes we started in an old-fashioned bathtub brimming with hot water in the bathroom next door. Then we rolled across the floor to the bed and under the blankets without drying off.

When I made it to a morning class now and then, my professor would say, "You're in this class?" Sue was good about getting out of bed in the morning when she had to get somewhere. I wasn't. Over the years I've forgotten how good that felt.

What usually happens when I meet and fall head over heels in love with a woman is she says, "I have a boyfriend." This happened with Sue, too. His name wasn't anything like Jim-Bob, but he did come from a farm town called Bucyrus, OH. They planned to get married after her graduation. That's when our relationship turned to sex only. Sex and beer. Well, sex, beer, and the Main Street Pub.

That was my last semester of school. I moved to Florida. I never talked to Sue again. I don't even know her name. I hope she isn't dying now.

Is John, the bartender, still alive? We had sex before and I regretted it. I guess I am thinking about this now because I am driving through town, barely five foot seven inches in tennis shoes, visiting from L.A. My old house is smaller than I remember it. So are the blocks leading to Main Street. Only the leaf piles look bigger. I had heard a few years ago that the drinking age went up to twenty-one and Main Street lost its clientele. I can't peek in the windows to see what the building is used for. I wonder if the bathroom John surprised me in by walking into is serving a different purpose now. Is it smaller than I remember? Is John smaller than I remember? All we did was have sex. I worked in a bar. It was the best semester ever.

MY DAY IN ABANOZ

Panos Christi

I check the equipment. It's working perfectly well, in full power. I'm meeting Taki at six-thirty at this coffee shop. Well, it's in Istanbul and it sells mostly milk products, pudding desserts, etc., so it should be called a milk shop rather. I've come a half hour early, because I wanted to eat two *ekmek kadayif*—a Turkish dessert saturated in syrup and served with thick crème fraîche. It is said to be a very potent aphrodisiac. So I had two, and then checked the equipment. Perfect.

Taki is taking me to Abanoz today. He has been trying to convince me for a long time. Abanoz, which means "ebony" in Turkish, is the red-light district of Istanbul, stretching four blocks on a street close to the center of the city. All entrances are blocked, and the two main entrances at each end are guarded by gendarmes, who check IDs to see that only people eighteen and over get in. Taki and I are both sixteen, and there is no way we can pass through, but Taki said that he knows of a side entrance that we can sneak in. He is doing it all the time, he says, and I know he has been going there regularly for the last ten months. He also has sex with me, but that's kid stuff. The real thing is going to happen for me tonight!!! I will, finally, have sex with a woman. When Taki first started urging me to go there, I was adamant in saying no. I wouldn't even walk near any of the streets leading to Abanoz. Somebody could have seen me and could have gone and told my mother, and then all hell would

33

have broken loose. But Taki kept on urging me and exalting Ayla's beauty. According to him, Ayla, who was a whore at house #34, was the most beautiful woman ever created by God; beautiful long black hair, a chiseled body, cupful of breasts, long legs, and a very tight ass. Well, I knew Ayla by heart by now, after listening to Taki's praises of her, trying to arouse me in having sex with him or after we had done it, explaining to me how different it would be with a woman. That would be the real thing that will make me a grown-up real man. So, after six months of hearing the same sermon over and over, I succumbed and said okay. So, we made a date to meet here at six-thirty. After school I went home and cleaned up, put on other clothes, and told my mom I was going over to Taki's to study.

In the days that preceded, I fantasized about Ayla and my first sexual experience with a woman that would take my virginity. I have already had sex with two old men and Taki for the last three years, but I didn't consider those encounters having taken my virginity because, I thought, my virginity could have been taken only by a woman. So, I fantasized about Ayla. Taki told me, step by step, how to behave, how to undress, how to lie in bed so that I wouldn't look green. I would go through the motions and finally end up in bed naked. She would walk into the room, smile at me, very excited that I was there. She would slowly take her clothes off and I would have the divinity of her naked body, right in front of me, for the first time, all mine. She would float into bed next to me and her hair would caress my face, my nipples. Her exotic perfume would go through my nostrils directly into my blood and increase my already throbbing erection. Her hand would caress my chest and slowly slide down. She would reach my erection, touch it, feel it, hold it, and would say that I was the biggest man she had ever seen in her whole life. She would get very excited and want me to enter her immediately. But I would resist, telling her that we should go slowly, for hours, get lost in our passion. Then I would touch her face softly, close her black eyes, and kiss her eyelids, her upturned nose, her ears, her cheeks, and her lips. I would move my lips farther to her neck, down her shoulders. My hands would be covering her cupful of breast and I would roll her erect nipples between my thumbs and forefingers. My mouth would move down to her stomach and for a while rest on her belly button while one of my hands would start to explore her Venus mound, her pubic hair, part the labia majora, reach to the labia minora and find her clitoris. (By then I had read every sexology book I could put my hands on, so I knew the anatomy of the female and male body inside out.) When I would touch her clitoris, she would shake and would demand that I be inside her now, but I would still hold back and continue brushing her legs with my lips, reaching her toes, and sucking each one red for a long time. By now I would be very excited myself and I would not be able to hold back anymore. I would gently part her legs and lie softly on top of her, being careful not to overwhelm her with my manly weight. I would allow my cock to find her opening on its own intuition and ever so slowly slide inside her. Her vagina would be the most perfect fit for my cock, enveloping it like a glove, squeezing its muscle to cover, feel every little surface of it. I would be inside her all the way and I would feel losing myself in a powerful vacuum that would eventually transport me to eternity. We would roll over all around in bed, always connected by our crotches, lost like leaves in a powerful hurricane, and finally I would explode inside her like a cannon. I would collapse over her, our bodies glued to each other by our sweat, and she would gently caress my hair, my back, my buttocks, asking me if this is heaven, and if it is, could we stay there forever?

At the end of my fantasy Taki walked into the coffee shop or milk shop. I was more than ready to go, wanting now to make my fantasy a reality. I paid my bill and we walked out. This place was fairly close to the Abanoz, so we didn't have to walk far. Taki took me to a side street that I never knew before and led me to an opening in the planked separation, and through a swift movement of our bodies we found ourselves inside Abanoz. My God, I have made it. Hundreds of men were walking up and down the pavements, sometimes stopping in front of a house, climbing a few steps to the front door and taking turns to look inside through a small square opening that was purposely placed on the door. Taki told me they were checking the merchandise. The whores would sit behind the door around a *mangul,* which was a brass container in which they would put burning red wood from the stove, to increase and localize the heat. They would sit around it with their legs open, warming and at the same time exposing the merchandise. And the men would look through the opening and if they saw a woman they liked they would go into the house.

We were afraid to be spotted by the patrolling gendarmes, so we ran directly into house #34 where Ayla was and knocked at the door. A woman opened and let us in. We asked for Ayla and were told that she was upstairs with a customer and were led to the living room, to wait there. The room was furnished in a lean way, with a sofa that had seen a lot of traffic, broken armchairs, and a table and chairs in the middle. The atmosphere was heavy with cheap perfume and cigarette smoke. We sat at the table excited and waiting. A whore of the household, a huge woman of about three hundred pounds, walked in. She was wearing an embroidered vest over her naked breasts and a skirt. Her breasts were huge, almost reaching her belly. She paraded in front of us, shaking her breasts by holding them from their nipples and lifting them up. Watching her made me get hard and I told Taki, who asked me if I wanted to go with her instead of Ayla, because the first time it was critical I go with someone who really excited me. I told him that he was crazy even to think that I would like to go with her. I would be afraid that she might roll over in bed and asphyxiate me beneath her. So, we each gave her ten liras and waited for Ayla.

Finally, she came down and was told by the other woman that we were waiting for her. She came into the living room and told us to go up, one at a time, to the room at the end of the first landing. Now I was scared and got hold of Taki's hand, pulling him with me, saying that he should come up and wait outside the door. Which he did. We climbed the stairs and found the door. Behind it was my paradise. I looked at Taki one more time, took a deep breath, opened the door, walked in, and closed it behind me. The smell of stale sex and burning kerosene oil hit me in the face. The room was semidark, with a black iron bed in one corner. The mattress was covered by a black-and-gray-striped sheet that looked like something out of a prison. There was a dresser with nothing on it, an armchair with a hole in the brown-red faded upholstery, and in the middle of this tiny room a portable gas heater providing the skimpy warmth. The cheap whore-perfume was everywhere in the air as if emanating from the small bulb that hung from a wire in the middle of the ceiling. The place was a disappointment for paradise to take place, but I thought when Ayla would come in, it would change. When I saw her downstairs, she was really the beauty that Taki had described. I started taking my clothes off, and when naked, I lay down on the bed and waited. The door opened and Ayla walked in, her long black hair flowing behind her. She was wearing a black turtleneck sweater and a black skirt. My moment had come, I would finally see my first naked woman. She approached the bed and my eyes open as wide as they can because I don't want to miss anything from her image. I am waiting. But all she does is pull her skirt all the way up to her waist and move next to me. My dream cracks. I want her naked, but cannot say anything. She starts playing with my cock, rubbing it on her vagina. The more she does that the more my cock shrivels and limps. I have absolutely no control over it. She tried all her simple technique on and on to no avail. Finally she said, "Is this your first time?"

"You must be kidding," I answered, summoning every inch of sophistication I could muster.

"Did you masturbate before you came?"

"Why should I masturbate if I was going to pay you ten liras?"

She smiled faintly. "I have an idea. Why don't I do it with your friend, and you watch us. Maybe that will excite you."

The idea seemed interesting so I said Okay, and as she went to fetch Taki, I moved to the armchair where I had laid my clothes.

She came in with him and lay on the bed while Taki was trying to rid himself of his pants and his underwear in a great hurry. When they were off, not bothering to remove anything else, he jumped on top of her and started humping her. The whole thing seemed so ridiculous to me I couldn't stop laughing. Before I could settle into what was happening, he gave a strong thrust and stopped. I knew it was over. He had said he had been with her many times and knew his way around. She gently pushed him over, got out of bed, and left the room.

As we were starting to get dressed, I played back the tape of what I had just seen and felt a small stirring in my cock. I told Taki and he said I should call her in again, which I did. I ran to the bed, lay down, and started to pull on my dick, hoping to continue the initial stirring. She came into the room and to the bed. She lay down again, first pulling her skirt up, and pushing her vagina on my half-erection. The moment her body touched mine I felt this ice-cold flesh, and any blood that had struggled into my penis left in a hurry to return to my warm veins. She had washed herself with ice-cold water. Understanding that nothing could remedy my situation, she said, getting up, "Why don't you come to see me again. I'll make you a professor of sex in six months."

"Fine," I said, trying to retain some sort of dignity while having watched my fantasy shatter and lie in tiny pieces on the dirty carpet. "How about Wednesday at six P.M.?"

"I'll be here," she said, and opened the door.

I started getting dressed and I felt a fear envelop me like a dark, black cloak. She would now go downstairs and tell all the other prostitutes that I was impotent, and when they would see me, they would ridicule me and laugh at me. But there was no way I could hide in this room, and I wasn't going to jump out of the window. So I called upon my flattened courage and walked downstairs, anticipating the whole house to echo with deafening laughter of the whores. But Ayla was a together woman and obviously didn't spill out the secrets of her room, because no one ever looked at us as we crossed the hall, opened the door, and left.

Once at home, I ran immediately to the bathroom and began playing with myself. I just wanted to make sure that this atrocious incident had not damaged me for life, as I had heard it happened. But the equipment was working perfectly well, and there was a smile on my face.

The following Wednesday at 6 P.M. I was knocking on the door of house #34. I was on my way to a classical recital but had decided to stop and see Ayla, as I had promised. I must have looked pretty ridiculous to the woman who opened the door and saw this sixteen-year-old kid, dressed in an evening suit, white starched shirt, tie, white silk ascot, overcoat over the shoulders, grasping his gloves in one hand, holding the doorknob in the other.

I asked for Ayla and was told she was in the living room. I knew this time everything would work fine, and even if it wasn't going to be anything close to my fantasy, I was at least determined to have my first "real" fuck. When I entered the room, Ayla was sitting on the sofa with a plate of spareribs on her lap. She was chewing on a rib; the sauce was running down the sides of her mouth, down her fingers. She was a total contrast to my clean, impeccable freshness, a definite jadedness to my innocence. She looked at me while still chewing on the bone with her teeth. "Oh, I'm sick today," she murmured. "I'm not working."

I wished her well and left before succumbing totally to the nausea that started in my stomach. I left Abanoz never to return again and carry a belief for life that, if I ever paid for sex, I would not be able to get it up.

THE PLUTONIUM STORIES

Bob Doyle

One year, sometime before I was born and when we still lived upwind of all that local nuclear bravado called Hanford, the plant that made the bomb dropped on Nagasaki, the local Jaycees thought it was time to honor the very mushroom cloud our town was so famous for. These junior chamber-of-commerce types decided to make a harmless chemical bomb that, when detonated, would form a mushroom cloud rising above the annual Atomic Days celebration.

Their plan was for the usual—speeches, music, and gathering at the new shopping mall—and for the unusual: the detonation of their chemical imitations, their Thank You, Mr. Atom, for making my carpet shop possible, right in the middle of the Mid-Columbia Symphony Orchestra's rousing version of "Stars and Stripes Forever." These junior chamber types could almost hear the oohs and aahs of the crowd gathered there at the brand-spanking-new Uptown Shopping Center.

Never ones to scrimp on a celebration of such commercial importance as Atomic Days, the Jaycees made sure plenty of chemicals were packed tightly in the red, white, and blue canister made to look like Hanford's own Fat Man bomb.

On the day of the celebration everything was marvelous. On time, atomic time no less. And everything was American. As the orchestra played, the Jaycees detonated their bomb.

The blast was spectacular even if the cloud wasn't. Windows

40

wobbled and groaned and shattered into a million sharp, tinted shards of glass. Windows at Newberry's, JCPenney, Atomic Launderland, Atomic Pets, and even at the National Bank of Commerce shook and spewed out on the sidewalk, and on the cars and the crowd beyond.

The orchestra had stopped playing and the musicians took cover under the bandstand. Nearly everyone else had run for cover, too. The only sounds were startled children crying and the grinding of gears as people got the hell out of there. The cloud, such as it was, drifted over all this and out toward the river.

The following year the Jaycees replaced the Mushroom Cloud with a Kiddies Parade.

∽

I was told a little radiation was good for me. Not those golden rays from the sun, but those from that blue, glowing plutonium I watched from my bridge crane on yet another graveyard shift were good for me. The stuff you can't see or taste or smell that shoots through you at any time, at random, in one side, dashes through your cells, jangles that DNA (or is it RNA?), and flies out the other side faster than it takes to bite, chew, and swallow a mouthful of bologna sandwich.

They, and when I say "they" I mean the epitome of the word *they,* the federal government, brought in one of their scientists. Well, that is what they called him. They invited us all in to their richly carpeted lecture hall to be told by their scientist, simply, that radiation is a cure for the common cold. He said radiation will put zest back in your sex life. Then they took their scientist away.

I had my doubts, particularly about the last part. I never felt horny after eight hours hanging on a bridge crane over a basin filled with spent fuel rods—blue-glowing plutonium radiation blasting its way up through thirty feet of cold, contaminated water, blasting through my rubber shoes, my canvas booties, my cotton coveralls, my skin, my bone marrow, my balls. No, the last thing I ever felt after eight hours of red-hot exposure was horny, but maybe it was the wrong kind of radiation or maybe it doesn't work on queers.

One thing radiation wasn't good for was treating acne. They didn't tell us then, there in the lecture hall, even though they knew it and had known it for many years, but we found out by digging in their trash bins that radiation was not a treatment for acne. An operator—he must have worked at the separations plants—managed to steal some plutonium from work. Why it didn't kill him and how he did it weren't explained in the report. It seems this worker figured that a little exposure to plutonium would clear up his daughter's acne. Word got around the neighborhood and several neighbor kids came over for a radiation treatment. Her acne didn't go away. I think she must have been hospitalized at some government facility in Tennessee. Oakridge most likely, her face disfigured with radiation burns and skin cancer. No one knows what happened to the operator or the rest of his family or even if the government got the plutonium back.

When I was a kid growing up downriver from the Hanford plants, I remember reading all the cow-mutilation stories in the local newspaper. Some said it was the Communists or aliens from outer space. In our town it wasn't the aliens who cut up cattle, it was the Atomic Energy Commission. The AEC would go out in the evenings to dairies downwind and downriver of Hanford and check the thyroid gland of the milk cows. If they found a "hot" cow, they killed it and took the thyroid gland for testing. I don't know what they did with the rest of the cow. I do know that they didn't destroy the milk. It was sold to towns downriver and downwind from Hanford. Calcium is important to growing children.

At first they paid the dairymen for the cows they killed, but that made the dairymen suspicious. The dairymen wanted to know what was wrong with their cattle. Was the problem caused by Hanford? The public began to get suspicious. For a while the AEC just showed up at a diary farm, impounded the herd, slaughtered some of the cows, and took off with the carcasses.

That caused even more of a scene. Eventually they just stopped checking. No one—well, no one but the Atomic Energy Commission—was ever told the results of their tests.

We were told by the Atomic Energy Commission to use iodized salt. They said we didn't have enough seafood in our diets. The real reason was the hope that the iodine in the salt would beat the radioactive iodine released from the separations plants at Hanford to our thyroid glands. We didn't know the real reason until after all of the separations plant were shut down.

When I was little, I used to wait for the man from the plant to stop by and leave the mint green canister for my dad. The man from the plant drove a plain truck, a lot like a bread truck, and even wore a hat a lot like a milkman. He always said hello to me. Anyway, my dad had never fought in World War II, so having the man from Hanford stop by with the mint green canister for my father made up for it when my friends and I were swapping stories about our dads and what they did in the war. I could cool the fiercest fight by simply saying, "The man from the plant brought another one of those mint green canisters by our house today."

Once a month that canister would appear on our front porch, and once a month my father provided them with a bottle of urine and a tub of shit. I was told never to touch the canister, but that was asking too much. In the heat of one of my biggest my-dad-is-cooler-than-your-dad fights, I used the mint green canister one time too many. I got double-dared into switching my pee and some dog shit for my dad's samples. For a while the canisters came every week. Eventually they just stopped coming. No one ever said why.

Years later, when I was older and desperate for a job (and oddly, against the wishes of my dad, who had retired from Hanford), I worked at the plant. I went through the security gates just outside Richland, past the guard station, and then twenty miles out to the one reactor still operating at Hanford.

On the graveyard shift, after we packaged a set amount of spent fuel, our radiation monitor, Billy, a man too big for any pair of coveralls, with a glistening crew cut and not a tooth in his head, would bring out the big book of radiation burns. The pictures in the book were a sequence beginning with radiation sickness and ending with an autopsy. He'd usually do this just after, and he would always close with the standard line, the company line: no one in America had ever died from radiation exposure.

Actually two guys in Idaho did die of radiation exposure, but that was due to a fight over a girl. To settle the fight one of the guys allowed the reactor they worked at to go critical, causing a partial meltdown. The incident killed them both. The government didn't count this incident since it was a murder-suicide and not an accident. The pictures of the guys from Idaho weren't in the book.

The pictures that were in the book weren't of Japanese at Hiroshima or Nagasaki. These pictures were of people like us; some looked like soldiers, American soldiers, and most of the people were calm, some even smiling, at least in the early pictures . . .

SHAVING CUT

Paul Canning

Shaving cut
red dot all day
wrote about this once in a teenage journal
when shaving was novelty
dots of days some with little pieces
of toilet paper attached to them to
stop the bleeding
I learned that from my dad
it seemed crass
but he insisted it was ok to
leave the house like that
I wondered how many men at work
or boys at school would have
little red-dotted pieces of toilet paper
stuck on their faces
didn't believe him
I wanted a "skeptic" pencil
it had more dignity
stop the bleeding
and no one would have to know
blood is too intimate
to accentuate on your face
in public when you do
blood draws the gawkers

the lookee-loos
the window-shoppers
there's dignity in that
when we were little
my dad would clean our faces
with his saliva
like a cat cleans his paws
it was so intricate I think now
then it made us shudder and recoil
mothers teach grooming
and suggest when it's time
to use deodorants or Kotex or depilatories
these animal
memories of Dad I don't think I ever saw him shave
but I guess I must have sometime
before Manson's girls shaved their heads
sometime after Delilah
that leaves it wide open
lots of dots of days
in between even now occasionally
days are as insignificant
as dots nothing extraordinary
happens as you imagine it should
days start with shaving
all right—I'm careful to
put my razor away now
so Stan won't share it
and when I cut my face
I use "antiskeptic"
no mixing of spit and blood
or casual dabbing with Kleenex
all my moves more studied
my face
I was a small boy
copying his dad
the bus driver
I would go on long rides

circumventing the boroughs of Boston
we didn't call them that
but that's what they were
Southie was Mom's hometown
she worked at Gillette there
world shaving headquarters during world
war two Dad was on leave met and married the
Gillette factory working girl
Hyde Park Jamaica Plain
these weren't tea-biscuit neighborhoods
but Dad was so worldly
then on his bus
knew his way around everywhere
and when he wiped
my face off with his spit
I felt embarrassed and proud
at the same time
maybe that's where I learned
to share body fluids.

2

JOURNEY

I first met him on the bus to Provo, we talked about needlepoint.
He had a boa constrictor named Vicky . . .

—Cary H.

Sometimes I want to close my eyes and go far away.

—James G.

(FRAGMENT)

Robbie Hilyard

It was the first time I kissed a man in public holding you close on the Pont Neuf bridge. Did we all have that same experience? Some of us ventured under the bridge—that was an education and entertainment for tourists when the Seine tour boats passed with their klieg lights and we were caught in their illumination. Isn't it redundant to say "pont" and "bridge"? Chestnuts, I can't remember your name now and I was thinking of you this morning as I passed the Berber, my importer, my Berber tribesman. The best was in the grounds of the Mosque when you placed your hand in my pants and told me they would cut off our conjoined parts if they found us like that in the sacred precinct. Tea afterwards. Your fierce religion. Food poisoning. Not going to Italy. Your care, your disappearance. Where are you now? The Parisian autumn. Food search. Hanud was your name and love was your game. How you cried when I went away.

With whom do I travel through life?

PIPELINE

Jack Beard

He loved that little airplane, a 1948 Piper J-3 Cub beautifully restored with its original sixty-five-horsepower engine. No electrical system, no lights, radio, or electrical starter. Each time he flew he faced the arduous and dangerous task of hand-starting it by turning the propeller. He would carefully go through the litany: magneto, off; fuel, on; turn the propeller two turns. Magneto, on; fuel, on; throttle set to idle. Then a hard, fast pull on the propeller—followed by a sputter or cough, or, hopefully, the roar of the engine coming to life with a cloud of blue smoke from the cowling and the propeller becoming a whizzing blur. It's a dirty and dangerous way to start an engine, but there's a feeling of accomplishment you don't get by simply pushing a button or turning a key.

The Cub was awkward on the ground; with its long wings to provide lift with so little power, and small wheels set close together, it exaggerated every turn. When he sat at the end of the runway and gave it full throttle, it would rattle and shake and ever so slowly begin to roll down the runway, but after only a few yards, going what seemed much too slow, the vibration would cease and the runway, most of it still ahead of him, would drop away. "She climbs like a homesick angel" was the inevitable comment from pilots who flew it for the first time. Ungainly on the ground, it became limber and graceful in the air. The Cub was very slow, cruising at only seventy miles per hour. He would watch cars below pass him. But what a feeling. Only a few thousand feet above the ground going so slowly he experienced things he never could hurtling along at five hundred miles per hour, eight miles up in those big jet buses.

Plane and pilot had found a perfect niche. He was flying pipeline patrol. Three days a week he would follow the oil pipeline from the refineries at El Segundo, across the San Fernando Valley, through the Santa Clarita to the wells and port at Oxnard. He would cruise along looking for the telltale stain that would indicate a leak in the pipe. Cruising over the Santa Clarita Valley, his favorite part of the run, he was thinking about lunch. A few miles back he had flown over the tangerine groves. On calm summer days like this the warming air rose straight up, and the drafty cockpit of the Cub filled with the sweet aroma of the fruit. He was passing over the onion fields now and his eyes smarted and his mouth watered thinking of the taste. He felt a growling in his stomach as he thought of the fat, juicy hamburger he'd have in the coffee shop at Santa Paula Airport when he stopped to refuel.

In the midst of this culinary reverie, the engine quit. No warning, not a sputter or a cough, just silence. It took a few seconds to comprehend the situation. He checked the fuel, both tanks indicating one-quarter full. He switched the selector valve to the right tank, then to the left, back to both. No response. He switched the magneto off, then back on. Nothing. "Okay, stretch your glide," he thought, and pulled back gently on the stick, bringing the speed back to fifty-five. "Now, where to put her down?" He remembered an abandoned training strip built by Moorpark College. It was just over the ridgeline to his left. Could he make it over the ridge? What other choice? Turn now, every second was costing precious altitude.

He went into a gentle bank and his heart beat faster as the mountain loomed closer and seemed to rise up at him. He could see the detail of every bush as the narrow summit passed below, and he was presented with the vista of a mountain valley falling away ahead of him. The valley was shaded from the sun and still filled with morning haze. "Damn, where's that runway?" he thought. He set up an approach for where he thought the runway should be and hoped he was right.

Slowly the runway materialized out of the haze, spectral at first, flirting with his eyes. He wasn't sure if it was really there or if he wanted it to be so badly that his mind created it. It became darker, its edges more clearly defined, and it took on substance. It began to look hard and rough and the reality of it pushed his fear up a level. His palms were sweaty and the seat felt hard as his muscles tightened.

He began to relax. The glide was just right. He would come down right on the threshold, not much to spare, but with only a quarter of a mile to go he knew he'd made it.

He saw the coyote before it saw him. It stood there at the end of the runway devouring a rabbit, casting furtive glances this way and that for any threat to its meal. It would occasionally look straight up where a hawk or a buzzard might fall on him, but he had no reason to look thirty degrees above the horizon, the approach path of the airplane, and consequently, it was only at the last second the coyote became aware. Maybe it was the wind through the control wires or the sound from the windmilling propeller, but suddenly, like a shot, the coyote was heading straight down the runway. His tail was tucked between his legs and his back was hunched as if he were trying to draw his body away from his pursuer even faster than his legs could carry him. His head was slightly cocked, keeping a frightened eye on the great yellow beast descending on him. "Turn little fellow, right or left, just get the hell out of the way," the pilot thought. And turn he did. Probably an instinctive, desperate move to attack the attacker when all seemed lost, he whirled in his tracks.

The airplane floated in at fifty miles per hour. Very slow, but it made for a closure rate that didn't allow the coyote time to fully turn. The right wheel strut struck the coyote with a sickening thud that the pilot felt as much as he heard. The airplane weighed thirteen hundred pounds, the coyote barely thirty, but their meeting affected the paths of each other. The coyote went tumbling toward the side of the runway; the airplane slewed to the right and the right wing dipped. The pilot tried to correct but immediately heard a scraping as the wingtip contacted the ground. He saw the horizon twirl, then the windshield was pointing straight at the runway as the plane cartwheeled, its nose slammed into the ground, and it came to rest on its back.

The first sensation was sound, a metronomic drip-drip-drip that brought him to consciousness. He was aware of an overpowering smell of gasoline and knew he had to get out. Movement felt strange and it took him a moment to realize he was hanging upside down by the shoulder harness. He released the buckle and was immediately sorry. He crashed downward, hitting his head and shoulder on the top of the cockpit. He wriggled out of the broken window, cursing as his feet caught on the inverted instrument panel. Once free of the airplane he got to his feet assessing himself for damage. His head and neck hurt, probably from that hasty exit. He saw blood on his shirt and felt his face and head for injury. His nose throbbed when he touched it. He assumed it was broken, had probably hit the instrument panel on impact. Otherwise he seemed unhurt. He walked a wide arc around the airplane looking at the damage. One wing was broken and lay back against the fuselage, control wires and fuel lines snapped. Fuel dripped from the exposed tube. The propeller had sheared both blades. That would mean an engine rebuild and replacing the mounts. His gaze drifted across the runway to the coyote. It lay twisted and broken also and the pilot felt sad looking at him.

He turned and walked across the blacktop to the tin shack that had served as an operations office. He sat with his back against the wall to await the rescue he knew would come when he didn't arrive on schedule. He thought about the work it would take to get the plane flying again, maybe six months of evenings and weekends and a few thousand dollars' investment. The tough part would be trucking out the wreckage. He sighed, thinking of the task ahead, then smiled. He loved that little airplane.

(FRAGMENT)

Jim Rudolph

I had just dropped off to sleep when I was awakened. The sound came from beyond the cloistered house, from beyond the shuttered window above the dirt street outside. It was music, rudimentary sounds of instruments and voices singing out of key—revelers in friendly competition with the sounds of a flute, drum, and *puerco,* a gourd that vibrated in a grunt when a stick was passed through the tight leather cover. The grunting, drumming, whistling and singing voices approached until they were beneath the window of my bedroom. Between the cracks of the shutters, the light of the full moon shone, the only light in La Jagua, a tiny village I called the town without names: no street names, no store names, no name sign pointed from the main road down the trail toward the village sitting above the Río Magdalena in south Colombia.

I had wanted a good night's sleep. The next day a driver would take us to Melgar, eight hours away, to the *finca,* a family ranch near Sante Fe de Bogotá. We had said good-bye to the family friends with whom we had become acquainted, to the Batemans, the Nicholses, and all the other third- and fourth-generation Colombians who still recalled the Welsh background of their immigrant forefathers.

Disconcerted and groggy, I turned on the hard mattress, a heavy cotton bag stuffed tight with straw. The frame for the mosquito netting gave form to the gossamer sheets that protected me from insect bites. Somehow, as always seemed to happen, a mosquito had found its way around the netting and buzzed me time and time again, threatening to land on my naked, sweating body.

I surrendered to the annoyances of the noise that seemed to be rhythmically rapping against the shutters. Carefully, so as to not tear it, I slipped beneath the netting and into my slippers. In the smoky darkness, I put my hand on my travel robe, drew it onto my arms and shoulders, and went toward the light entering under the shutters.

As I eased up the ancient latch and pulled open the enclosures, the noise flooded into the room, as if riding upon the bright moonlight, filling the room with life. I looked over the adobe sill and down into the street. My astonished eyes met with scores of other eyes looking up from the faces of villagers, staring at me in anticipation. With even greater vigor, the voices sang, surrounding the house and me in sound and joy.

The whole village—children, grandparents, fishermen, housewives, and even the ninety-year-old street cleaner—stood below with faces uplifted and mouths moving in unison as they sang Spanish love songs. Suddenly I realized what was happening. It was the first time. I was shocked to find myself being serenaded. They were singing a song to ask me to return. I was honored by the most romantic of moments, an all too infrequent moment of unreserved public adulation . . .

THE RIVER

Jack Beard

I watched them emerge from the jungle. They moved slowly, silently, single file. One or another would occasionally stop, listen, scan the areas with his eyes, then resume his slow, careful pace. Predators! I felt a chill that birds must feel when they see a cat stalking. I felt small and helpless lying there. The wound on my back throbbed. I was feverish. I knew the wound was infected and these guys could save me, but I was afraid to show myself. I had been trying to stay hidden for several days, since I crawled out of the river. I walked when I could, a little each day, but any movement that caught my eye or the slightest sound would send me to the ground hiding in the leaves for hours, shivering and sweating.

They came toward me but didn't see me. They wore ripped and tattered tiger-stripe battle dress. With the dirt and grease on their faces they were well camouflaged. They seemed part of the jungle, and as they moved through the leaves and shadows and splashes of sunlight, they would appear and disappear as if they possessed magic. I watched them silently gesture to each other, subtle hand signals, slight nods of the head, and I remembered how my father and I had done the same thing when we were deer hunting. I remember once a large doe approached me; I sat perfectly still, thrilled that I was able to fool this wild animal. The deer came within three feet of me when it caught my scent, snorted, and stopped. It was beautiful, the shiny black leather of her nose, the dark liquid eyes, large ears swiveling and trying to get a sound fix. She was big and powerful and I noticed how sharp her hooves looked. I was afraid she might charge when she realized I was there, so I thumbed back the hammer on the Winchester in my lap, ready to shoot if necessary. The metallic click of the hammer sent the deer bounding away from me in six-foot leaps.

Another wave of pain went through my back and it was all I could do to stay still and silent.

I had been manning the forward fifty on a PBR: a Browning .50-caliber machine gun mounted on the river patrol boat. We were working the lower Mekong, traffic cops really, stopping barges and sampans, boarding and searching for war materials or insurgents. It was a joke. Charley was too smart to send shit out in the open, and how could you tell an "insurgent" from a gook farmer or fisherman? It was hot out there on the deck: the same heat I had felt as I stepped off the chartered Pan Am when I arrived at Tan Son Nhut air base. It slapped you in the face. It choked you. It was unrelenting, even at night and in the rain it was hot.

As the bow dipped and cut through waves on the river, some fine spray would come over the deck. It gave the impression of cooling, but it was brief and didn't really help. Spook was whining at the skipper to move away from the bank and back toward the center of the river. His name was Kessler, but we called him Spook because he was always worried about something, spooked. Peterson, listening from the stern, let out a hoot of laughter and in a show of bravado dropped his pants and mooned the shore. The chief told them to "knock it off," keep their mouths shut and their eyes open. I stifled my laughter, fished a cigarette from my shirt pocket, and had just passed a stretch of jungle on the close bank. It streaked at us, five feet above the water, paying out a smoke trail like a white string unwinding behind it. I swung the fifty toward that point on the bank. Already there were muzzle flashes in the leaves and the chatter of AK-47s on full auto.

I remember a huge shove and a pressure in my ears. I couldn't get the water out of my mouth. I could taste mud and I didn't know which way was up. When I finally got my head above the brown water, the firefight was going strong; AKs chattered, M16s answered in a staccato rattle, one of the fifties opened up with its deep booming. A line of tracers arced across the river like a stream of liquid fire; where it struck, it tore ragged holes in the vegetation and left great splashes on the mud bank. Around the boat the water churned white from a hail of bullets missing their mark. The boat was moving away from me, toward the opposite shore. There was a blackened hole on the bridge directly behind where I had been. The wood hull was burning. I tried to raise my arms to wave to the boat, but cramped with a searing pain in my back. I had to force myself to relax just to take a breath. I drifted with the current, glad to be moving away from the firefight, then I saw Peterson on the stern, pointing at me and shouting to the skipper. I felt relief. I knew they'd swing around, once out of range, and pick me up downstream. Then the boat exploded! One moment my rescue, my buddies, my crew, than a huge orange flash as a hundred gallons of diesel fuel ignited and a *ka rumph* that reverberated across the water. Debris rained down. Then just a big ball of black, oily smoke clung to the water. It drifted downstream with me, my personal black cloud. I let myself drift for over an hour, wanting to be well clear of the ambush site before I climbed ashore.

As the soldiers drew closer, I noticed how laden they were. Each guy carried a backpack and had cloth bandoliers slung over each shoulder, heavy with rifle magazines. They had frags hung all over them. A few carried claymores. One guy carried the radio, its antennae bent in an L and swiveling above his head as he walked. As they filed past, a low moan escaped me. The two closest to me froze. When I rolled my eyes and looked up at them, they were pointing their weapons at me. I stared up at them still mute. They stared at me. The others in the squad had stopped, too. Some stood, some squatted. Weapons pointed in different directions, covering all sides. A sergeant approached the man closest to me and softly muttered, "What's ya got, Murph?" Murph, not averting his gaze or his weapon, answered,

"One of ours. He's alive." The sergeant squatted down, looked me over, and asked me if I could stand. When I spoke, my voice didn't sound like me, I hadn't used it in so long. I said I could stand, but when I tried, I couldn't. A couple guys helped me to my feet and supported me. They stank! Not just sweat and jungle rot but something really fetid, putrid like death. Then I saw the scalps on their flak jackets and the ears they had collected on the dog-tag chains around their necks. I recognized who they were: LRRPs, (lurps) long-range recon patrol. These guys were fucking crazy. They went into the boonies for several weeks at a time, carrying everything they needed, freeze-dried rations and ammunition, about sixty pounds on each guy. They staged ambushes and kept track of enemy movement and troop strength. Stealth was everything. But for all the ordnance they carried, they seldom returned to base with ammunition. They all had hollow cheeks and a vacant look in their eyes we called the thousand-yard stare. One guy checked the wound on my back, dressed it, bandaged it, and gave me a shot of morphine. I protested about the morphine, saying I didn't need it. But he gave it anyway, without comment. I asked him for a drink. He pulled a canteen from his belt and handed it to me. It tasted of iodine from the Halizone tablets, but I didn't care and drank half the quart without taking a breath. I asked him if he had a cigarette. He looked at me without expression and said, "We don't smoke in the bush. Charley can smell it." He took his canteen back and walked away.

The sergeant and a couple of guys were arguing about what to do with me. They wanted to hump me back to the river and radio for another PBR to pick me up. They didn't want to call in a Medevac chopper and give way their presence. The argument was settled when they radioed their base and were told to meet the helicopter in two hours at a clearing one klick north that would serve as a landing zone. The sergeant called them together and told them they were all going to pile into the slick when it landed, whether the pilot liked it or not. Their position was compromised and they were scrubbing the mission. There was grumbling on the walk to the LZ. When I stumbled, weak and loaded from the morphine, they gave me black looks, pissed that I wasn't as quiet as they were and that I was the cause of their mission being called off. In the chopper they continued to glare at me and talk about me as if I weren't there. A few started playing a game. They'd pull the pin on a frag, let the spoon fly off, then toss it, underhand like an apple, to the guy by the door. He'd swat it out the door, open palmed, like a tennis racket. A second or two later the thump of the grenade exploding could be heard over the rotor chop. It scared the shit out of me watching this. The pilot and medic looked pissed but no one said anything, knowing they would just do something more dangerous. I closed my eyes and let the morphine take me.

The rest was just brief excursions into consciousness: the field hospital with all its commotion, the real hospital in Yakuska, Japan, being prepped for the operating room. On a Military Air Transport plane crossing the Pacific, I woke with the buzz of jet engines in my ears. A pretty young nurse was sitting beside my stretcher. Her starched uniform was pure white. Her skin and hair were immaculate. At first I thought she was an angel. "Hi," she said. "How are you feeling?" I looked into her clear eyes and began to weep. I cried, unashamed, right in front of her. I realized I was going home.

MY BOY BILL

Frank Wang

Survival training in the jungles of Luzon had left me hard. The fires of survival on the most primitive level had changed me. Going in, I was soft, malleable, trusting. Coming out, I was firm, hard, and obdurate. I had been shaped.

I did not know this, that day in Sasebo. I was only grateful to be out of the mud and back into the cleanliness of my sick bay aboard ship. When Lieutenant Bill, as I used to call him in our postcoital cuddle, and I first met, I was struck by his fastidiousness and the fresh, unspoiled complexion of a newly graduated, recently commissioned officer. His face, so sharply planed and handsome, threw the light from the porthole into his eyes, brown, softly luminous. His voice was soft and the words falling out had been gently caressed. I was entranced. As he turned and left, he exposed his slender body tapering down into the most agreeable curves of buttocks, inviting and promising delights only slightly hidden by tautly stretched summer whites.

Our evening's scheduled conference of major brass, Washington heavyweights, Bill and me, was both frightening and fascinating. My lust for the unknown overruled my fright of being the bottom rung in the hierarchy of firepower. Fear left me feeling small.

That meeting took me to Saigon. Our ship sailed from Sasebo to the Gulf of Tonkin. There, I spent thirty-two days, and as my ship sailed for the Philippines, I was choppered to the Mekong.

Twenty frantic days of work-filled hours, sometimes long into the night, threw Bill and me into intimate proximity as we developed policies and procedures to handle intentionally inflicted death. I never questioned the morality of what I was doing. It was my job. We were consciously plotting to break the Fourth Commandment of God. We were obeying the commandments of those holding political power and bloodlust.

We could only express our love in our private times together at Nadine's, a fine French restaurant, elegant setting, great wines, and assignation rooms for rent upstairs. They could be had by the hour, by night, by week, or by month. There at the end, we had just paid for another month, four days before Lieutenant Bill was killed. One of the most difficult days of my life was the day I bagged up his body parts to be sent home and I went to Nadine's alone. Alone, I climbed the stairs entering the room that reeked of Bill and me. Alone. I breathed deeply of the essence of sexual effluence that marked our love. I let no one else enter. Maids forbidden to clean. For twenty-six nights I returned. Alone. Each evening upon arriving, I would call for room service; eating our favorite foods, drinking our favorite wines, and smoking our opium-laced Marlboros between pipes of Soi Eighteen. And each night I relived those moments when we explored each other.

I remembered the way the lamplight would give his errant eyebrows a luminous, lightly oiled shine. Lust-slaked perspiration lubricated our bodies as we lay encoiled, helplessly laughing as we slid down from our orgasmic high. At last we grew conscious of faint breezes stirring the mosquito netting shrouding our life bower as whiffs of jasmine and kerosene brought us back to earth.

> *Of what use is recounting each moment?*
> *Quickly the flowers faded*
> *Quickly the dust grew thick*
> *Slowly the lamplight lowered*
> *As each night the fuel was sucked out by the wick.*

On the twenty-fifth night of my vigil, after hours of biting clouds and many dragons chased, my mind, so heavily drugged, opened up to the day I could never erase.

It was just another day. I had overslept. Too late for breakfast. A quick cup of coffee, a cigarette or three, I grabbed my med kit and ran to the wharf for the duckshoot gallery's galley boats. The usual duty roster had brought the five of us together: Mike, the engineer below, Lieutenant Bill at the con, Jeff on bow gun, Paul on the stern. Myself disheveled, my med kit unlatched, a grin of joy-filled satisfaction thrown at Bill's smiling eyes as we cast off heading up the Mekong. We all chattered amiably, teasing and cursing each other's foibles as we cruised away from the base. I dropped my med kit to the deck and all the morphine slap-shots spilled out. I had not latched it shut, unlike my usual neat habits. Bill laughed aloud as he knew the source of my distraction. Grinning back sheepishly, I dropped to my knees and began gathering up my gear. As I turned to make a witty retort to Bill's all-knowing laughter, the sounds of machine guns chattering . . . shattered the morning. Time slowed. At one twenty-fourth of a second my ears heard bullets individually smacking into flesh like large, fat raindrops splatting against windowpanes. At one twenty-fourth of a second, frame by frame, the bullets erased Bill's smiling face. Each splat became a vision of blood, bone chips, and brains. Fragments of him covered me like rain. Time stopped. I watched the remnants of that beautiful body crumple, then fall; drained of those living rubies that geysered up from severed arteries . . . where once pulsed love, now . . . pain. I heard a terrible screaming as I crawled to that red, rumpled heap. The screams stopped as I gathered that heap into my lap, pulling his heart to mine. A low moan rose and fell as I rained kisses on still perfect lips while only his left eye remained to stare at the sun. His wet warmth saturated my uniform and warmed my ice-cold flesh. Time and training took over. With dripping hands I grabbed the con, turning hand over hand bringing the boat

about, heading back to base. I noticed the morning's perfect still-
ness broken only by the increasing tempo of chugging from the
engine room below. Mike knew the skirmish without seeing and
up-throttled us back home. Jeff and Paul crouched; silent behind
their gun shields. Eyes and guns sweeping port, starboard, port,
starboard, port, starboard, and I noticed that my heart was beat-
ing to their rhythm. Port, starboard, port, starboard, and I saw
the control wheel red with blood.

Quietly the maid entered our room. Warm, scented water and
small towels covered the tray. She left and returned with coffee
and cigarettes, proffering them with a smile and a nod. Still silent, she picked up my uniform and disappeared. Two cups and
six cigarettes later she returned, shaved and uniformed me and
put me into a cab. It appears that she was performing an accus-
tomed routine.

That night, the twenty-sixth of my vigil, I returned. The lamp
was empty. I threw it out the window. With a single sweep of my
arm I cleared the bureau. Lighting two candles, I tipped them,
watching them bleed hot wax onto the wood. Thrusting their
bases into their own puddles, I righted them, placing a large blue
bowl of cooked rice between. Into the rice I stuck a handful of
burning incense. I added a Lincoln-head penny and a mangosteen, then knelt and said good-bye. Prayers completed, I rose
and picked up the mangosteen. I took the heart-shaped fruit, the
color of oxygen-starved blood, and tore it open with my teeth.
Inside, six creamy segments wept. I crammed all six into my
mouth and bit hard. Sweetness burst out, followed by hard bit-
terness. I chewed flesh and pits, swallowing both. I stepped back
and looked at my reflection. It had not changed. I pinched out
the candles' flames slowly, searching for pain. There was none.

I left, not looking back. I went down to the sidewalk café. Jeff,
Paul, and Mike were waiting for me. As I joined them, picking up
the martini, they toasted me. I returned the toast. This became
our nightly ritual.

Kennedy was shot and a week later I left Saigon. I have never
returned.

(FRAGMENT)

Scott Riklin

Hugo was a hero of the revolution. He drove a motorcycle and hated the government as viscerally as he breathed air.

He was slightly crazy, probably even slightly off, taking chances where none were necessary.

But I'm running ahead of myself. I was in Central America to see— tired of the rhetoric of the left and the rhetoric of the right—to see what revolution was. And wasn't.

Hugo had a lot of rules. He'd given me a helmet and I rode behind him for several hours up to Quiche, the home of his family and the center of revolution. He'd given me a book by Lenin, as if that would settle a point we'd been arguing, which I promptly left behind in a store.

He was furious at me for something—I never learned what—and locked me out of his family's guesthouse as punishment.

But most of all I remember the birthday party. A girl of six who happened to live across from a military base was having a party, to which Hugo and I were invited.

I was under strict orders (from Hugo) not to speak a word, which I misinterpreted as not to speak bad Spanish. Suddenly the girl's mother was hysterically rushing out me and Hugo—the colonel didn't like my answers and she wanted no blood shed at her house.

I almost got shot. I was almost an American casualty of war . . .

CONFRONTATIONS

Darian Walker

It's November 1959, almost the end of a new decade. The past few months have been frightening. The United States Air Force has chosen to release me from my contract of service. My sexuality was the catalyst. Now, this morning I am about to have another life-altering experience. I'm sitting on my bed, surveying my old room, my safe haven for privacy. My art supplies are here, my books, the snapshots of my friends and my car, a 1949 Plymouth convertible. I had preened it until it sparkled. The interior was a two-toned blue that went with the metallic blue exterior. Convertibles weren't the norm in Pennsylvania and I was proud of it.

But then these fleeting thoughts were overshadowed when I glanced at the blue Air Force uniform hanging on the back of the door. Airman second class, that insignia announcing my meager military accomplishments. I had been so proud that day when sixty of us had graduated from Weather Equip Tech school. We received our stripes and our orders. I was elated, my request had been granted and I was off to Japan to serve the remainder of my tenure. Maybe I'd forget some of the follies I'd created.

Love was never a consideration in my sexual antics in those days. Quantity and Style over Quality was my thought for the day. I enjoyed masculine company and had immersed myself in all the nationalities, attitudes, and physical differences available to me. Even the smells were erotic.

Was love ever an issue? No. Larry was just a hunk from Arkansas; his size and Southern mannerisms made me smile. I was an adventurous soul and this poor naive farm boy fascinated me. Who knew he'd become so violent when my interest moved from him to a '58 Corvette? It all came to a head in an explosion in one of the private rooms of the barracks. The barracks held about fifty men, but a military dance was taking place and it was empty that night.

He pummeled me with fists and rhetoric, a jealousy I had never experienced. His screaming brought scores of men including the military police. I was rushed to the hospital and only later found out that Larry had admitted our affair, saying that I had "made him gay." How do you make someone gay? Larry was whisked out of the service, without even a good-bye, and I was left to face the military courts alone. I fought to stay in the military but was subsequently discharged. I was undesirable but not dishonorable.

Last night I arrived home late. I'd been told that my commander had mailed a copy of my trial transcripts to my family, and I knew my father would be devastated. Fearful of running into him, I crept silently to the solace of my old bedroom. The room was in an upheaval. My cherished poster of James Dean had been ripped from the wall. I dreaded the confrontation that would take place in the morning.

Slowly I descend the stairs. The house is surprisingly quiet. The smell of breakfast and coffee almost make me forget that this is not one of the cheerful mornings from my past. My father sits silently at the head of the table, the table we always called the conference table, the place where so many family decisions and crises have been resolved. I am looking at the table, dark and formal with its three long mahogany leaves. I find myself admiring the silver tea service that my parents received for their twenty-fifth anniversary.

My mother busies herself, on guard for the tirade to follow. But there is no screaming. In fact, the encounter is surprisingly civil. All the suspicions he had harbored and my mother knew were now confirmed by the Air Force documents lying open in front of him. How many parents have an official government document proclaiming their son's homosexuality?

Then my father says it. "I have no son." I feel this sinking in my heart. I am being disowned. He orders me to leave the house and have no contact with him. I may correspond with my mother, but he will not want to hear news about me. My mother and I cry then, she for her helplessness, me for the loss of the life I have known.

This is the last face-to-face encounter I will have with my father for years. By 6 P.M. this evening, I will be en route to Los Angeles. I will have $60 in my pocket and a sheaf of addresses, hurriedly collected by my mother, of people to call. She also gives me her love and support. I do not have to request it.

PASSPORTS

Stan Brodsky

The excitement of it was hard to contain. The day I received my first passport, back in January of 1971, marked the culmination of months of planning my great escape from L.A., and the beginning of my upcoming adventure abroad. After going through the necessary steps to find the cheaper fares available to students, I booked a one-way flight to London with another one-way fare to Israel—all of which cost less than $200. I remember taking an ID picture, making sure to pull my long hair back into a ponytail, so that I wouldn't look like too much of a hippie on my passport. I went for my draft physical, already having prepared the groundwork to be dismissed due to homosexuality. I had gone to a draft counselor, who sent me to an Army psychiatrist, who then wrote me a letter declaring my sexual practice a "perversion," as it was labeled then. This supported my choice to "check the box" on the intake forms. After that, all that was left was the matter of having four wisdom teeth pulled and getting inoculated for typhoid fever and malaria . . .

. . . International travel has declined for me since HIV has progressed to AIDS. My passport expires next year. It rests unused in the bottom dresser drawer. Today, *passport* has an entirely new meaning for me. Having an infusion device implanted under my skin, which is sometimes referred to as a "passport," has created an entirely new and foreign form of traveling. My nightly infusions of a life-sustaining nutritional formula, containing vitamins, minerals, proteins, lipids, amino acids, and glucose, reach the most remote cells of my body, providing an absorption that my digestive system has proven less capable of accomplishing on its own. This new "port of embarkation" for a quite different form of adventure—sort of like the movie *Fantastic Voyage*—feeds my body in the same way that traveling abroad always fed my spirit.

I'll probably renew my passport. Maybe, just because I want to believe I'll be able to visit friends and places in Paris or London again. Perhaps I will—before it's really too late. At least I have records as reminders of all the adventures I've enjoyed. Together with my new passport, permitting entry into inner worlds and providing the continuation of the most precious adventure—*life*—these objects are cherished possessions I didn't realize I valued so much—until today.

3

RAPTURE

New Year's Eve, 1973. The samba palace above the mortuary.
(I heard the place collapsed later.) I'm wearing the silver lapis
bracelet you gave me at Christmas. I feel like a star in the jungle.
I miss you so . . .

—James G.

Let's call him Alfario . . .

—William M. Franklin

"You call? You call? See again?" "No," I said.

—Dave Knight

CHRISTOPHER STREET

Ezra Litwak

"Three."

"No, you're being too generous"

"A three out of ten too generous? Where'd you get your standards?"

We're sitting on the stoop of my apartment on Christopher Street. It's a hot, muggy New York night. The kind that has a certain New York City romanticism about it. The night is a parade. A parade of men. We sit at crotch level and rate them. We eat our Häagen-Dazs cones, neither one of us in any sort of physical shape. Going by are men, each more perfect than the next. Muscles in every conceivable place. And some inconceivable ones, too, no doubt. They are all dressed alike, it is a uniform. It says, "Yes, I am."

We're rating them to bring them down. Let's dismiss them. But what if I could be like them. What if I could transform myself by moving pieces of iron up and down, up and down? What if I could transform my little-boy body into that of a man. What if I could wear such tight jeans without enduring internal organ damage. What if I could travel *parks* and look like I knew how great I looked. What's it like to be wanted, to have turned yourself into a fantasy object and know it's working. There'd be lunch dates, dates every Sunday, the bars every night, patio parties that you had to say no to because you were already booked at another patio party. What would it be like to go to the gym and feel like you belonged?

"I hate these guys," I said, "they all look alike."

"But look how they look. *Wouldn't* you want to?"

"It's a club, a clique. It's supposed to keep people out. People less than perfect."

"You'd like it *if* people walked around with pumped-up brains, their IQs pinned to their chest."

"Oh, come on, I'm not that bad."

"You're an intellectual snob. You can't stand being around people who aren't witty or sophisticated or glitteringly bright."

"Okay, okay, I'd trade places for one night. Preferably a Saturday, just to see what it feels like to be part of a group to conform. For once not to feel one always has to be different."

We watch the endless procession. He tries to get back into the spirit of things.

"Four, two, six."

"Six?!"

"We have to be a little less judgmental or we'll just feel depressed at the end of the night. Think of them as statues that are on parade. Why do they have to be reflection of you?"

"That's the problem, they're not."

Two perfect specimens cruise by. One turns back, offers a little smile, then turns away.

"They *knew*."

"Yaah . . . sometimes I really hate myself."

(UNTITLED)

Darian Walker

I t was as if an omen appeared and I knew I must embrace it.
It happened to me one morning when I was hungover and
feeling in the dregs. I stood in front of the mirror and turned on
that awful ceiling light and there she was, this vision: blond hair,
red lips, and voluptuous tits. Her arms were open.

"Welcome to the seventies," she screamed. "Get your act together and roll a joint. We have some partying to do."

The sixties had been just the preparation, opening up my
mind, putting in perspective the rigid thinking and restrictions
of my past. Suddenly I believed that I was "all that" and my social
and private life took a new turn. Slowly, without obvious intent,
I had been gathering a group of friends who would become the
Disco Divas of Studio One.

Psychedelics had a way of making everything right. Preparing
for a night out together was almost as exhilarating as the evening
to follow. We calculated the "Come on time, how long is it before
the drugs take hold?" It was LSD, mescaline, whatever your pleasure.

We had to be at the right parties, the right clubs. We had to
arrive at the optimal moment, not too early, but at that moment
when most of the dancers had begun to develop circles under
their armpits and sweat across their brows. We would be fresh,
our patchouli still pungent, and the little gleaming silver bullets
of amyl dangling suggestively around our necks. Fashion was

abominable but we wore it with a passion. We were a fashion front.

Some of our excursions left lasting memories. I remember our first trip to the Canyon Room. The Canyon Room was a private club in Topanga where beautiful men danced together and the hours went way beyond 2 A.M. Before this place existed, in Los Angeles men had not been allowed to dance together, to touch one another. Gay social life was, how shall I put it, restricted.

That night we dressed to dance. The body was the objective and nothing was left to the imagination. Bell-bottoms flared down and out to completely envelop platform shoes, shoes I could not drive in and had to put on as I lay across the bed; these shoes that were the only fashion statement I ever fell off of. And those pants we wore: tight around the glorious buns of youth, shirts snug and transparent with huge sleeves and lapels.

Six of us were getting ready together. Everyone brought his drugs to my apartment where we were putting it all together for a total effect and stirring in a little attitude for the kickoff. These excursions cemented our relationship as *sisters* and we lived for them. I don't think there was a masculine moment in the group. The friendships were solid. We weren't inhibited by the world around us. We just blocked everything else out until we were forced to deal with it.

We drove to Topanga and arrived in the place of the beautiful men. From the parking lot, we could see the lights filtering through the trees and hear the pounding music that filled us with anticipation. We shared a joint and joined the entrance line. We had arrived at prime time.

When we approached the doorman, the person who screened new arrivals, I was asked to stand to the side. We knew they checked out people's clothes, but what was the matter, I knew I looked fabulous. I was a bit taken aback at being singled out and started to feel a bit anxious being stared at by the other guests.

My friends were admitted but waited with me to make sure all was well. Then I was called aside. The club did not allow blacks, I was informed. I'd have to leave. Talk about bursting a bubble.

God, how we'd prepared for that evening. I'd been the one to plan it. My friends all rallied around me; we decided to split. We didn't think we had another choice then. And who wanted to make the long drive to Studio One? Racism had raised its head in a sneaky manner. On the surface, in the limited avant-garde world of homosexuality, we prided ourselves on our social diversity. But underneath the gaiety, it was festering.

Now, years later, I look through my closet and see that gold-lamé Eisenhower jacket I made and so effectively wore to Bette's "Half Shell" concert. It reminds me of all those evenings including that night in Topanga. Well, I could never let go of the exhilaration that jacket gave me. I wore a black rhinestone shirt beneath it reflecting light on everyone.

Maybe I'll give away a few other things, like the velvet pants I made in the early seventies. I tried them on recently. The mass that once filled them and made them alluring has somehow vanished. Probably best to give them to the blind; the Salvation Army might be offended by them. But it won't be easy.

MEETING BARRY

Ezra Litwak

We met in a bathhouse on Fifteenth Street. We had sex (this was a long time ago). When it was done, there was something I noticed: he was gentle and he didn't seem to move as per the unspoken rules of the bathhouse. He said, "Do you want to get something to drink?" We went down to the juice bar. It was kind of awkward. We were both eager to extend this good feeling. It was so innocent in light of what we'd just done. I felt like a little boy. He asked if I wanted to go to this restaurant that was popular after the baths. We got dressed. It was almost more intimate seeing each other in our bright white Jockey shorts. I was glad he didn't wear boxers. We trudged through the night-time street. I noticed he was carrying a bright green vinyl briefcase. I asked what was in it. He said he sang with a local theater. I thought that was kind of queer. But he had big welcoming eyes. He admired my black cowboy boots, which had been a real liberation for me when I bought them. I sensed he wanted a pair, too, but was still bound by the twenty-four years of his mother saying cowboy boots were bad for your feet. How does she know? Did she used to wear them?

The restaurant was closed. It was Monday night. He invited me to his place. Big moment of decision. He could be a killer, who knows. But this time it was too late. The experience had taken on wings of its own.

We got to his apartment. He had a big Naugahyde couch. Did

80

this guy have a vinyl fetish or what? We started making out on the couch, but I kept sticking to it. He suggested the bed. I started to undress while he put on some wretched Jane Oliver, Helen Schneider, and Liza Minnelli. I was appalled, almost ready to leave, but I liked him so I forgave him. We made love several times and I was very contented. I assumed I'd spend the night. But he told me he had to go to New Jersey very early in the morning. But then he said, can I call you tomorrow? I said yes. I waited the next day by the phone. He called. After five dates he asked me to move in. He was very in love. I told him I thought we should wait. I wasn't as quick to realize my feelings. After a couple times I moved in. We still like each other thirteen years later. He still has borderline taste in music. But I did get him to lose the green vinyl briefcase and the Naugahyde couch.

STAN STORIES

Paul Canning

I.   The Miss Galaxy Pageant of last night

I have not laughed as hard as I did last night (and on into this morning) as I think of Stan describing his idea for a wild intergalactic beauty pageant: "Miss Universe to the nth power, with each contestant representing her planet— delegates, I think they call them. Miss Mercury, red and angry. Miss Venus, touching her multilegged flesh with delicious narcissism. Miss Earth, the girl next door. Miss Mars, no Dunaway here, walking backwards, her moons wobbling shamelessly in front of her. Miss Jupiter, very overweight. Miss Neptune: the rest of the gals smell something very fishy about her during the production numbers. Miss Pluto, a small girl-cyclops, eye heavily mascaraed and shadowed, soft purple hair growing below her waist like a grass shirt. Miss Uranus—can't touch that . . . not safe. Is that nine? Nine planets? Oh, dear, I forgot Miss Saturn, returning this year to capture her crown—a gorgeous ice ring—measurements: 7, 14, 28, 35."

My sides splitting, I butt in, "Yeah, and in the talent portion each contestant would be required to name the planets in order of distance from the sun!"

My joke falls flat, but I'm so grateful for the chance to hear one more Stan Story anyway, every dog man who shot me up with his toxics worth it 'cause they led to him.

II.

If I had not met the red-haired boy in the parking lot a block and a half away from Studio One, on a thick-aired night in L.A. in '88, hadn't been drunk and asking for direction, hadn't restrained myself somehow, or hadn't been restrained by somebody from kissing him dirtily on the mouth, made a quick hit-and-run back to the long-distance runner who never included me on his route when he said he would, hadn't been later held by the light-toast copper arms of a red-haired boy-girl, the fleshy one with eyes too close together and a halo of baldness on his crown (I thought then), hadn't said yes-yes-yes to the dogs and birds and in-laws, hadn't postponed my HIV test for seven more years, waiting until I really knew he wasn't going anywhere near that parking lot again, I would not have lived long enough to make it to here today, would not have had a blue-blocked ride west on the Hollywood Freeway, preventing the searing of my eyes in the wind, hadn't decided that today was the day to write the Stan Story—to take him out of the realm of colorform boyfriend and flesh him out, attempting a truth.

Here I write for only the self, listen to bird-by-bird, bead-by-bead, asking for directions to my revisiting, careful to conceal the closest-to-the-core things like Stan and the guilt I feel for having him—for having made love in a lake in Northwest Arizona in the glare of a family Labor Day weekend, or on a desert mound seventy-five miles from mid-Wilshire with wave-aid one claiming the silences after it turned dark, having somehow been restrained from infecting him with my unknown toxics . . . the red-haired boy-girl Mormon missionary man to everyone, caregiver never care taker, who glances away for a microsecond before every kiss without fail, this is the reason I love him so much, that he won't ever allow a highwayman to leave him crumpled on the road's shoulder, if I had not stopped, glanced away for just one microsecond myself before inflicting my love pattern upon him, if I had forgotten to be intrigued by a Bullhead City story from the seventies, or the adventure in Salt Lake with his sixth trick, if the money thing became too undesirable or the east-west void became the Continental Divide, if the Thrifty-aisle blond that I was seemed too real and exposed that night in the parking lot, or if my disdain for Jell-O or Miracle Whip was just a little harsher, if the Cancer-Scorpio-Leo connection was a little weaker, augmented by different units of latitude and time, if I hadn't been so sure that he was my imaginary childhood play-mate ages three through seven, it was really him! just as I'd crafted him twenty-eight years prior, for Saturn's return, and it returned for me, if the baggage hadn't been AIDS or alcoholism or child abuse or repressive religion or fear of flying and dying, if the plane crashed on my short trip from Logan to LAX, if stars weren't still in my eyes long after they should have gone, if we ate at some less embarrassing restaurant than the French Market on our first date, or if I lived on June instead of Cherokee, or if he waited tables at the Ivy instead of Kate's, if he was the second last of nine children, the athlete instead of the class president, if he still had his garments on underneath the ivory cotton sweater, or was any less a holy man, without the fez on, staring across from me over his halibut, if I discovered he was three inches shorter and it was only those damn gray cowboy boots, if I didn't accept his trickery as he looked down on my shaded face and into my red-rimmed eyes, if I didn't make it to here today be-cause a seven-year-old darted his bicycle in front of my Miata, maybe I'd never write about this Stan/Paul glue, the only glue I ever knew would hold this collage together, holding what was shattered together for a very particular mosaic to be seen by just a handful of souls here, instead of those that think they know us well, I'd never "accentuate the positive," never scream "hooray for Hollywood" without three kamikazes under my belt, if I had never learned that sacrifice was holy, I could never write for forty minutes, giving up my urge for nicotine, bolting away from what was too real or close to the heart or home for me, offering it all up, if I already knew that sacrifice was holy before these lessons, gotten a much stronger lesson in this on-earth stuff not matter-ing, if the red-haired boy decided to be a Thrifty-aisle brunette, or had distorted his body at the sports connection, or had spoken in an octave lower, or had hailed from Idaho instead of Utah, or had needed me more than he seemed to, none of this, this wild write, this pen meeting paper, this rubber meeting road, would have found me.

THE VOICE
(FRAGMENT)

John Mulkeen

CPW and Seventy-seventh Street was the best place in the city to hear the voice. Dan had been in New York three years and never grew tired of it. Never. It was a beautiful spring evening. Six P.M. He had to be on the East Side for a dinner appointment, but thought he would go hear the voice first. It never took him very long. This time he heard it almost immediately.

"In here," he heard. "Come in here."

He walked to the entrance of the park. "In here. Come in here."

Dan loved the voice. He felt at ease, relaxed his tie, and said aloud, "I'm coming." The voice was one of his best friends.

As he walked into the park, he saw joggers go by. People walked their dogs. He smelled the lilacs that were just beginning to bloom.

"In here. Come in here."

He walked quickly across the road inside the park. Into a thicket of trees, fresh with the buds of new leaves. The light was fading, but in this section of the park there was a special glow. A sex glow.

Tonight is the night. He's in there, Dan thought. Under one of those trees, behind one of those rocks, he's in there. Dan glanced at his watch. Six-fifteen. Forty-five minutes to find him.

"In here. Come in here," the voice called. It sounded impatient.

The Rambles was busy tonight. Several other men with relaxed ties strolled around. Dan was careful not to make eye contact with everyone. That would spell disaster. Dan only wanted to find the one the voice belonged to. The voice of the past three years. The voice that loved him and would always be there for him. The one that continued to elude him.

In a clearing, he saw a park bench and decided to sit for a moment to see if the voice would seek him out. Six twenty-five. The light grew dimmer, but Dan was calm, although he hadn't heard the voice for ten minutes.

He's teasing me again. Just like the last time. I always fall for this little game of his. Wait till I get my hands on him.

Dan was fully erect. He adjusted himself and enjoyed the sensation. He was ready. Six thirty-five. Six thirty-seven. Six forty-one. Maybe tonight wasn't the night after all.

From behind the bench, a hand touched Dan's shoulder. Dan tensed slightly. It was an odd feeling. The hand gently grazed his neck below his ear. Without looking back, Dan placed his left hand on top of the stranger's. Their fingers intertwined.

"At last," was what Dan heard. It was the voice.

"Oh my God," was all that Dan could whisper. Tears rolled down his cheeks. "Oh my God. Oh my God."

"What should we do?"

"Do you know how long I've been looking for you?"

"And me you?" asked the voice.

"I want to look at you. I want to pull you close to me and tell you everything."

"But," said the voice.

"But it seems so silly now. I knew tonight would be the night." Dan looked at his watch. "And now I don't know if I'm ready, if I can, if I have the time."

"Go," the voice said, without any trace of anger.

"No, you don't understand," Dan was pleading. "I don't have to go.

I have to stay here and be with you and never turn and look at you and never let go of your hand."

"That's what I want, too."

There was a long pause.

"Are you real?" Dan asked.

"Very real. And you?"

"I think I'm real. I think I have a life outside this place . . ."

SHOW HARD-ON FOR BLOW JOB

Jeff Cohen

I

Show hard-on for blow job. It was scratched into the wall of the toilet stall, three feet from the floor, just above the three-inch-diameter hole. There were notes all over both walls. Another note, written in blue ink on white toilet paper, was passed from one stall to the next through the hole.

II

He was walking along the sidewalk and saw the bicyclist riding his ten-speed. Running shoes, no socks. Strong, athletic legs, gym shorts. No shirt, masculine, muscular chest and arms. The expression on his face: "I want it . . . I need it . . . let's do it!" You know the look.

A few minutes later he saw the bicyclist in the passenger seat of a car, with a lucky driver who had successfully cruised him. Oh, well. He walked home. His heart began to race as he realized that the biker had chosen as his bicycle parking space a tree right in front of his door.

He wrote a note, folded it neatly, and placed it securely onto the handlebars. Then he went into the house, to the window with the best view of the bike, and waited. The note said: "If you want to suck a big dick ring the doorbell directly behind you."

III

I had been in Barcelona only a week, long enough to have discovered and begun frequenting La Morera, a small restaurant on one of those narrow *calles* near Las Ramblas. Ernesto was by far the sexiest waiter, and each time I went there I made sure I sat at one of his tables. He was masculine in that Spanish way: serious expression, erect posture, strong hands, smooth, dark skin, and that face, that look. I wanted him, and each time I made sure he knew it.

In my broken Spanish I wrote a note on a paper napkin asked him what time he finished work and slipped it into his hand as he hurried by. I sat there waiting, feeling my stomach moving toward my mouth. In a short while that felt like forever Ernesto returned to me a slip of smooth white notepaper with his response: *"Trabajo hasta las seis. Nos quedamos en la plaza delante."*

IV

I was the first to board the *autobús* at Plaza Catalunya, its point of origin, and sat in the bank of five seats at the back. He boarded the half-empty bus ten minutes later, just as it was departing, and sat in the same bank of seats as I. Then tension between us was thick, the glances subtle yet direct. The passengers in front of us, boarding and departing at each *parada,* seemed oblivious to us, as we were to them. My hand moved to my crotch just as his hand groped his own. He opened his pants and removed his cock, displaying it in all its glory, erect and firm in the grip of his fist. It was long, thick, and perfectly proportioned.

After a few close calls with passengers directly in front of us, he hid it away. He quickly returned it for my viewing pleasure as soon as I showed him my equally, glorious, erect cock. As my *parada* was approaching, I placed my still-hard cock in my jeans.

I stood up, walked to the *salida,* and waited. We continued returning each other's glances. The bus slowed to a stop. I gestured to him to follow.

V

Top stud. Big Dick. 10x7 uncut. Hot ass. No attitude. Mark. That's what the photo ad he had chosen from the models/escorts section read. He called the number.

"Hey, Mark, your ad's really hot. Tell me about yourself."

"Sure, dude. I'm six feet two inches, two hundred and five pounds, real tight, muscular body, masculine face, and like the ad says, a great cock. What about you?"

He intently described himself, and his attributes, to Mark as if he were the one in the ad. When he knew he had the model turned on, he asked more questions, like: "What do you like to get into?" "What turns you on?" "What's your cock like when it's hard?"

When he was confident it would work, he said, "So, wha'd'ya think about getting together with another hot guy without charging?"

The model paused a moment, then replied, "I don't usually do that, but . . . What the hell, let's go for it."

He gave Mark directions to his house. He dimmed the lights. He stood in the window, half-naked and half-aroused, waiting and watching.

VI

The boy was just thirteen, but he was not a kid. He knew what he wanted, and he thought he knew how to get it. He would lock himself in his bathroom surrounded by a layout of photos of men, all very masculine, in various states of undress. At his side were the Yellow Pages and the telephone. He thought he was safe and nobody would discover his secret.

The boy blended his fantasy with reality as he called gas stations, mechanics, and sometimes X-rated movie houses, anyplace he would be guaranteed of talking to men. Men that sounded like the ones he was looking at in the photos. One time he didn't end up just masturbating. The boy got lucky, he thought.

"La Brea Chevron," answered the deep voice at the other end. The boy began his questioning. He started with, "Is your penis very big?" The man's voice did not give the usual enraged, homophobic response. Instead, without pause, he gave a straightforward answer. The boy aggressively proceeded with his extensive collection of questions, each one answered favorably, from his point of view. When he heard the man's offer, the boy hesitated a moment. Then, he accepted. All he had to do was come on over, and the man would give it to him.

The boy quietly put everything away. He quickly slipped out the back door. He removed his bicycle from the garage. He was on his way.

VII

It was our first night in Istanbul. We had hit the streets thinking we blended in. It wasn't long before a young man appeared at our side, as if to escort us down the street. He was too friendly, and much too forward. It wasn't difficult to figure out he was a hustler, who thought he had found his next two clients.

We walked together for hours, through labyrinthine streets, thick with foot traffic, reminiscent of a scene from *Midnight Express*. Our Turkish escort eventually realized we would not be his next paying customers, but fortunately, at that point, he agreed to grant our wish. We wanted to see a real Turkish gay bar. I began to question our good fortune as we found ourselves winding through narrow, dark, and deserted streets. We stopped at a door, nondescript except for the dimly lit doorbell, in what appeared to be a residential neighborhood.

He rang the bell. The door opened and we went in. First I noticed the two seductively handsome bartenders behind the U-shaped bar. Then my eyes were drawn around the room in complete amazement. I looked into the eyes, the Turkish eyes of each man. I felt their sensuality and an attraction I knew I could not resist. The men were posing against the walls and casually chatting with each other as they charmed us with their glances.

Apparently respectful of their competition, the alluring men waited for our escort to leave before making an approach. At that point my friend Bill reminded me of his recent vow of monogamy to Miguel, his lover waiting in Barcelona. "This is a hell of a time for you to decide to honor that farce!" I said. He called for a taxi and wished me a wild night.

As I watched him go, I felt inside I should be leaving with him. Instead, I turned and looked into the eyes of the man at my side.

VIII

Today is one of those hot, January L.A. Sundays. Where else could I be driving with all the windows down in shorts, no shirt, no place to go, and loving it. Any other day the traffic on Sunset Boulevard would make me crazy, but today feels perfect. I'm heading west down the Strip. Carneys' Hot Dog Train. Bigger-than-life billboards. Body Shop Burlesque. I can't believe it's still there. Damn, I remember when I was ten years old riding in the backseat. I swear my head used to turn 180 degrees as we drove by. Just the same, Body Shop Burlesque, teased my imagination and made me want whatever was considered taboo. I still do.

Stopped at a red light at the intersection of Sunset and La Cienega, I see it all. I thought I had already seen it all, but I'm wrong. In the fifteen seconds stopped at this light the guy in the car next to me has opened his sunroof, opened his shirt, and now he is opening his pants. We're looking at each other, talking that talk with our eyes.

The light is green now and it didn't just change. We forgot all the cars behind us that are waiting to be in a hurry. I know it's me driving because I'm alone, but I'm not watching the road. I'm watching him, and he's watching me.

I pull in front of him at San Vicente and get into the left-turn lane. He follows me. The West Hollywood Post Office parking lot is deserted. That will work.

He pulls in behind me and parks next to me. He just opened his passenger door and is showing me what he wants. I want it, too.

BATHHOUSE

Donald Colby

One night my lover Jamie and I were walking home from Club Paradise. It was snowing. We stopped outside his place and he looked at me; his eyes were wide. We were both high on MDA. All he said was, "You wanna go to the baths?"

I looked at him. He said it softly, but firmly, like he'd given it some thought and might go anyway, whether I wanted to or not. I heard myself say, "Yeah, okay." Then I thought about it. I had never been to the bathhouse before. Never. I'd always thought of it as a sinister place, dirty, like an old Texas whorehouse. But I always passed the place with a sense of wonder, longing almost. In the daylight it looked Cloroxed and clean. And harmless.

We stepped into Jamie's apartment and I watched while he packed his gym bag. I could tell he had done this before—he knew exactly what to take: lube, a cockring, poppers, and an extra cockring for me. We were, after all, going as a couple.

We walked along in silence. The snow was silent, too. We stepped inside and paid; it cost more than I expected and there were papers to sign. It took much too long. I worried that someone from work would drive by and see me standing there in that bright lobby. Inside, we undressed at the lockers. The place looked like a health club except the walls were black. It sounded like a party; disco music pounded through the ceiling. The smell of poppers mixed with mouthwash and sweat. Jamie showed me how to keep track of my locker key by looping the elastic band around my wrist like a bracelet. He demonstrated how to drape the skimpy towel so it wouldn't ride too high and make me look like a dork. He didn't smile during any of this, and his eyes had that look they had when he knew he'd let me down.

We walked upstairs where all the rooms were and I saw Jamie catching glances, cruising. That's when he suggested we separate; we'd split up and find each other later. Somehow I'd assumed we'd stay a couple, but I didn't say anything. He seemed to want this so badly.

I watched him go off with a couple we'd seen at the bar earlier. The three of them went into a small room and closed the door. I walked past that room at least a half dozen times straining to hear what was happening inside, afraid I'd hear Jamie moaning. Then I realized everybody in the place was moaning. I gave up and decided to practice cruising on my own.

I knew how to smile and I knew what kind of guy I liked, so it didn't take too long to rope a man who was big as a bear, blond and furry. And solid. We went to his room. He wrapped his body around me like a huge fist. He talked rough and dirty, when he talked at all, and he ordered me in a coarse whisper to grab hold of my ankles. I hated to admit it, but he was everything I loved about Jamie, only distilled, nameless, exaggerated. Perfect. He went at me forever; at least the drugs made it seem like that. Before we were done pumping in very corner of that room, I was screaming. I wanted Jamie to hear me. I wanted everyone to hear. Something had changed—I had changed—and something horrible had been planted in me. I was already blaming Jamie.

Afterward, this bear held me in his rock arms and I sank into him. I felt him breathe, his stomach rising and falling against my back. "You're great," he said. "Real hot."

"You are, too," I said, thinking I sounded like a porn star. He kissed the top of my head. I kissed his arm, tasting salt, and smiled. We were both slick with sweat. I could feel his cum dripping from inside me, escaping.

He shifted, then said tentatively, "Are you lovers with that guy you came in with?"

It was as if he woke me from a dream. "Yes," I said. "Yeah,

we're lovers." But I didn't know what that meant anymore, or what it was worth.

The bear straightened. "Oh," he said, "Too bad."

"Yeah," I said.

We put our towels back on and took a shower. Then I dressed and sat by the lockers alone, waiting for my lover.

LIST

(FRAGMENT)

Philip Justin Smith

Baths
Needles
Boyfriends
Bill G
Robert MacP
Drag Queen from Des Moines
Born with it
Toilet seat
Lipstick
Sprayed at birth with HIV
My consciousness listened and heard
Wayne S
Omaha
The man who's listed in my phone book as stud—and I meant it
Robert MacP

SECRETS

Jeff Sullivan

"Secrets? You want one of mine?" He looked from face to face with uncertainty, lightly wringing his half-folded hands as he leaned back on the syrup-brown sofa. Most of the group in therapy that morning seemed buoyant, playful; and we all politely stared back while the sunlight splashed in through a large open window, warming the attic and its mismatched furnishings.

"It has to be a secret that you feel guilty about," someone said.

The man on the brown sofa gazed beyond the human circle seated about him. He then bowed his head, his fingers cradling his temples, while he squinted shut his eyes. He remained in this pose while the group grew curious.

"If this is too painful for you, you can always think of another secret," someone else said. He didn't answer, but opened his eyes and gazed at the wall, oblivious to everything. He took a deep breath and planted his foot on the floor as a dead silence descended on the attic. Then, looking down, he said, "I was seventeen. I was a junkie, and one time, while hustling in Chicago, I was offered a lot of drugs to torture someone to death. Back then I had a very serious habit. I was not who I am today; I was capable of anything, and I was desperate. They'd offered me a lot of heroin among other things, so . . . I did it."

All anyone could say was, "Are you serious?" We did not

need an answer. The ex-junkie sat there looking down with red eyes. He started rocking slightly back and forth in acknowledgment. And we saw his tears.

There were questions and answers, and he talked on, sometimes with reluctance. He found it hard to look at anyone. I most recall his hopeless red stare; and as we sat there in the peaceful, sunlit attic, astonished listeners, he sat in the darkest corner of his world, alone, condemned, ripped down the middle by what he believed and what he knew. When he'd finished, there was a moment of serenity before bodies began to move, stretch, and breathe audibly. It was in those peaceful seconds that he looked most alone, the only soul on a train bound for hell. With screams in his ears, blood stench in his nostrils, and death in his red, distant eyes, he sat in his shadows, turning away from where he'd just been.

Later in the afternoon, I was alone with him in his room. The light was now soft; venetian blinds throwing misty stripes on him as he sat on the bed, hunched, as if in front of a campfire; head thrust forward, facing the floor. Only his eyes faced me, gray-blue, with traces of red. They gazed over his glasses, unobstructed. The rest of him, his body, his face, fell into the pit between us on the gray carpet floor.

Earlier, in group therapy, he'd revealed his deepest secret, like throwing an anvil into the middle of the room. I was as shocked as anybody. He had the nature of a lamb.

"I just can't imagine you doing it," I told him.

"You didn't know me back then," he said. "I was a completely different person." He always confided in me. I did not like to judge or hurt anyone needlessly; I tried to listen instead. And I liked him. We talked; I asked him questions about the manner of killing, how it was contrived, who was the victim. Private questions. His answers were as repellent as my questions, but I was morbidly intrigued.

"I started by cutting off his fingers," he said. "It was for a snuff film, so it had to take some time. I would cut off a finger, and he would scream for a while, then wait for me to cut off the next one. He liked it, I could tell. He was really loaded on methamphetamine, and probably other things as well. After he stopped screaming, he would goad me on, and we would do it again. There were other things I had to do; and then he finally died. But that's really what he wanted—to die."

"I thought they only did snuff films in South America," I said.

"Oh, no. They were doing this one in Chicago, USA. Didn't you know the Mob is into snuff films? They've been doing them for years. At first I thought it was a trick when they picked me up. They said, 'We want you to do some porn. We'll give you all the drugs you need, and lots more when you're through.' I didn't know I was going to have to kill anybody until I got there, and the victim was already there, high as a kite and ready to die. Afterwards, I used up all the drugs just trying to forget it, but I never could, and I'll never stop regretting it."

He paused, but I was speechless and could think of nothing to say for comfort. He had my complete attention.

"People like him, the trick I killed, they're not hard to find. Some hustle, some are whores, and they all use lots of drugs. There are people out there who look for people like him . . . and people like I used to be. You wouldn't have liked me back then. You would've been scared of me."

With that he stopped talking, and I did not press him. He looked sad and tired, and I wanted to tell him that somehow he could forgive himself, that he had repented enough, but I felt it would be pointless, and I said nothing. After a long period of quiet, he said, "Can I tell you something?"

"What?" I asked.

"I love you," he said.

"You do?" I asked in amazement.

He smiled sincerely. "You have no idea how hard it was for me to say that," he said.

&

His parents buried him in the corner lot of a freeway cemetery, outside the city of L.A. At his funeral, I stayed a respectful distance from the bereaved family standing around his white coffin and the hole in the ground. The reverend delivered a sermon about the wayward son finally coming at last to walk the last few steps of the righteous path.

Afterward, I watched his father, standing over the coffin, staring down at it, saying whatever he had to say over and over in his mind. I felt for his family in their grief, but I could not approach them or shake their hands knowing the part of him that was a disgrace, an aberration in their eyes. For he had confided in me, and I know about the very straight and narrow path from which he'd strayed so far. Most of his life he'd been afraid of that path. Afraid he couldn't walk it, because of one thing. Something which they told him would condemn him to a burning hell: he was gay.

The words *I love you* stayed in my mind, and I knew they would not understand. And I didn't want to share anything at all.

A LETTER

Tony Gramaglia

Dear . . . I'm sorry. I have forgotten your name. My therapist would say I was blocking. My doctor might say dementia. I think I have just forgotten.

I was writing to see if you were still alive. You see, I am dying . . . and I was just wondering if you were still alive.

Okay. It was short and stubby and different. Your name, that is. It was four, maybe five letters long. Italian. I think.

Tori. Tony. Toby. Aah. This is so frustrating. Considering I used to fantasize years later about the sex I had with you. Touching myself. Repeating your name. Calling you into me and then feeling you ooze out. I can't believe I can't remember your name.

Names. Butch. Brad. Bob. No, too common. Not Italian.

Well, anyway, are you alive? I think that our encounter is the source of my dying like this. I'm not writing to blame. I'm not even angry with you. That was 1982 and no one really knew. It was New York City and my town in Ohio did not know this disease yet, and I've always just had this feeling.

Sometimes I feel like I took that tour bus in college from Cincinnati to Manhattan just to meet you so I could die like this. You know. Unfortunate destiny.

Victor. Vince. Vito.

I promise I'm not writing to blame you. You were my first, but certainly not my last. If I'm angry with anyone, it is the county prosecutor of Cincinnati. A notorious man. Remember the obscenity trial regarding Mapplethorpe?

Well, anyway, that man shut down a radio broadcast before I took that trip to New York. He closed down the radio station while a gay man was on the air talking about some new disease and instructing about what he thought might be safe sex. It was really just about condoms. But I never got to hear that broadcast. That news. Because this man said it was obscene. This man stopped this man on the radio from telling us. Telling me. Maybe I could have known before I took that trip. Maybe then things could have turned out differently. Maybe not. But who is this man who thinks he can kill me? He is whom I blame. He is the one who is killing me. Who killed me.

I know we wrote at least twice to each other after that night together. If you are still alive, I would like to see those letters. I would like to remember what I was like when I was first coming out. First having sex with a man.

Okay. It's on the tip of my tongue. Lou. Mario. Bari. Roma. Florence. Oh, God, I'm sorry.

I will never forget seeing you at that piano bar just off Forty-second Street of all places. I was there with a group of college students and a couple of professors. You were standing at the piano. Short and dark with thick black hair, singing "I Feel Pretty." And in the middle of the song we saw each other. I knew at that moment we would meet. What I didn't know was that from that night on I would be dying. I didn't even think about dying when I walked home from your apartment at four in the morning to the cheap hotel I was staying at. I was just thinking that I was really living. Really living for the first time.

All right, I'm not even going to try to remember you name anymore. And I won't apologize again. I hope you understand.

I remember sneaking back out of the hotel that night and coming to you. Coming back to that bar. And you were waiting. I didn't realize it then, but you were so much like my father. Funny, in a way I was making love to my father and it killed me. Talk about Greek tragedy. Even the cigarettes and beer on your breath smelled like him. Tasted like him. The dark beard stubble against my face. Your thick hands. That deep smirk.

When we got to your apartment, after running through that

December drizzle, I didn't for a moment feel unsafe. Thanks for that.

Within moments, my body pushed against the kitchen floor, your dick was inside me. I came right then. You not much later. We exchanged addresses. You wrote directions to get me back to the hotel, and on the way there I remember thinking that a cold December drizzle never felt so warm.

I fantasized about you for years. I remember you went from looking like you to becoming the most handsome man in the world. Funny how your memory works.

Well, not much else to say. Like I said, I was just wondering if you were still alive. I hope you are. I mean, if you want to be. Sometimes I'm not so sure about myself. If I want to be alive, that is.

So I'll end. I guess I could title this letter "Bus Trip to Death" or "Killer Bar" or "Destiny to Disease" or just "I'm Fucked."

Maybe when this is all over, I'll see you later. And you can tell me your name. Until then . . . my best to you.

Tony

4

SOMETHING

This is the season to keep sharp objects away from me.

—*Scott Riklin, line crossed out in his notebook*

. . . I remember a little old lady palm reader once told me back in 1966 that I would experience a complete change in the middle of my life. Holding open the palm of my sixteen-year-old hand, this woman pointed with her finger to my lifeline, which, sure enough, was completely severed in the middle. Even now as I study the wrinkles of my left palm, I can remember her telling me the meaning of this break in the crack of my left hand.

"Your life is going to end here," she said, "and start all over again here."

"What?" I cried out. "My life is going to end where?"

"Right here"—she pointed—"in the middle of your life there is a break. And then your lifeline starts all over again right here." With her index finger she pointed to the beginning of a new

—*Alan Erenberg*

NOTHING

Michael Martin

Once I had discovered it, I could see that all my other endeavors had been just false starts. No longer did I want to drive a cab, be a lawyer like Perry Mason, or a chorus boy. Thoughts of the priesthood, soda-jerking, or playing second base evaporated. I wanted to do nothing.

I was elated with my new choice, but perplexed. How does one train? And if you're training, then you're no longer doing nothing, so you have a problem. I didn't know where to begin, but I talked a good game. The daily dialogue with my mother went along these lines:

She'd say, "Where were you?"

I'd say, "Out."

She'd say, "What were you doing?"

I'd say, "Nothing."

Nothing. How it just rolled off my tongue, how it made me tingle and light-headed.

Soon I learned about freelancing. This freelancing sounded more substantial, but still being noncommittable, and it helped in tight situations. When teachers or other adults asked, "What are you going to do when you grow up?" I had no longer to say "Nothing," which usually drove them crazy and started them into lectures on responsibility and commitment. Now I could just say, "I'm going to freelance." This caught them off guard and it gave me time to escape.

I struggled for a time trying to perfect doing nothing. The distractions of high school were endless: dances, good grades, boys, just showing up at school. But I was fortunate to meet others who possessed the drive, the courage, the fortitude, to do nothing. We began to work on this, but to do it well, you couldn't really work on it. One of the main ingredients was the proper place to do nothing. Front stoops and street corners seemed to work best. It wasn't a seasonal thing either, and your perseverance showed during rainy and cold New York winter nights, especially school nights. If you could get out of the house, avoiding homework, chores, TV, and just meet on the corner and just hang, hang out, you were successful.

Planning ahead or setting goals were pitfalls on the road to doing nothing. You could dabble in these areas, but only if you knew that they wouldn't come to fruition. Then you were safe.

But time was not kind to we doers of nothing. Vietnam, marriage, babies, careers, all broke through and we were scattered. I especially felt lost, for I still wanted to do nothing. Years went by and I found myself living in San Francisco, just another town in a series of towns. The skill in moving was to do it quickly, no investigation as to where you were going, leave most of your stuff and go.

It was there that I met my guru, Gerald. I was once again going from one living situation to another, moving in with three guys I didn't know so I could save rent. That first morning over coffee I asked Gerald, "What do you like to do?" He said, "Nothing." Yes, he said it. "Nothing." No one had ever been that up-front about it; I mean, I was almost a total stranger.

He said, "It's what I do best." I knew I could learn from him. I had met my champion. The word would be revealed to me.

Over the next several years I studied with the master. He stressed it was important to have the right attitude. Even when forced to do something, your attitude must reflect your deep-seated desire to do nothing. *Nonchalant, laid-back, unruffled,* these were adjectives you cultivated as descriptions of yourself. Coffee and cigarettes helped, and when I stopped smoking, I wasn't sure I could do nothing with the same fervor.

A few years after meeting Gerald, I found myself, after another quick getaway, living in Los Angeles. We would visit each other and give support over the phone, but I knew that when I started working out, doing aerobics, and watching my diet, Gerald would begin to worry abut my commitment to doing nothing. He felt I was lost to the doers.

To prove to him and myself that I still had what it took, I spent a week's vacation in Los Angeles doing nothing. When I returned to work, there was a message from Leonard, a friend of Gerald's and one of our roommates in San Francisco. I had been waiting for him to call. Gerald's fiftieth birthday was approaching, and I knew that there would be a celebration. I also knew that Gerald would do nothing to arrange it, but since Leonard was a doer, he'd work out the party details.

I called Leonard.

"When's the party?" I asked.

"I have bad news," he said. "Gerald died yesterday. He went into the hospital last Sunday, seemed to bounce back, but slipped away."

I was stunned.

Leonard continued, "They don't know what he died of, they'll be doing an autopsy this week. The memorial service is on the thirtieth at his apartment."

In the world I live in AIDS is always the villain, but with Gerald none of us knew his HIV status. Plus, it happened so quickly. All the doctors could come up with was that Gerald had died of a massive body infection. What's that? Seems pretty inconclusive to me, a cop-out. Everyone was outraged that the doctors couldn't tell us more. Friends wanted to get to the bottom of this. But I figured dead is dead. And then I thought, how perfect for Gerald. For it seems that Gerald had died of nothing.

I'm jealous of Gerald. It's too late for me. The chance of dying of nothing has passed. I already have something.

NOTES WHILE WAITING

Tony Gramaglia

I am with my friend and he is waiting to get tested for the third time. I am thinking about what it would feel like to just once see the X in the box marked negative. I pray my friend sees it again for the third time.

We sit on a thinly cushioned bench, against the wall with the others. The wall is at least fifteen feet high with a row of narrow windows at the top. They are covered with blinds, slats of aluminum. But they seem useless, as there is no one tall enough to look in past them from the outside. Not even the sun wants to look into this room. They are there, those blinds, because there are windows. Windows that do not even open.

I imagine that I am in a holding cell. Even if I could claw my way up that wall, to the window, I could not escape. He can though, my friend. Escape that is. Negative. He will see that X in the box on the paper marked negative.

There is a double door at the end of the hall. It is marked EXIT. PLEASE USE OTHER DOOR. But I still could not escape. I have never seen that box marked negative. I am really trapped here, in this waiting room.

I look up to the pale blue walls to see if there are any scratch marks, any claw marks from others like me who may have escaped. There are none. I see in the room the others who are waiting to be tested. Today they will be counseled by a man who greets them first by asking, "How are you today?" A question the

Latino boy wearing the high-cropped shorts and white T-shirt would rather not answer. But instead he uneasily responds, "Fine, thank you."

Those people here today will not see that box on the paper marked one way or another for a week. Some may not even come back to find out. They could not bear those fifteen-foot walls again.

There is another man, who I am not sure is not a woman. He goes to the room marked LAB 6. A man greets him at the doorway while pulling on a pair of latex gloves. He will do the actual test. The actual needle stick.

Next to me is a large woman with thin, stringy blond hair. The air in the room is perfectly still, but the paperwork in her hands is shaking as if a thousand tiny breaths are blowing onto it. I want to tell her that it will be okay. That she is brave and smart for being here. But who am I to say? I've had seven years to deal with it.

The couple across from me, a man and a woman in their late twenties, are holding hands. They are Nos. 1603 and 1604. I can see it on their papers. I see two men sitting down farther on the left. They, too, are holding hands. I remember then that it is okay to hold my friend's hand, too. To touch him here. I look him in the eyes and they tell me how he is today. I don't have to ask.

I reach out to take his hand. I wonder if the woman next to me is angry. As if this is our fault, that any of us are in this room to begin with. The video in the next room is blaring safe-sex instructions. How to roll the condom on. How to take it off. It is old news to me. News that came too late.

I look up at the row of windows again. Too high to see out of. I know that there is a sky beyond there. I want to fly up there. Crash through the glass and never come back.

Instead I will walk out the door with my friend. He will have a small cotton ball pushed down with tape on the inside of his arm. We will walk through those double doors marked EXIT. PLEASE USE OTHER DOOR. But I will still be trapped inside that room. Always looking for a way to get out.

MOM AND ME

Jim Rudolph

A few days after Dad's funeral, Mom and I drove to East Eagle Creek. It was early summer. I drove the three-quarter-ton pickup because Dad had never let her drive in the mountains and she wasn't ready to do so.

By afternoon we arrived at the old tailings of a long-defunct gold mine. There the road became a footpath trailing up the steep slopes of pine-forested mountains until the trees became dwarfed and disappeared above treeline. I took the aluminum lawn chairs from the back of the pickup and placed them under a couple of pine trees, trees so young the bark was red instead of the gray of the broad-trunked and ancient pines along the nearby river.

We sat down with a thermos of coffee and cookies, as her Swedish mother had always done when she talked to someone. There Mom told me the events that had occurred on the long night before Dad died. "He said I had taken good care of him, but he never said he loved me," and she cried. In a way, she was scraping clean the open wound.

After that day, I waited two years for her to recover from Dad's death. Then I knew I had to tell her my news. There is never a right time to say some things, and I had to tell Mom before anything worse happened. I went back to my hometown to visit Mom.

It was natural for me to want to take a drive to Eagle Creek—

after all, wasn't it a kind of family sanctuary, where we had hunted and fished and camped throughout all the years we kids had been growing up? For me, the end of the road was a sacred place, a mountain meadow above which towered the granite cathedral spires that topped the Eagle Cap Mountains. Few people went up so far, unless to leave their rigs and trek up to the waterfalls, snowpacks, and unlogged forests along the upper trail.

When we arrived, the crimson Indian paintbrushes, the creamy blue lupine, and wild strawberries were still in bloom. For Mom, this pilgrimage was still just an outing.

As if retracing my footsteps when we had come after Dad died, I pulled the lawn chairs from the back of the pickup. I unfolded them and set them beneath a couple of long-needled pine trees, the same trees under which we had sat two years before. The air was clean. The sound of water moving over boulders in the river played with the breeze moving in the treetops. From the pine-needle carpeting on the forest floor arose the soft odor of rotting vegetation to mingle with the acrid smell of the tree sap pliable from the midday sun. I pulled a string of sap off one of the young trees, rolled it between my fingers into a small amber ball, and held it to my nose.

Had I thought of everything? Was it really necessary to tell her? Had my secret built a wall between us? Was I being fair to give her such news? She was always worried. When she had asked if I was okay, I had told her I was being careful.

Mom walked over to our spot with a thermos of coffee in one hand and a box of cookies in the other hand. The chairs sat at a forty-five-degree angle, positioned so we could easily look at each other—or look away.

Mom put the open box of oatmeal cookies between us. I held the mugs while she poured the coffee. We were quiet. I didn't know how to start. "Mom, I've got to tell you something. I've been lying to you. Six years ago, I found out I have HIV."

"Oh, Jim, no," was all she said before the tears overflowed her old blue eyes and struggled down her soft cheeks crisscrossed with lines that impeded the flow. Tears came to my eyes and I tried to blink them away, tears considered by Hindus to be the only sacred body fluid. But even my tears, the scientists said, contained the virus, though in such small amounts so as not to be contagious. The burning tears stung my eyes. Finally Mom broke the silence. "No matter what happens, I love you."

Then, as though my words could never be untrue, she said, "But you told me you didn't have that virus. Oh, how I prayed you would never get it. How long have you known?"

"Six years," I repeated, and felt the guilt of having violated her trust. "I'm healthy and I take good care of myself."

"But then why did you quit work?"

"The doctor thought the stress of work was making the virus more active." Again I had lied. I didn't tell her about my diminishing memory or periods of disorientation.

"Since I quit work, my immune system has improved," I tried to reassure her. But the damage was done. After that, I wasn't sure she heard much of my explanation. I remembered when I was first told I was HIV-positive—what more do you hear after being run over by a truck, dropped from a plane with no parachute, caught in a riptide and unable to swim back to shore?

The news could not be made pure and clean even at the end of the road along East Eagle Creek. The clouds passed in front of the sun, turning the afternoon cool. We got up. Mom took the thermos and cookies and I folded and took the chairs. "I want to drive," Mom said, and she did.

Behind the steering wheel of the big pickup, Mom didn't look so small. She was a strong woman. If need be, she was capable of picking up an unsplit section of firewood and wrestling it into the back of the pickup. As we drove down the narrow mountain roads, I realized that during the last couple of years the pickup had become hers, not my dad's.

I remember little about the trip down the mountains or the rest of my stay with Mom. I do recall stopping on the lower bridge across the creek. There I photographed the cloud shadows and sunlight as they played across the river channel, forested banks and mountain caps in the background.

Dad died five years ago. Three years ago I told Mom I was HIV-positive. Now Mom is eighty-one and I am forty-eight.

Sometimes she still wants to know about my T-cell counts or the new viral-load tests. Occasionally she sends me a clipping from the *Baker Democrat Herald* about this or that AIDS drug. Mostly we enjoy my visits home by traveling together across Oregon in her pickup, seeing new places for the first time. In October of this year, when I went to Baker for her birthday, Mom and I drove to Eagle Creek to see the fall colors, but we didn't go all the way to the end of the road. Neither of us felt we could spare the time.

WHAT I HAVE

Marc Wagenheim

I've just turned thirty-four and I've got things in my life I never imagined I'd have. I have a doctor of internal medicine and infectious disease, a gastroenterologist, a radiologist, an oncologist-hematologist, a home health-care nurse, a hospital I've spent so much time in that I know which floor and wing to ask for. I have a basket of pills that I keep bedside and take throughout the day that includes medication that costs hundreds of dollars. I have a catheter that is inserted in the right side of my chest through which I infuse a nutritional supplement for nine hours each night. To accompany the catheter and the infusion process, I have a cart full of medical supplies—tubing, syringes, needles, clamps, etc.

I have a Monday-afternoon support group. I have a remarkable creative-writing group that meets on Saturday mornings. If you haven't guessed by now, I have AIDS.

I have people who love me and care for me and support me. I have a special person who'll hold me at night sometimes when my temperature soars and the chills invade my body. I have a mother who loves me and believes in keeping our lives separate, yet who's always there when I need her to work mother's magic. I have some friends I really don't talk to anymore, maybe because they're scared of the sadness, maybe because they're just scared.

I have a golden retriever whom I've had since he was just a fluff ball whom I adore and who will be ten years old this summer. I have a sick sense of humor and tell people that he and I have the same life expectancy, though his blood work looks a lot better than mine.

I have a comfortable, warm, Spanish-style house that often consoles me and gives me a place to which I cherish returning. I have "things"—objects and knickknacks and souvenirs of a life that mean something but also mean less.

I have times when I'm very brave and strong and manage to climb out of a seemingly bottomless pit. And I have times when I'm very afraid.

(FRAGMENT)

Panos Christi

I want to write about my life, about the events of my life, not because my life has anything extraordinary or exceptional about it—it has been and continues to be a full life—but because I want to investigate once more how our childhood formative years create the recurring experiences for the rest of our lives. How the play is the same but the cast changes. Different forces, same events . . . and how regularly the patterns are being repeated until, hopefully, one day they are healed.

I want to write about how my longing for my father, who was almost never there—busy with his other family—created my constant attraction to constantly unavailable men. I want to write about how from the age of thirteen I sublimated intimacy with sex—particularly in my relationships with men. I want to write about the nonexistence of time and how we can go back and forth at a moment's notice, how everything happens maybe simultaneously. I want to write about my mother and the good and horrible things that she gave me, and how my relationship with her colored and shaped my relationships with the women of my life. I want to write about me and how I touched others. I want to write about my wounds and my nirvanas, and how I picked up the pieces and started, all over again, every time I fell. I want to write about my journey to understand me better, and about my excitement and my boredom, and maybe at the end I'll be healed.

BOLERO NEGRO

Leonard Mosqueda

AIDS Andy Bactrim Barry Catheter Colby DDI David Eyes Erik Fever Frank Gancyclovir George Hickman Hal Intravenous Ivan Joints John Kaposi Kal Lymphoma Larry Misery Michael Neuropathy Ned Obsolete Oliver Pneumocystis Paul Queer Quackery Stop

WARTS AND ALL

Joe Hogan

I t began with one small wart. On the lower side of my nose, where the nostril meets the upper lip. I noticed it while shaving as I tried to get the razor as close as I could to the top of my lip. I cut the hard, fleshy bump with the blade and it wouldn't stop bleeding. I thought it was a pimple at first, but the wart was still there two days later when I cut it again.

I was concerned, more at the thought of having a wart on my face than the reality of it. I could hear a wicked-witch cackle inside my head. No one could really see it as small as it was and where it was, but it bothered me all the same. I stood looking at my reflection in the mirror with my head turned to the side and then straight on to see if anyone would notice it. An uncontrollable shiver swept over me as I looked at the irritating, little white bump. I made a mental note to pick up a bottle of Compound W at the drugstore.

One morning a week later, I felt another bump as I washed my face in the sink. I surveyed the new wart in the mirror. This time it was in the middle of my left cheek. It was bigger than the first, definitely noticeable. "Shit," I said to myself. It wasn't there last night when I brushed my teeth. I felt sick to my stomach as I examined the two warts and wished I had remembered to go to the drugstore. "That's it, you're calling Dr. Miller today," I said to the face staring back at me.

"Warts are just a virus," Dr. Miller said as he wrote on the prescription pad. I kept wondering what he used on his hair to make it so shiny. It looked like patent leather. "It's no big deal. We'll do some blood work just in case, and in the meantime, this should clear them both up in a few days. Just be careful when you apply this stuff that you get it only on the warts, otherwise it'll burn the surrounding skin."

"Yeah, sure, Doc, and thanks for seeing me on such short notice," I said politely.

"That's what we're here for," Dr. Miller said with a wink.

The next day at the department store where I work, my friend Sandra asked, "John, what are those bumps on your face? They look like warts." I was helping her pick up some shirts that had fallen off a shelf.

"You mean you can see them? Are they that noticeable?" I ran over to the dressing-room mirror to take another look. "Can you believe I'm getting warts on my face?" I asked a little too loud. Two customers browsing the sale rack quickly looked my way. I immediately felt my cheeks flush red.

"I had a wart on my thumb when I was thirteen," Sandra said, ignoring my questions. "It took forever to go away. No matter what I did, it kept coming back, and then one day, just like that, it was gone. But on your face, I don't think I could wait. Can't you get 'em frozen or burned off, something like that?"

"My doctor gave me this stuff that's like battery acid, but he said it would take a couple of days to work. Do you think Mr. Sheridan will say anything?" Mr. Sheridan was the floor manager, who gave new meaning to the word *fastidious*. He was always talking about image consciousness and how important first impressions are in making a sale.

"What's he gonna say?" Sandra replied. "It's not like it's your fault or anything. Besides, remember that girl in housewares? What was her name? Peggy or Penny, you know, the one who had the huge boil on her neck? Nobody said anything to her?"

"I thought she got fired."

"She did, but according to Marge Seely, it was for stealing a toaster oven, not for the boil."

"Sandra, promise me you'll not mention this to anyone else. I don't want people asking about them. Okay?"

"What am I going to say? 'You should see the warts on John's face!' I have better things to talk about." She laughed. "Besides, you can't really see them unless you're up close, and from the way you talk, you haven't been up close to anyone in a long time."

I turned around without saying anything and began tagging the new shipment of dress shirts. She was right, of course.

My girlfriend, Denise, had left six months ago. Our fight started when I unexpectedly told her that I didn't want to get married—"not today, not next week, not next year"—and that "maybe we need to spend some time apart." The words came spilling out before I could stop myself. She tossed her copy of *Bride* magazine onto the coffee table and, with contempt in her voice, said she didn't know me any better today than the day we first met. She went on to say I was the greatest actor she'd ever known who wasn't in the theater. Her last words as she picked up her purse and slammed the door behind her were, "Goddamn faggot." I sat on the couch and laughed at her choice of words. In the final months of my parents' seventeen-year marriage, the words *queer* and *whore* were thrown around like dice on a craps table.

I continued checking the warts each morning to see if they were shrinking, but by the end of the third day of using the medication, there was little change. "They actually look worse," I thought as I moved my face as close to the mirror as I could without losing focus.

That afternoon on my way back from lunch, I approached the mirrors outside the men's dressing room to straighten my tie and comb my hair. I saw a new patch of white bumps covering my left jaw. I quickly counted ten new warts beginning at my cheekbone and running down to my chin in no particular pattern or sequence. I felt nauseous. How could they have just appeared out of nowhere? I wondered as I looked around to see if anyone was watching.

As I hurried past her, I yelled to Sandra in the Young Men's department that I was leaving and to please cover for me. I ran out the employee exit with my hand on my face and got in my car.

"Goddammit! Why is this happening?" I yelled at my reflection in the rearview mirror, tears welling in my eyes. It had been a long time between cries. . . .

∽

I stood crying on the playground of my new school. It hadn't even been a week and I was afraid. I'd moved with my mother to a new town after the divorce, and already a group of kids were making my life hell. It seemed that the whole fourth-grade class was out to get me. At lunch, on Wednesday, Robby Stewart, the ringleader, grabbed my lunch sack out of my hands and threw it over the playground wall. It landed in the backyard of a Doberman pinscher as Robby dared me to go get it. I watched helplessly as the dog tore into the bag and ate my bologna sandwich, wax paper and all.

That afternoon, three boys shoved me from behind into an open locker and shut the door. A skinny girl with thick glasses and long braids named Kimberly let me out when she heard me crying. She had a high-pitched, squeaky laugh, and when she opened the locker door, she asked, "So, what are you doing in there, stupid?" She took off running down the hall. The other kids stood by the locker, shaking their heads like disapproving adults.

It was only Thursday and I knew something was up. I watched my tormentors talking in the lunch room. They'd look my way, point, then laugh. Kimberly and Robby appeared to be doing most of the talking. I got up from where I was sitting, walked outside, and stood by the monkey bars, pondering how I could convince my mother that we had to move. I began to cry.

Before I could turn around, I felt a pair of hands wrap around my ankles and lift me off the ground. "Get the crybaby's hands," I heard someone yell. I recognized Kimberly's squeaky laugh and knew she was close by, but I couldn't see her. As they held me off the ground, I counted six faces. Then Kimberly stuck her head into the circle and said, "We're gonna take you out in the field and throw grasshoppers all over your face until you scream for mercy."

I felt the long grass whip against my skin as they carried me out into the field, away from the playground. I had recently read Lord of the Flies. *I hope they ate enough for lunch, I thought.*

"Please don't do this, I won't tell. Just let me down. Come on, you guys, I haven't done anything to you," I pleaded.

"Grasshoppers, big, slimy grasshoppers that are gonna spit on your face, just like this," and one of the boys spit on me.

"Yeah, only there are hundreds of 'em," another yelled.

"He's probably gonna piss his pants like a big baby," said Robby, who was holding one of my ankles.

Something about the way their faces looked through my tears, big and distorted, like cartoon characters, and Kimberly, with those thick glasses, sticking her head into the circle like an ostrich, struck me as funny. I began laughing.

"What's he laughing about?" one of them noticed.

"Aw, he's not laughing, he's crying."

"No, man, he's laughing. Look, he's laughing."

"Hey, buttface, quit laughing," another yelled.

But I couldn't stop and the more I laughed, the madder they got, until finally Robby said, "Oh, just let him go. There aren't any grasshoppers out here anyway," and they dropped me on the grass. One of the boys kicked me in the side before he turned and followed the others.

"Assholes!" I yelled out, still laughing. I lay there for a few minutes, holding my side, feeling the coolness of the grass against my bare arms and neck, aware of the quiet of the open field. I watched a plane fly overhead. I don't want to go back to school and I don't want to live in this stupid town, I thought, but I could think of no alternatives. I finally, stood, dusted off my clothes, wiped my face with the bottom of my shirt, and slowly walked toward school.

I sat waiting for Dr. Miller to come into the examining room. I had driven straight from work to his office and demanded to see the good doctor. The receptionist started to say that he was booked solid, but she looked at my face and told me to wait just a minute.

"So, John, what seems to be the problem today?" Dr. Miller asked as he closed the door behind him.

I was shaking as I removed my hand from my left jaw and said, "This is the problem. They're spreading. That medicine didn't do shit. Look at my face."

"Okay, calm down. Let's take a look and see what we've got here."

"*We* haven't got anything, Doc. I'm the one with the warts."

Dr. Miller ignored my sarcasm and continued reading my chart.

"Your white blood cell count is low, but I'm sure you're fine. I'll give you an antibiotic, which should clear this whole thing up." He spoke quickly, as if he wanted to make a fast exit.

"Yeah, well, that's great, but what'll I do in the meantime?" I demanded.

He handed me the prescription slip and opened the door. I heard him mutter as he left the room, "You might try changing your attitude."

I called work when I got home and explained the situation. I told Mr. Sheridan that I needed to take some time off, a week or two, until the warts cleared up. Mr. Sheridan agreed, but only after reciting verbatim the section in the employee handbook that stated a doctor's note was required to return to work. I remembered back to when my father died last year and I took a few days off. I nearly had to produce the body as evidence. This guy made Little Lord Fauntleroy look like James Dean, I thought as I hung up the phone.

I laid down on the sofa and lightly ran my fingers down the side of my face. It felt more like a rubber mask than my own skin. I squeezed the hard bumps until they hurt.

As the days passed, the short space between sleeping and waking became my only peaceful moment. It was in those few seconds that I felt whole, unmarked, as if the warts were unreal. As my mind became alert, I would automatically fit my hand to my face and realize it wasn't a dream. It was reality.

The antibiotic wasn't working. The warts kept coming. There were five new warts on my forehead, eight on the right side of my face, and two on the bridge of my nose. I counted twenty-eight warts all together. I wondered if they'd soon cover my entire head. Would my hair fall out? I grabbed a towel off the shelf and covered the bathroom mirror. I was tired of counting and recounting the warts.

Dr. Miller referred me to a dermatologist, who referred me to an immunologist. Although both were intrigued by my strange condition, neither offered much hope for a quick recovery. The dermatologist said they could freeze them off, but they would most likely return and it could cause scarring. The immunologist said that it could take months, possibly years, for my body to recognize the virus and begin fighting it, but that I was healthy in every other way, implying I should be grateful.

I asked for a leave of absence from work. Mr. Sheridan insisted that I come in to fill out the appropriate forms. As I entered the store, an obnoxious little girl pointed at me and said, "Look at that man's face, Mommy." The mother frowned at me as if I had made the child say that and she pushed the girl toward the exit. I turned around and got back in my car.

I spoke to Sandra on the phone every day for the first week and a half. We laughed at what a certain customer had said or how the store was falling apart without me, but we never spoke of the warts. She vaguely offered to drop by, but never did. The last time we spoke, she was making fun of Marge's new hair color when I suddenly became infuriated. I screaming into the phone to either be a friend or quit calling and slammed down the receiver. The phone rang twice after that and then, nothing.

The thought of killing myself came to me as I was chopping an onion. I cut my finger and didn't even feel it. Maybe death was that unfeeling, I thought. Not to feel sounded comforting to me. I stared at the knife in my hand and pictured samurai warriors impaling themselves on their swords. I decided it wasn't long enough as I imagined the blade pushing into my stomach.

I put the knife on the counter and walked to the tiny balcony off the living room. I looked down over the railing. Would a fall from the third floor be high enough to kill me or would I just be a paralyzed man with warts? I wondered with amusement. I saw my body writhing in pain on the pavement and decided it wasn't worth the risk.

I woke that night to what sounded like a gun going off in the street below my bedroom window. I lay in bed, rubbing my face and speculating about how much someone would charge to shoot me. I figured I had nearly $600 in the bank. The newspaper was full of people getting shot for a lot less than that. Where would a person find a hired assassin? I wondered. I pictured Denise standing over me with a gun, yelling like James Cagney, "You dirty fag!" and frothing at the mouth as she pulled the trigger. No, better to do it alone, I thought, and yet, guns seemed so messy, so violent, to me.

Pills would be the only way, I thought coolly, as I shifted my pillow. I could call Dr. Miller's office, tell the nurse I wasn't sleeping well, and could the doctor please prescribe something strong? Dr. Miller would send horse tranquilizers just to keep me and my bad attitude out of the office. Pills were nice and neat. Just drift off to sleep and wake up dead.

∽

I walked home from the bus stop, continually looking over my shoulder. Someone had pushed me as I got off the school bus, knocking me down the stairs and onto the pavement. I heard the bus explode with laughter as it drove away.

"Yeah, go ahead and laugh," I shouted as I picked up my books.

The youngest of the Sutton kids, Jeff, yelled out to me as I approached my house, "Hey, what happened at your house? There was an ambulance and everything."

I ignored him, thinking it was a trick, then opened the front door and shouted, "Mom, hey, Mom, are you here?" as I ran from room to room. She never left without leaving a note or at least locking the front door, I thought. I was heading next door to see if Jeff was telling the truth when the phone rang.

"Johnny, this is your aunt Lois. Now listen, honey, I want you to brace yourself. You know how your mother has been lately, how she's not been herself at all? Well, she tried to kill herself this afternoon, but she's going to be all right," she said without taking a breath. Her voice grew higher as she talked.

"She did what . . . ?" I whispered.

"She took too many sleeping pills, but now everything is going to be just fine. They pumped her stomach. She'll be as good as new in no time. Thank goodness I stopped by when I did, otherwise . . . Now you wait there until your uncle Jack and I come over, and stay inside so the neighbors don't ask any nosy questions."

My aunt was still talking when I hung up the phone and ran to the bathroom to vomit.

Mother succeeded on her third attempt. I found her when I came home from school on a Thursday afternoon. She was lying in bed, her fingers and lips were blue. She was barely breathing. By the time the ambulance arrived at the hospital, she was dead. The thing that made me the maddest was she didn't leave a note; she just checked out. I went to live with my father the day after the funeral.

∽

The blaring signal of a garbage truck backing up woke me. I sat on the edge of my bed for a moment before walking into the bathroom. Maybe suicide isn't the answer, I thought as I splashed water on my face. I gently ran my fingers over the warts as I dried myself with a towel, touching them almost with reassurance. "What's a few lousy warts anyway?" I asked out loud.

I opened the front door and grabbed the newspaper off the mat. I imagined the headlines as I unfolded the paper. "Man Commits Suicide over Warts!" or "Man with Warts Found Dead!" At least my sense of humor remained intact.

I showered and combed my hair. I put away the towel that covered the bathroom mirror and shaved as best I could without cutting the warts. I called Mr. Sheridan to tell him that I'd be coming back to work the next day. He asked in his usual annoying tone if everything was all cleared up, taking great care not to mention the word—*warts*. I told him matter-of-factly that I would be returning to work, warts and all.

I walked to the park at the end of my street and lay down on the grass. It was quiet; a light breeze was blowing, just like that day on the playground. The grass felt like a thick carpet. A plane passed overhead. I propped up on my elbows and watched a woman pushing a child on the swings. I suddenly remembered the sound of my mother's voice. A man in yellow running shorts with tan, muscular legs jogged by, nodding to me as he passed. I nodded back. I watched him disappear over the ridge, then fell back on the grass laughing. Maybe Denise was right.

HAIR

Stan Brodsky

Hair
here today, gone tomorrow
Once dark black, then salt and pepper
Finally grey.
Sparser with time and mega-doses of meds
Meant to keep me here.

But where does the lost hair go?
Is it a weakening of power, as Samson and Delilah discovered?
Or is it truly the basis of genetic life,
Reproducible in test tubes to clone another me when I'm gone?

Am I colder now with the loss of body hair?
More aware of my return to some type of prepubescent stage
Before I grew hairy?

One could say I'm in a hairy situation
More scary than hairy really.
Each morning after showering, I bend over to collect
Yet more of these vanishing friends.
Perhaps I'll start saving them and have them woven into a ring
Or pendant to leave my partner after I'm gone.

Jerry Rosenblum

None of us complains that his hands are going. Our eyes go. Our feet hurt. We can't eat keep our bowels intact, but our hands work. We hold books we can't read, spear food we have no appetite for, and coddle our dicks long after we can get excited enough to enjoy it.

Scabs and broken nails become ordinary; cracked skin no longer responds to even the most expensive emulsions. We blame our brains or our inner ears or our softening muscles whenever we drop something.

We scratch. Even when we break skin and blood starts seeping and dripping, we go after that itch, that rash, with unflagging determination and increasingly skillful contortions.

SKIN STUFF

Phil Curtis

One

I've tried to write about the guys I work with, but what I had to say embarrassed me. I felt like I was feeding off their suffering.

But if I did write about them, I'd start with the skin stuff. That's what my friend calls it—skin stuff.

He said it once; he was talking about the pimples and lumps and rashes that he's had all his life. He said, "I'm a skin stuff kinda guy."

When he said it, I thought, "You're so clever." And then I thought of all the lesions, funguses, and growths I've looked at over the past few years. And then I looked at him and saw his first shingle and his first lesion. And then I didn't want to look anymore.

I'm squeamish about skin stuff, but better than I used to be. The first guy I was a buddy to, he had skin stuff—white pimples called molluscum sprayed across his face. When our cheeks touched, I was afraid that I'd have white pimples sprayed across mine.

I had one client—that's what the agency likes us to call them—named Frank, and Frank had big skin stuff. Something called congenital Reiter's syndrome. When his immune system failed, the syndrome blossomed, and for over a year Frank's body was covered with inch-high stalagmites of yellow-green fungus.

People said he looked like a mushroom farm.

I was afraid to touch Frank and I think he understood. He stayed in his apartment all that year, till the doctors got the fungus under control. He laughed his way through it, made peace with the family he'd been estranged from, and came out, finally, still laughing.

The last time I saw him he couldn't get out of his car. We hugged through the window, and I couldn't take my eyes off his fingernails, which were just lumpy deposits of yellow-green scales.

The skin stuff scares me for the same reason it scares my clients. It's external and on the move. It makes me think of Jung, talking about the gods having become diseases. I see these guys, must be thousands by now, bursting out of their skins. And I wonder.

I had another client, Ray, who wore a full face mask of purple KS. He looked like a skier, or an Indian fresh out of the rain forest.

Someone I worked with warned me ahead of time, but when I met Ray, I just stopped in my tracks and my mouth dropped open. Ray came to the rescue, said something straight away about his KS—I don't remember what, exactly. But soon he seemed to be very comfortable, hiding in there behind his mask. Almost proud. At least that's what I thought.

KS is the Zeus of skin stuff. The lesser gods range from shingles to herpes to the molluscum to something called itchy red bump disease.

The red bumps swarm over the body and sting it with non-stop itching that clients say goes right to the core.

My friend Bill had itchy red bumps for almost a year before he died. He barely slept and never stopped scratching. Bill was a pink-skinned, redheaded guy, and when it was really bad, when he couldn't sleep at all, he'd come into my office and I'd see these red storms in his face.

He had a series of strokes before he died. I went to see him in Cedars. He could barely talk and had lost all movement on his left side. But his right hand still itched reflexively at some psychic bump that wouldn't go away.

The last time I saw Bill he was sleeping. Just sleeping. The itching right hand had stopped, and someone kind had powdered him with talc; the red storms were gone from his face and he looked like a big, beautiful baby, and I thought, "Oh, great, he's ready to go."

Two

Sometimes I envy them, these men with wounds so red and so visible; envy what I see as some rage to live or to escape the body.

Sometimes, I wish I knew some words to say, words that would hurry them on their way.

Sometimes, I pray silently to myself that they'll find a way to appease the gods and save themselves.

Sometimes I'm angry that they're leaving, bailing out early, leaving me behind to do what they can't or won't. And what I'm not certain I can do either.

Sometimes I think that if all the rage and itching could just turn itself around, find some other vent, the whole thing would just be over.

Sometimes I'm afraid of thinking what I think, afraid that what I'm thinking about them I should be thinking about myself. And that if I'm not careful, then next year or the year after I'll be them, coming in to see me. And I wonder what I'll be thinking then.

Sometimes I think, "It's just a virus."

I have plenty of time to think, sitting there in my office.

It's dull work, really. And I wouldn't do it for any other tribe. I haven't got that big a heart.

I love the way people say they can't imagine how I do the kind of work I do, as if I were the one who was sick.

Sometimes I milk it when I'm after something. Mostly I tell people it's really not so bad, as long as I remember who's doing the suffering.

The same people always ask me if I do what I do because I'm

just another guilty survivor. I tell them it's more complicated than that, but I'm not really that sure.

I've often thought I'd write a story called "What I Did at Work Today."

I'd describe the plain old mechanical dreariness of the way I opened the folders, make my calls, do what needs to be done, write up "Progress Notes"—I love that concept—and put the folders away again. There's nothing dramatic about it all, except that everyone I talk to is young and dying.

When clients die, I get to put black dots on their folders and send them back to the archives, which are a bunch of cardboard boxes in the warehouse.

We have a stash of stick-on black dots in the clerical office, but I like to ink in my own dots with the cheap black pens we use.

Sometimes when I'm black-dotting a folder (we made a verb of it), I dream about someone going through the archives, years from now. So when I write up my last progress note, I include something personal—like, "I really liked this man," or even "Adios, asshole"—something, anything, to let my future archivist know that I was watching and thinking and feeling and that the men in these folders were more than just, well, more than just a bunch of guys who died.

Sometimes I get real anal with the paperwork. It happens so fast and I get too busy and some need for order and completion overwhelms me.

There was a client I hadn't heard from in a long time, which is always suspicious, so I called. His mother answered the phone—another bad sign—and told me her son had died just that morning.

As she said it, I was inking in a neat little black dot on his folder and thinking to myself, "Oh, good, now I can send it to the warehouse and get it out of my files."

So the whole time she's telling me about her son's death, I'm saying unconsciously but out loud, "Great, terrific, good . . ."

This was some mom. She turned her perspective on a dime and was right there, with me. It was as if while taking care of her son, she had learned to focus so intensely on the other that nothing could stop her now.

I apologized and explained. She said she understood and could not imagine how I do the kind of work I do.

And I said the same to her.

(UNTITLED)

Dave Knight

I want to rest
No
I want to eat
No
I want a Cola
. . . something with cold bubbles
to fluoresce my teeth
so I don't have to brush them

I need a toothbrush
the last one fell into the toilet
after the nail file

I don't file my nails
I'm trying to file a wart off my dick
so someone will love me

It wasn't my fault
I got the wart
I was drunk and tried to love someone
I guess it was the wrong person
a wart-person

How could I have done that?
there wasn't a wart in his eyes

that's what drew me in
the eyes

I hope I don't get any warts in MY eyes

I suppose that if he didn't, I guess I won't
but if I do
I'll have to go to an Ophthalmologist
or should I go to a Dermatologist
because when I had a wart on my foot I
went to a Podiatrist.
It's so screwy, I'm unsure

I'm also unINsured
That's why I'm sitting here
filing a wart off my dick
instead of consulting a Urologist.

I called my brother
he said, "Lawry's season salt works."
I never asked if it killed the wart or
just made it taste better

I hung up on him
my brother
I've been hanging up on
a lot of people
lately

TEETH

Jerry Rosenblum

I have all my wisdom teeth
All four of them
They grew in straight and solid
With no problems
I don't think about them except
When I brush
And then
I struggle to get off all the
Gop and goo of the day
But it's tight in there and
My dentist questions my sincerity
And skill.

My father lost his teeth when
He was forty
I watched him bleed and spit
But he didn't cry
He was a soldier
A veteran of the Great War
Stationed in South Dakota
He said it was the only time in his life
He was happy.

I try to be good
Drink milk and juice

And brush and clean myself
Most days
Some days I don't feel like
Getting out of bed
So I swish around the water
I keep on my nightstand
For when I'm too tired to
Go to the kitchen
To take my pills.

My teeth haven't ached for a long time
I remember once in the fifth grade
The dentist hurt me
I wanted to cry
But didn't
He gave me a red lollipop for being
A good boy
He's dead
So is my father.

We buried him with his teeth so
He'd look good in his box
He did
I shivered as I peeked in on him
Sleeping
Only his sister and his kids
Saw him lying there cold.

He wanted me to be a man
To play basketball and bowl
Go out with pretty Jewish girls
He wanted me to smile
To bathe and brush and
Eat meat and potatoes
He wanted me to be strong
To join a gang so I could
Fight off bullies and knock their teeth

Out
He told me how the Nazis killed wimpy Jews and gypsies
And burned their bodies and
Took their gold fillings to make
Bracelets and rings.

He told me how my grandmother would
Put ice on my sore gums when
I was teething
Feed me Zwieback to make it better
After he left us
He said he'd give me a buck
For each tooth that fell out
That there was no tooth fairy
That bodybuilders and Rock Hudson
Were fairies.

In the Ural Mountains there are
People who exist on
Yogurt and apricots
They live until about one hundred
And ten
They don't fuss about their mouths
I bet it's no big deal if a tooth
Falls out.

My friend Jim wore away the edges of his teeth
Until the yellow inside oozed out
His teeth almost got me clean
Every time I get high
I check my teeth
I hope I give out before they do.

I notice a guy's teeth
Especially when he's dressed
I hate gaps or unnecessary adornments like
Gold caps or diamond inlays

When a man's naked
I'm less particular.

I used to go to parties where
Guys would share their brushes
I didn't
Even then
Now I see little germs and viral flakes
On mine.

The day I got my test results
I came on someone's teeth
He swished it around and told me
How good it tasted
I cried when I got home
I didn't see him before
He died.

FOUR STORIES ABOUT SKIN

William M. Franklin

First Story

Monsieur Garbarz, who ran a small handbag and shoe repair shop in Paris, took Sundays off from his long hours of retooling shopgirls' purses and regluing wayward high heels to spend the day with his only son, Jean-Jacques, a handsome young man with a shock of reddish blond hair that cascaded over his forehead like one of Monet's brighter haystacks.

Sundays, Jean-Jacques and his father would head off to one of their favorite restaurants in the Algerian section of Paris. Monsieur Garbarz loved couscous, and on this Sunday, since I was visiting for the weekend, they promised to take me to one of their favorite dining spots.

After a short ride on the metro we emerged above ground into the sweet-smelling neighborhood favored by North Africans. The pungent odors of cumin, saffron, and turmeric wafted through the air. Street vendors hawked colorful leather belts and woven bags.

Suddenly, Monsieur Garbarz's face turned into a tightly clenched fist. A few feet away, three tourists, replete with cameras and a street map of Paris, were bargaining with a Moroccan vendor. Without hesitation, Monsieur Garbarz approached the little delegation of tourists, a graying, middle-aged couple and their teenage daughter.

"Excuse me, are you from Germany?" Monsieur Garbarz inquired, forcing a broad grin on his tightly knotted face. The Germans nodded innocently, curious as to what might motivate the question.

"Have you found any interesting souvenirs while visiting our fair city?" Monsieur Garbarz asked. Jean-Jacques, who clearly had heard this question before, stood frozen, expressionless.

The German tourists shook their heads in the negative and tried to disengage from the conversation, assuming Monsieur Garbarz was simply trying to sell them something.

Monsieur Garbarz persisted. "*Quel dommage,* what a pity, no souvenirs yet, because when I visited your country, I was given a beautiful souvenir." At this point Monsieur Garbarz pulled up the sleeve of his jacket, exhibiting a small line of crudely tattooed numbers that snaked along the inside of his forearm toward his wrist.

The German tourists stared for a moment, transfixed. Then they moved away, quickly, yanking their teenage daughter, who still seemed paralyzed by the encounter. We headed on toward our restaurant. Monsieur Garbarz, who ordered heartily, ate with great enthusiasm, as if he hadn't eaten in a very, very long time.

Second Story

Peter, who is always a little sad, runs a second-rate art gallery in Los Angeles. As soon as his artists gain a bit of a following and start to sell their works, they leave Peter for a more prestigious gallery. Peter's boyfriends, who are usually from Lynwood or Hawaiian Gardens and are struggling with drug problems, end up leaving him, too—either for a prison term or a richer boyfriend.

During one of his unusually well-attended openings, Peter announced, "You must meet the artist, Gregorio." He pointed. "In the corner, by himself." My eyes travel along the wall decorated with huge wood panels painted in oil. Beautiful Renaissance figures with three-quarter profiles and heavy lids stare out in defiance.

In the corner, partially obscured by several dozen gallery regulars, Gregorio stands, or rather leans slightly on something. His perfect olive skin seems to radiate vitality, his slightly wavy blue-black hair pulled back in casual disarray. I have never seen anyone look this way. He is the most startlingly, not quite human creature I have ever seen, one part Renaissance painting, one part mythical faun.

"Gregorio, this is Bill, he's a writer," Peter intones dramatically, then instantly departs. I am looking at my boyfriend-to-be. I had never seen anyone so exotic, so untamed, so at peace.

Our eyes lock for an awkward moment. I've fallen and he's right there with me. We are sailing off alone, together. "What do you write about?" he asks, inquiring with a smile that says I want to lick you all over.

"Profiles, design . . . art," I say in my most casual yet seductively engaging manner.

"Perhaps you'd like to write about me?" He smiles. I am lost in his blue-green eyes.

And then he moves; he shifts ever so slightly, and suddenly everything changes. Gregorio takes a step toward me and for the first time I realize he is leaning on crutches. Not the kind people borrow after skiing accidents, but the kind of crutches the disenfranchised in downtown to slowly catapult themselves up the steps to board a bus.

Part of me wants to rewind, to rethink this thing, to start over, but we have stepped way over the line. Part of me wants to reel myself away, but it's too late. I'm fascinated, and terrified.

"You're not one of those cripple groupie freaks?" he challenges as soon as we get to his place, removing his shorts to show me where his spinal cord snapped, bodysurfing at the Wedge four years ago. I trace the knotted line of his spinal column down to the small of his back where his cool, soft flesh wraps around the thick braid of scar tissue. I kiss the spot lightly and tell him I don't think I'm a cripple groupie, but I'm not really sure.

Third Story

"You get a seventy percent reduction on all cosmetic surgery by our editorial consultant, who is board certified," I am told on my first day on the job. The art director of this most famous bodybuilding and fitness magazine has just had the sides of his nose thinned and sports white bandages that crisscross his face and give him a permanently bewildered expression. An editor in the next cubicle has just had his abs liposucked and is forced to stand at his desk all day while the sites continue to drain. The publisher, who has recently undergone painful pec-implant surgery, is wearing a wool cap even though it's the middle of summer. He has had another round of hair plugs placed and is waiting for them to take.

The skin here is different. Since they have long since eliminated even the tiniest amount of fat from the diet, most employees' skin is dry and chalky, and the tones are of an otherworldly orangy-mocha hue, achieved through the religious application of self-bronzing creams, pills, and on tanning beds. The skin here is very different. It's pulled drum tight, stretched over bodies until veins pop.

Month after month printed images are sent out, illusions of men and women whose bodies are posed and oiled and artificially lit in ways that are both hypnotic and frighteningly unreal.

And then, just after blueline one month, our senior editor is discovered curled up napping on his carpeted office floor, a result of too much AZT and too many margaritas at lunch. Before quitting time that day, from the mailroom to the CEO's inner sanctum, news of the editor's break with office decorum spread.

Diagnosed soon thereafter, the popular editor who had directed with style and humor is jettisoned into the publishing gulag. Yanked from the top of the masthead, he is never mentioned again in the glossy pages of flesh and muscle. When he is hospitalized, no one from the staff visits. And when he dies, not one person from the company attends his services.

Fourth Story

The night I met Robert he was stripped to the waist, his perfectly chiseled body responding to every beat in the cavernous nightclub. He wore his body like a trophy, not so much the narcissist but more Incan high priest and Spanish warrior. His skin glistened with just the right balance of light, moisture, and muscle.

Little did I know that night, mesmerized by his otherworldliness, that I would explore every millimeter of that richly textured skin. Wearing his skin like my own, I would wear it as armor and as signpost. It protected me from the world.

I spent thousands of nights pressed up hard against the buoyancy of Robert's skin, which covered so much, and revealed so much. I nestled into the soft indentation at the nape of his neck and marveled at the tiny hairs that curled and teased their way up the back of his head. This was my safe harbor.

I watched Robert's skin change like a dangerous, unprecedented season: force majeure despite man's feeble efforts. Robert's first lesion was like a searing acid bath. He bore it with quiet dignity. First, just a little discolored speck, the flaw that underscored the beauty, like the aged and marred face of one of Giotto's frescoed figures. Then tiny little flecks on his personal landscape that grew to states and then continents and finally to whole galaxies. His beautiful skin turned dry and crackly like fine china. His beauty only deepened.

After months of radiation and chemo Robert's skin turned to charred ash, his legs half-burned tree stumps rescued from some terrible forest fire. The proportion of horror is unspeakable. With that horror Robert is transformed into something much more beautiful than anything possibly imagined, idealized, or dreamt. Robert's skin disappeared, like a black-and-white photograph bleaching out in the sun.

These stories are dedicated to Robert Leal.

USED TO BE

Ezra Litwak

I used to be healthy. I used to be stronger. I used to be a lot of different. Things have fallen away like snakeskin. It's screwy, when I look back and realize all the things I used to be and how quickly I had to give them up. Used-to-be is dead. It doesn't exist, it's unalterable and yet it haunts me all the time. Yearning, searching, reaching back. It's an unnatural position that could wrench your arm out of its socket.

"Those who don't remember history are condemned to repeat it," and yet imagine if we had no memory, no used-to-be. Would we be happier existing just in the present? Would we be inexplicably lonely for memories?

It used to be. There's a judgment trying to get out of that phrase. It says, "Things were better." Is that true? There is a terrible yearning for the past when the future is so frightening. There is an anger at the present for making me let go of what used to be.

I don't care. There's nothing I can do about it. I accept the present and won't think about the future. I tell myself these mantras and others tell them to me, but is it really true? Wouldn't I go back to the way things were? I think so. It feels weak to say so. I don't want to be sick. I don't want to die. Not yet. When you're dead, there must be one huge used-to-be to look back on. I hope I laugh at the courage and absurdity of a lifetime.

I hate people who say, "They just don't make 'em like that

anymore." Of course not. Why would you think they would? And who are these mysterious "they" who've grown older and suffered their losses? There is no going back. But it's a comfort. Used to be grandmothers with fresh-baked pies on the windows. There used to be cold, snowy nights sledding and screaming glee and sheer exhilaration. Used to be best friends and toy cars and everything warm and tender and in its place. And death couldn't find a way in. But that's not how it really used to be. Don't let them tell you that.

TUBES

Doug Bender

I t was late, and the room was dark. There was just enough light to see her outline. She sat in the chair next to my bed, behind the pole and the pump. She had brown hair, swept behind her head and held with a chopstick. Her face was round, and ruddy.

She told me many things that night. She lives in the desert somewhere—Lancaster or Apple Valley or Victorville—and drives into the city two or three nights a week to work her shift, but goes against traffic so it's not so bad. She explained how CMV, a life- and sight-threatening virus, affects body cells, and the procedure for implanting the Hickman. She likes to ride horses and has a husband, but no children. The Landers earthquake caused some damage to their home, but not as bad as her sister's home in Big Bear. She thought my boyfriend must really love me. She showed me the way to care for the catheter, how to clean it and apply the dressing, even though I hadn't had the procedure yet. She liked working nights and considered her job to be half-teaching and half-caretaking. She was sure that having a Hickman wouldn't make any difference to my boyfriend, because he obviously loved me. Occasionally she would get up and check the pump or throw something away or pour me some water, as if she knew I didn't want her to leave, that I needed someone there, that it was going to be a rough night, a life-changing night, my last night of freedom.

❧

It took me a year before I could take my shirt off in public. I was on a weekend away with the Chorus, a retreat at a camp in Malibu. The camp was old and rustic; the plumbing was in a separate building from the beds. There were three toilets, five urinals, and four showers walled in cracked tiles, the grout black from years of unscrubbed scum, with torn gray plastic shower curtains sprouting small tabs that read NEVER MILDEW, NEVER ROT. David, a six-foot-five-inch leather and uniform queen with a bushy mustache and a bushier chest, sat nude on the little bench in the shower area, because he had forgotten his clothes in the dorm room and had sent someone to get them. I walked into the shower area, saw David, and froze at the thought that someone would see my disfigured body, that someone would know.

The choice was simple: I could risk embarrassment and humiliation by baring my chest, exposing white tubes dangling beneath a white gauze patch, surrounded by dark orange antiseptic, covered with a clear plastic protectant the size of a three-by-five card, or I could make the mortifying choice not to shower, an unacceptable option because I was already in the shower area with soap and shampoo in hand, and I would have to divine an explanation as to why I had changed my mind. I was trapped.

I took off my clothes, chatting politely with David. We were careful to look at each other straight on, no eyes straying below the neck, as if we were obeying some unspoken rule of genteel homosexual society. He shivered. He seemed as flustered about being unclothed as I was about having tubes dripping from my chest. It is acceptable to be naked if you are changing clothes or showering or having sex, but to hang out in the nude without activity emphasizes the nakedness, the vulnerability. And I can't pass as a healthy person if the catheter is visible: it is one of the most obvious signs of illness, an unmistakable mark of the plague, as if I had been held down and branded as unsalvageable, a lost object of desire. I preferred to hide my affliction beneath a polo shirt.

I ran into a friend on the street last week. He was carrying a gray backpack that made a small mechanical sound, a whir like two revolutions of an eggbeater. The clear plastic tubing stretched from the backpack into his shirt between two buttons. The sound from the backpack made me nauseous. It made me remember a time when my guts had stopped working, and I used the backpack and the little pump to feed myself, hoping it wouldn't keep my boyfriend awake, that boyfriend who must really love me, that boyfriend who hadn't yet left. I only weighed 120 pounds then. Taking a shower was a major accomplishment.

I can eat now, but the infusions continue. I take my drugs out of the refrigerator at night, so they will be warm enough to use by morning. The two drugs, both treatments for CMV, are held in individual latex balloons encased in plastic. The device, called a home-pump, eliminates the need for an IV pole, and the big bulky pump used by the hospital. In the morning, the sacred ritual begins. I collect all my supplies: two red caps, two dispensing spikes, five 3-cc syringes without needles, one 10-ml vial of heparin, and anticoagulant that prevents blood clots from blocking my line, and one 10-ml vial of saline, used to flush the line. The dispensing spikes are inserted into the vials, the syringes screwed onto the spikes, and liquid drawn into the syringes. I think of how my nurse from the desert taught me to do the drugs: "Remember SASH," she said. "S-A-S-H: saline, additive, saline, heparin. Only use sterile supplies, and make sure you wash your hands and work surface properly. Be sure to clamp the tube when you are done." I do not want any problems. I follow the procedure meticulously, as I have done for the past three years. It is not difficult, more tedious than troublesome. It's as much a part of my day as Rice Chex and the crossword. Taking care of myself is my job—it is what I do, literally, for a living. Some days I like my work: it is interesting and challenging and meaningful. But some days, I want a vacation. Or at least a raise.

❧

I am becoming very well-known in West Hollywood. I'm the guy with the Hickman catheter who goes to the gym. And showers there. In public. Naked. Tubes and all. When I first went back to the gym, I showered at home, but as time passed, and I was able to do more in a day than just go to the gym, lift a few metal-plated Q-Tips, and go home to rest, I decided to shower there, so I could go somewhere afterward.

I know I am becoming well-known because I had dinner with a friend who also has AIDS. We talked about AIDS in the nineties. He said that the entire gay community is in denial about AIDS, that we don't see people with AIDS on the street because people don't want to be seen in public with gaunt faces and lesions on their cheeks. I reminded him, in case he had forgotten, that he and I have AIDS, and there we were, out in public, having dinner. He said he had been having the same conversation with an acquaintance who told him about this guy who goes to the gym and has a Hickman. The acquaintance said, "I don't think we need to see that." And my friend realized that he was talking about me.

I am the only person I have ever seen with a Hickman at the Sports Connection. The gym is in the heart of West Hollywood, the heart of gay Los Angeles, and this is, after all, 1995, well over a decade since the dark clouds first appeared, but I am the only person I have ever seen with a Hickman at the Sports Connection.

When I finish my workout, I have to steel myself as I'm getting undressed for my shower. What if someone says something? Not that I think anyone will; after all, no one has, so far, but what if someone says something nasty? So I collect my arsenal of retorts: "Yeah? Well, you have a hairy back, and a little dick" or "So I shouldn't come here because it makes you uncomfortable? Rub a lamp!" or "I prefer to think of it as a really exotic form of piercing." I don't think mine is the first Hickman people have seen. I have to assume that most city boys have friends, or have had friends, with catheters or have catheters themselves. But what happens is that people look at my chest, and at my eyes, and then quickly look away, like an impertinent child who stares at someone with a huge birthmark or without an arm, until the mother says, "Don't look, dear, it's not polite." I understand the curiosity, the freak-show attraction of my abnormality. After all, a chest is not supposed to have tubes hanging out of it. So people look, and look away, trying not to show any visible signs of disgust or shock or intrigue. But in all these months, in this new gay apartheid of sick and well, I've only been asked about it three times.

Once was by a man with a Southern accent who marveled at my willingness to go into the steam room. He had had a Hickman in an earlier, more severe stage of his own illness and was able to have the catheter removed, but had never been willing to use the steam room. He asked if I would like to be set up on a blind date with his friend, another Hickman-ized homosexual, because, after all, we have so much in common.

Once was by a man who I thought was straight, who said, "What is that thing?" I told him, and he said, "Oh, well, I figure everybody's got something wrong with them."

The third time I was asked by a man with a severe speech impediment and a disabled gait. I couldn't tell what was wrong with him; I thought he had cerebral palsy or multiple sclerosis or maybe a stroke.

"What is that?"

"It's a Hickman catheter."

"What's it for?"

"I have to give myself drugs by infusion every day, and this allows me to do it without a needle in my arm."

"What's wrong with you?"

"I have AIDS."

Pause. "Oh." Pause. "That's rough."

"Not always. Sometimes. Actually, I probably have less trouble day by day than you do. What's wrong with you?"

He proceeded to tell me, although I couldn't understand what he said, because his speech was so impaired. We stood there, naked and wet outside the Jacuzzi, toweling off, one with a catheter and a life-threatening illness, one with a severe muscular disability, surrounded by healthy-looking young men with well-defined muscles who averted their eyes from us as we played "Your life must be worse than mine."

≫

I was at the doctor last week for my regular visit. He thumped on my chest, looked at my tongue, and listened to me breathe. The nurse, an appealing twenty-eight-year-old with a graceful round butt uncommon for a straight man, has been drawing my blood from the catheter for many visits. "How long have you had your Hickman?" "Three years." He was astonished. He said it was amazing that I've had it so long, not only because I haven't had any problems with it, but because a Hickman is required only when the illness is serious, and people don't usually last three years.

It isn't as though it hasn't impacted on my life, or my personality. It has. I don't snorkel now or allow myself vacations in the sun. I have given up my dream of an Olympic gold medal in figure skating, although if pressed hard enough, I would probably admit that my chances against Brian Boitano weren't all that good before the catheter. And it isn't as though I don't wish that I didn't have it. I wish it every day. But I do have it, and somehow that's okay. This is reality, today's version of a life that gets redefined daily. I'm a forty-year-old, gay, Jewish man with AIDS. I pick my nose. I have dry skin, droopy buns, a decent sense of humor, and tubes hanging out of my chest.

And who knows? Maybe the day will come when catheters are a status symbol, an instant entrée into the world of wealth, fame, and power.

I'll be the first person they call.

THE HEADLESS BOY

(AN UNFINISHED WORK)

Marc Wagenheim

[*Editor's note: "The Headless Boy" began as Marc's remembrance of a visit to a carnival. When he came back to it at another Workshop meeting, the fictional voice of Joey, the "headless boy," emerged. Then, Ralph, Joey's brother, appeared. Marc hoped that it might become a novel. He wrote the last installment about ten days before he died. The sections have been printed in the order they were written.*]

One (Anything Headless)

I'm sure now that it was the rinky-dinkiest carnival ever. After all, this was Canberra, Australia, in about 1963. But to me it was magic the way it suddenly came to town and sprouted up. And the carnies, people different from any I had seen before. Rides. Smells of cotton candy and popcorn. Games of skill and chance. Sawdust and screams. That Saturday afternoon my parents let my baby-sitter take me to the carnival. Her name—honestly—was Skin.

Skin and I walked around and decided to take a ride on the Ferris wheel, no huge, colossal extravaganza but certainly in keeping with the fair's scale. As we lifted up, I threw my head back and my stomach flipped with that wonderful dizzying high. When they let some new riders on, Skin and I got stopped at the top. This gave us a chance to survey the entire carnival scene. And then I saw it.

It was a booth along the path where there was a mini–freak show: the strong man, the bearded lady, the fattest woman. But then there was a crudely painted tableau heralding the Amazing Headless Boy. In the picture he was on an elevated bed. Where his head should have been were two thick tubes through which flowed some viscous fluid. To make the painted scene even more real, two lab-coated attendants (a doctor and a nurse?) were watching over the boy, one actually touching one of the tubes.

I felt myself fill with unbelievable terror. An unknown horrible chill ran up and down my spine. I was fascinated but so repulsed. This defied anything I had ever known. Our Ferris wheel ride ended and Skin insisted on walking down the Freaks' Alley before we left. That was the last thing I wanted to do, but I didn't want to show any fear.

We approached the Headless Boy Exhibit and the hawker outside promised wonders within. "He's seventeen now, come in and see him breathe even without a head. Ask his doctor any questions you like . . ."

I felt such revulsion, the nightmares started that night and lasted for weeks. No head, just tubes. His chest expanding and contracting. Living to be a fifty-cent attraction. Where were his parents? What would happen to him?

Two (Joey, the Headless Boy)

"I ain't gonna be that Headless Boy every day anymore. I hate being in that contraption with my neck flung back, with the stupid sound of that fake colored water gurgling through those dumb tubes all day long. Sure I get breaks, but it ain't enough."

"Shut up, Joey," said Joey's dad, the hawker for the Headless Boy sideshow.

"And you let them touch me. I thought they weren't supposed to touch me. I can't see them, but I feel their hands all over me. Some people are scared and don't come near me at all—but other ones, the show-offs with their girls, they pinch and poke me trying to prove I'm just a dummy. I can't stand it. Then when the old ladies come into the tent—I can tell they're old 'cause I can smell their powder and perfume and rouge—one of them gets bold and then they all think tickling the Headless Boy is fun. Sure, I twitch a little to give 'em a thrill, but you said 'no touching.' "

"Listen, Joey—if they pay me a little extra, I gotta let 'em have a feel. You don't think that measly fifty cents they fork over to come in is enough to keep us on the circuit. This is show business and we've got to give 'em a show."

"I swear I'll run away if you let someone grab my dick and balls."

"That was just a nun from Brisbane, who gave me a dollar and that made her entire life!"

"Shit, no matter what you say, I'm sick of it. Why can't Ralph be on display and I'll play the doctor some of the time. I look old enough, and hell, I shave now every day. If you want, call me the young intern assigned to the Headless Boy."

"No way, Joey, Ralph is a real pro at playing the doctor. He's even talked to *real* doctors; people think the whole thing is real. And with Mary Ellen playing the nurse, they're just right together."

"Yeah, but, Pa, I hear his answers to the questions all day so I got them in my head:

"Question: 'How does he eat?' Answer: 'The tubes flowing into his neck give, I mean provides, him with vital nutrients that keeps him alive. They come all the way from Hong Kong and costs hundreds of dollars a day.' "

Three (Ralph, the Doctor)

When I put on that white lab coat, even I start to believe that I'm a real doctor. A healer. An expert on the functions of the human body. Why, one of the carnies came to my trailer the other day because he had some kind of infected rope burn. He wanted me to treat him. Me, Ralph, the keeper of the Headless Boy. And, yes, I have talked to and answered questions from real medical practitioners and convinced them of my own prowess as well as the entire concept of a living headless boy.

"Excuse me, Doctor," I'm asked by a medical student who is interning at a local hospital where our carnival has stopped, "but how are the boy's autonomic functions managed without a brain to direct them?" "I'm glad you asked that," I reply. "In the fluid you see in those tubes. I've developed a compound that permits the boy's spine to maintain control of many functions normally handled by the cerebellum . . ." The intern shakes his head approvingly, his brow deeply intent and furrowed. I don't know how or why I can engage in these kind of dialogues. I've always been the smart one in this strange family of carnival vagabonds. My father turned all his accounting chores over to me when I was just ten years old. I've always read everything that I could get my hands on.

At a used-book store in the city, I found some old medical textbooks and just absorbed them. The systems of the human body. The biochemistry of living organisms. Comparative anatomy. Physiology. It made sense to me. So when I got older, it was my idea to add the characters of the doctor and nurse to the Headless Boy exhibit. Before that, my father (who has always been vague about how he acquired the Headless Boy platform and paraphernalia) would awkwardly field questions from the patrons. Back then, I'd have to fill in for Joey and be the Headless Boy and I hated it. It was so uncomfortable and claustrophobic. I'd find myself breaking out in a cold, clammy sweat with a powerful nausea. At last I convinced my father that I looked old enough to be the doctor. It was exciting when we hoisted down our old exhibit sign and my mother painted in her crude rendition of a doctor standing by the Headless Boy's platform. I convinced her for balance to add the figure of a nurse as well. I had ulterior motives.

I had been wildly screwing Mary Ellen Capistrano, the middle daughter of the World Famous Tumbling Capistranos. Somehow, like me, she was an oddity in her family and could barely manage an ordinary somersault. She helped with ticket sales for a while but never truly grasped the concept of money and change. The family decided to leave her behind at a local convent's tuberculosis asylum, and that day I found her on a small riverbank at the edge of the carnival crying. I took her in my arms and comforted her and discovered that what she might have lacked in amazing tumbling skills or intelligence she compensated for in the sensuality department. Her olive-skinned body was ripe and bursting with bounties I had never known. She worshiped me and I realized that she was my ticket out of the family's hellhole into a trailer of my very own with room for my books and journals and writings (more about those later). We tried her out as the nurse for the exhibit, and her quiet, pretty way soon captivated my family. In her zippered white nurse's uniform and starched white cap, she completed our headless extravaganza. No one was surprised when we announced our engagement.

Four

The carnival left town and I never had my questions about the Headless Boy answered. I didn't want to ask Skin because she would have found it silly. Her main concerns were, in no particular order, her new boyfriend Ian and the Beatles. So I gathered up my nerve one Thursday afternoon in our kitchen and dropped this question meekly into a conversation I was having with my mother. "Mom, do you think someone could live without a head?" I think she pretended not to hear me. I asked again a little more forcefully and she looked at me oddly. "What are you going on about?" she asked. "You've been reading too many comics lately. Go out and play and let me finish getting dinner ready."

I sullenly left the kitchen and went out to the backyard and climbed my favorite tree. So much for the wisdom of the elders. I knew, even in the limits of my seven-year-old wisdom, not to bother broaching the issue with my father. Still, it haunted and perplexed and frightened and preoccupied me. At night, lying in my bed, I wondered where the carnival was and how they even transported the boy. How often would they have to check on his tubes? Would his body squirm if the road got too bumpy? Did he sleep? All those questions bounced around my brain . . . .

Five (Notes)

I want to take the Headless Boy further. During some of my wild fevers I imagined the story going back in time to the company that originally made the headless contraption. It's the late 1800s and the company is located along the wharf in Portland, Maine. Its current owner is third generation to the business, which produces magician's, sorcerer's and illusionist's props and cabinets and secret devices. There is, or was, some family connection to Joseph Guillotine in France, but that will only be explored briefly. The proprietor of the magic workshop is a bachelor who, despite numerous offers, has refused to greatly expand it. Much pressure has been placed on him to move the enterprise to Boston or New York. Further, expanding trade with the Orient has created new competition for the magicians' market.

(1) Go to magic shop (Pasadena). (2) Go to the Magic Castle? (never been there, heard it's ehh). (3) Find a different environment in which to write.

Six (Ralph, the Doctor)

It was a few days before my wedding with Mary Ellen. I had almost finished reconstructing our trailer. It was magnificent. The owner of the carnival had a dingy old wagon that he used mostly to store animal feed. I convinced him to let me have it as the more modern metal food trailers they had were better deterrents against vermin and pests. Seeing the enthusiasm in my eyes and being of generous spirit, he presented it to me as a wedding present.

I became obsessed with restoring it. First we peeled off old crusty layers of hideous paint. It turned out there were dangling mirrors circling the top of the perimeter of the wagon. I could tell what the original colors were and let my imagination go wild. The other carnies were flabbergasted and gathered to watch me work. They oohed and aahed as I added pieces and restored an intricately detailed section. When I was almost done, I decided to reward myself and spend my first night in the trailer. I had gone into the nearest town and picked out a new bed and a few modest furnishings and by that evening felt quite comfortable in my new home. Exhausted after the evening meal, I got into my new bed and the comfort soon took me away. It was then that I had the dream.

I awoke to find myself somewhere else. I opened my trailer door and stepped out. Then I could see it wasn't a trailer at all but a small, innocuous house. I was wearing my doctor's lab coat, and to my surprise and horror most of the people I saw, walking down the street and doing what people do in towns, were all headless. There were men and women, young and old, children, even a headless dog scampered by. Some had tubes extruding from their necks of the kind of which I was familiar, while others had tubes in their chests or arms or abdomens or legs. Many wore simple white tunics while others wore nothing at all. As a way of primitive communication, they had different ways of touching each other with their hands or feet. Every so often in the distance I spotted a white-lab-coated person like me complete with head though all with the same faces. . . .

FIRE ISLAND

Stephen Jerrom

The men at the meat rack
On Fire Island
Don't know he has AIDS,
But in the darkness
On the foggy nights
When shadows shift like vapor
And the clouds of heaven
Crash down hard against the dunes
The hungry man still searches
Tall grass prickling
At his swinging hands—
Perhaps a canvas parka
And a higher boot
Warding off the late-day season
Still he comes to walk, to cruise.

His shadow is his secret
Carried hidden like the poisoned blood
Running in his veins;
Moonless here this early night
And in the distance, waves—
A muffled thunder—are his rhythm
Deep,
Like a heartbeat,

As his penetrating eyes
Scan the shifting mist in silence:
Perhaps a promise in the rising breeze
Foretelling of an Arctic winter
That he alone in darkness sees.

December 1993

5

HOMO PHARMACEUTICUS*

2:42 A.M., too late to take a sleeping pill.

—*Tony Gramaglia*

How does one describe this particular brand of hell?

—*Doug Bender*

*coined by Robbie Hilyard

CHEMICAL MAN

Robbie Hilyard

This is how his days begin.

He's out of bed and at the dresser where he tugs open the bottom drawer. His pharmacy, he calls it, containing his stash of precious relics of five opportunistic infections—and two years on the HIV circuit.

There are pills to help him breathe, pills to make him cough things up, pills to smother his coughing so he can sleep at night, pills to make him sleep when it isn't the coughing keeping him up, pills to mask the itchiness when the combination of other pills causes his skin to erupt in nasty-looking red bumps that no one can identify, pills to smother the nausea from that same combination of pills so he can keep them all down, pills to shield his white blood cells from the ravages of other pills, further pills to ease his withdrawal from former pills. Pills to calm his nerves so he can go about his day and look the world in the eye.

Pills enough to kill any presumptuous microbe rash enough to come within spitting distance of him.

There is even a section of pills that he will never take again, pills that didn't work for him but are too expensive to throw out. A constant reminder and a silent reproach, for he has seen his medical record and it never says, "This medication did not work for this patient." It always states, blamingly, "Patient failed drug." Like computers, he figures, modern medicine is incapable of making errors. It is the human in him that has failed.

Today his hand lingers over these last. Perhaps, one day, he will gather them all together and take them to his doctor. Maybe someone who can't afford to buy them can use them, will not fail them.

But to the task at hand. Here is his little blue plastic pillbox with the six sections—one for each day of the week with a rest on Sunday, except that he does not get a rest on Sunday, and his regimen for the day more than fills the little blue pillbox so he has a second one, in pink, that he keeps at home with the pills for the end of the day, and a third, in white, with a beeper to remind him to take the pills that must be taken apart from meals.

He puts so many pharmaceuticals into his body that he no longer feels quite human. He's evolved into Chemical Man. He knows he's not alone. There are others like him. Is this the future of mankind? he wonders. Are they the first of a new race? *Homo pharmaceuticus.*

He reaches for the pills that will forestall the fungus from crawling again inside the lining between his brain and his skull—that mysterious region the doctor calls the "meninges," with almost lip-smacking satisfaction, as if these were somehow the Bahamas of the body—and all the little microbes who want to go there for some R and R.

It was last winter when the fungus took over the area, reproduced enthusiastically, and tried to squeeze his brain out his ears. He'd suddenly understood then how it could be that people could get headaches so bad they banged their heads against the wall. But every time he moved to get out of bed, he barfed convulsively and never made it to the wall.

The treatment, when he'd been carried to the hospital, had been nearly as lethal as the infection itself. The doctors called it "shake and bake." During the daily four-hour infusion, his temperature would plummet and his body would be racked with uncontrollable shivering. Just when the nurses got him packed under a mound of blankets so thick and heavy his body didn't dare to shake anymore, his temperature would rebound and soar off in the other direction. He would suddenly break into a full-body sweat and be drenched by the time they got all the blankets off him, and still he would be tearing his gown off because it made him warmer than he could stand to be.

The only reason he isn't still on this drug, or dead from it, is that the government—only five days after they isolated the fungus in his spinal fluid—finally granted approval to the little pills he is now shaking into his hand as a "maintenance therapy." Maintenance therapy. That means he will have to take these pills every day for as long as he lives.

As long as he lives . . .

The lifesaving, life-sentence tablets are little pink trapezoids; they look like Flintstones vitamins. They are the driest thing he has ever had to force down his throat, worse even than the time his mother force-fed him saltines until he choked because he'd whined, "Mom, I'm hungry!" one time too many. These dust-bombs, he feels sure, could be used to drain swimming pools. He takes two a day.

And the doctor can't say why he suffers from dehydration.

Now he counts out the pills that are to prevent yet another episode of that garland of burning blisters that has come twice to clasp him off by the waist more warmly and tenaciously than he's ever been held in his life by parent or lover. Sleek capsules of robin's-egg blue. State-of-the-art, high-tech looking. They slide down his throat easily, comfortably. They even have their name and the name of their manufacturer printed right on them in a high-gloss black—presumably edible—ink.

Black and blue; he won't even think about the implications of this color combination.

Sometimes he hopes there is magic in this printed information, for it is his understanding that a virus is not, after all, a living organism, but a free-floating coding of information. And, he likes to think, even if the virus can't read, there is a certain comforting logic, or at least symmetry, in fighting information with information.

The pink and the blue lie side by side in the To Be Eaten With Breakfast section. Pastelish. Easter-egg tones. These are, coincidentally, the colors he has picked as his healing colors. The colors of babyhood, the colors of new life. The pink and the blue help him reflect on the paired opposites of his life. The old conflict of the masculine and the feminine elements of his spirit, still unresolved, certainly, but no longer so important to him in the face of life and death, hope and fear, love and anger, body and soul.

He tries to wear the pink, or the blue, or both together, as often as possible. They are his uniform of healing. His signal to the world that he has accepted the challenge, that he is living with this impossible thing in his life, that he is not satisfied with being told there's nothing he can do.

Kneeling before the dresser now, he counts them all out in their established order. The succession of pills disappearing into the little pink and blue pillboxes is like a rosary, an ornament of his devotion to keeping alive. The line of pills is like a rope by which he pulls himself through the day, a week, an abbreviated lifetime. But it is also the chain that binds him to the earthly and the daily when he wants to fly.

These white pills here represent another time that he went into the hospital. On this occasion, for five days and nights, he floated suspended between this world and the next, buoyed up by Demerol and weighted down by pain, while he waited for the baffled doctors to determine what was the cause—this time—for the return of the headaches, the nausea, the convulsive vomiting, the extreme fevers. He was also losing the sight in his right eye.

He wanted to die.

Finally someone on the hospital staff took his hand and said to him, "I just don't think it's your time to go. Why don't you step back into this life?" And, coincidentally, on that day, the doctors began treating him "presumptively"—that is, "as if" they'd identified an actual causative agent for his mystery ailment—and he soon began to get better. But he believes still that he is alive today not so much on account of the treatment, but because somebody bothered to invite him to remain in this world.

Shortly after the presumptive treatment began, his eye got suddenly better, or at least stopped getting worse.

It happened like this.

Still in the hospital, he was watching the *Ryan White Story* on TV one night and for the first time in a long while he cried for someone else as much as for himself. When he drew the tissue away from his eye, he found on it a large rusty blot, the color of old blood. When he looked around the room, the world was suddenly bright as it used to be in the old days, but the picture was still distorted, and two large areas were missing. Black hairline floaters still swam across his field of vision, but there were fewer of them. He felt that he could see again, although it was rather like looking through running water or broken glass. He calls that eye his shattered opal.

The little white pills are to keep the infection from crossing into his left eye and taking that one from him, too.

Having lost his eye makes him feel like a hero in a great book or a fairy tale, who loses something precious to him in the accomplishment of his quest. But he is not a hero in a book, he lives in the real world, and he will have to live here without his eye.

What he has gained, anyway, in exchange for his eye? A certain wisdom, perhaps? He's learned, for example, to feel homesick in the hospital when he's never before in his life felt any connection to any place he's ever lived; he's learned that it is more fun to surprise the world with how healthy he can be, rather than with how sick; he finds, to his surprise, that the more connected he feels to his life, the less afraid he becomes of leaving it behind. He is learning to love his own life, just the way it is, and not desperately want somebody else's.

He never asks himself if the lessons were worth the price.

The ritual of counting out his pills concluded, he proceeds automatically with the unvarying routine of his days. In the kitchen, he puts the oatmeal on to boil and mixes up that day's batch of his nutritional supplement, the substitute food that gives him nourishment when he can't keep down—sometimes can't even take in—enough of the real thing, and he fills with water the two plastic pitchers that he will keep beside him throughout the day and try to empty into himself.

But today he will do something different.

Today, drawn by the music of the wind chimes on a neighbor's porch, he will linger at the open window over the kitchen sink. He will notice the softness of the air, its sweetness; he will see the red bells unfurling on the trumpet vine across the alley. Sometimes he forgets that he wouldn't have these things if he didn't work so hard to hold them. Sometimes, immersed in the struggle, he forgets that this is what it is all for.

So today, after a while, he returns to the dresser—to his pharmacy—and he gathers up all those strays and leftovers, those pills that no longer work for him, and he puts them all into one of the lunch bags with the picture of the rabbit being pulled out of the hat. Today, he decides, is the day he will take them to his doctor for redistribution. Perhaps their magic will work for someone else. Perhaps they will give someone what he has: a chance to live.

LITANY

Christopher Gorman

1995   I live beyond the cure. I will die of AIDS, I say to my-self. I know this like I know my phone number when asked—or the way I can pick out my car in a crowded parking lot. I have lived through all the medical breakthroughs in the war against AIDS. Still, not long ago, I threw a shovelful of Connecticut onto the casket of a friend who once wrote a Broadway play. The week he died, his doctors informed him he was cured of lymphoma—but the fevers got him anyway. Old joke: Dentist says, "The teeth look great, but the gums gotta go."

1987   Fortified with nine hundred T cells, I receive the break-ing news about AZT with buoyant optimism. My sister calls to ask excitedly if I've seen the *New York Times*. I joke that now I might be alive for the publication of the sequel to *Gone with the Wind*.

1988   Infused with the spirit of my ancestors who had sur-vived the potato famine, I drive through a rainstorm to Tijuana with six hundred dollars stuffed into my Calvin's. The latest AIDS treatment is available in Mexico without prescription. Searching frantically for the Regis Pharmacia, I am pursued by small children who implore me to buy small packages of Chiclets. Fearful and determined, I speed on, past mothers rummaging in trash cans for discarded french fries and hot apple pies from McDonald's. One hour later, I drive through border customs with a three-month supply of ribavirin and Isoprinosene. "Anything to declare?" snarls a uniformed official who reminds me of Mandy Patinkin as Che Guevara. "No," I answer (flatly), having rehearsed several versions: "No" (detached); "No!" (emphatic); "No" (nonplussed); "No" (quizzical). He writes down my license plate number and glares at me through the dirty windshield of my Suzuki. I stare past him into the gray sky over San Diego. He waves me through—not knowing I am smuggling the AIDS cure into the United States wrapped in a brightly colored, hand-embroidered tablecloth.

1989   I meet a friend of a friend at a restaurant on Beverly Boulevard. He knows an airline steward who is sneaking dextran sulfate into his luggage on return trips from Tokyo. I slip $400 across the table to this stranger. One month later, he completes the transaction, turning the drug over to me in the lobby of the Sports Connection.

1990   My physician studies my most recent lab work and looks at me through a pair of glasses I recently admired at Oliver Peeples. "You have failed AZT," he says sternly, signing a form that would enroll me in a community-based trial of DDI. "This is a turning point in the treatment of this disease," he says, handing the form to me across a desk littered with phone messages. "A turning point," he repeats for emphasis. On the way home, I stop at Video West and rent the movie starring Shirley MacLaine and Anne Bancroft.

1992   The Federal Drug Administration approves DDI. I have relocated to New York and am enrolled in a study of DDC—in combination with protease inhibitor and the aforementioned

AZT. Every third Tuesday I join the masses at Bellevue Hospital. Among the crack addicts and schizophrenics, I feel comparatively healthy and comfortably superior. One Tuesday, after spending an hour in the waiting room seated next to someone with penicillin-resistant tuberculosis, I treat myself to lunch at Arcadia, washing down the protease inhibitor, AZT, and DDC with a California cabernet.

∽

1993   "You failed dapsone," the emergency-room physician admonishes as I lie on a gurney in a basement hallway at New York University Hospital.

"Don't say I failed dapsone," I croak. "You sound like my high school guidance counselor. Dapsone failed me."

"Be that as it may, you have a mild case of *Pneumocystis*—or possibly, a severe case of asthma. We'll begin treatment with pentamidine immediately. I'll see you again Monday morning."

Delaying his exit, I whimper, "But . . . this is Friday."

Looking at me directly for the first time, he sheepishly explains, "I have a share on Fire Island. This is my weekend," and he's off, practically skipping down the hallway past linen carts and infectious-waste containers. I am left alone on the gurney to contemplate his diagnosis. Behind Door #1 is a ten-day $15,000 hospital stay. Behind Door #2 is a year's supply of Primatene Mist. Behind Door #3 is a full share in a house at the Fire Island Pines.

∽

1994   Back in Los Angeles . . . "I have the results of your viral sensitivity test," says the doctor with the thinning hair and the bulging biceps.

"Oh?" I respond tremulously—sounding like Mary Richards being interviewed for a job by Lou Grant.

"Yes," says the doctor with the thinning personality and the bulging bank account, "and the results are less than dazzling. Your particular strain of the virus has mutated to the extent that it is resistant to AZT, DDI, and DDC. Also D4T."

"Wait! I've never taken D4T."

"Well, now you won't have to," he answers without a trace of comic intention.

Driving away from UCLA, I recite the litany of drugs I am no longer sensitive to: AZT, DDC, DDI, D4T. Can R2D2 be far behind?

Today   Recently, the *New York Times* broke the news that interleukin-2 therapy represented a significant breakthrough in the management of HIV disease. The article specifically mentioned that researchers believed the drug would not be an effective option for people with less than two hundred T cells. My T-cell count is now compatible with the song "One Hundred Bottles of Beer on the Wall." I've lived so long with this virus that I'm no longer available for the latest cure. My future is behind Door #4.

Was it Greta Garbo who said, "I'm tired?" Or Madeline Kahn?

I'm tired.

There.

Now *I* said it.

TURTLE MEAT

Jim Rudolph

"Turtle," Dr. Chang told me, "make you moist." According to Chinese medicine, my body was dry because of the HIV residing within me for at least the last ten years. The young-looking Chinese doctor, his abdomen protruding from bottom-bowel breathing, said, "You eat cow, don't you? Why not eat turtle? I eat two or three turtles each month." I guess Dr. Chang must also be dry. "Any store in Chinatown sell turtle. They cut up for you," he said in a tone full of exasperation with people who didn't eat turtle.

Modern medicine had failed. I had tried all the antivirals—AZT, DDI, DDC, and D4T—each with a miserable side effect: anemia, neuropathy, or pancreatitis. My T cells dipped into the realm of two hundred and I needed more than the depressing options at the AIDS clinic.

So I took the plunge down Sunset Boulevard until it became Caesar Chavez—the new street, not the man. I crossed traffic, entered Chinatown, double-parked in front of an herb store, and popped in to ask, "Where can I buy turtles to eat?" No one knew.

Finally, in a side-street market at the end of the meat counter I discovered two boxes of live turtles. One turtle type was shaped like a Mongolian yurt; the other had a peaked pagoda-roof shell. I chose the Mongolian yurt, which looked more like turtles I had seen.

The Chinese butcher spoke no English. I chopped one hand

against the palm of the other and pointed to the turtle. He grabbed it and chopped it with a cleaver before I could avert my eyes. A paw pointed at me and pulsed.

I turned my back and wandered through aisles of tea canisters and bamboo shoots. Why was I so squeamish? I had grown up in eastern Oregon hunting and butchering wild game, gutting and skinning rabbits we raised, and cleaning trout so freshly caught they danced on the skillet. But California had changed me with planetary nonviolence, vegetarianism, and karma, and with Meher Baba, Sai Baba, and Swami Beyondananda.

About five minutes later I returned to pick up my turtle, but suddenly a woman grabbed the plastic sack off the meat counter. Aghast, I stood while she carried it away to the cash register. I had been robbed of my turtle, and the turtle butcher had disappeared. A Spanish-speaking beef butcher explained to me that his colleague had gone to the rest room. He, he pointed out, did not butcher turtles. Dr. Chang's frustration came to mind, and I wondered, if he can butcher cows, why can't he butcher turtles?

Another Chinese butcher walked behind the counter and I asked for another turtle. He told me to pick the turtle I wanted, but said he would not butcher it. Why he would not butcher it, he did not explain. When I asked for the store manager, he pointed to an old white-haired Chinese man watching me as though I were a shoplifter. Although success seemed unlikely, I walked over to him and asked to have another turtle butchered. The manager turned his back on me and walked over to the ginseng counter.

"Now what's happening?" I asked myself, wondering if the old man did not understand English. If I were brave enough to cry in public, I would have. I did not like having turtles killed, I did not want to despair, and I did not want to die of AIDS. I was as happy as I'd ever been with my loved ones, friends, travel, and work. I hated searching for ways to live a little longer, but I loved my life. I felt caught in a trap.

While looking at some ceramic rice bowls, I flashed back to 1957 when I was ten years old. Dad had arrived home, his arms holding several identical sealed jars. He had driven across Dooley

Mountain, along the Malheur River, and all the way to John Day City a hundred miles away to buy herbs from the Chinese doctor with a reputation for miraculous cures. "It's got toenails in the brew," Dad said. The quart jars, like ones Mom used to preserve peaches and huckleberries, were filled with dark brown liquid, herbs, and things that looked like toenails.

Dad didn't trust our family physician and town surgeon: "All he wants is to cut on me." Most ailments in our family were treated by Mom, but all the bland foods she fed Dad didn't make his stomachache go away.

Dad's stomach hurt as never before. Was he remembering his own father, who died of stomach cancer on the family ranch in Colorado? The doctor had opened up Grandpa to see what was wrong, then he just sewed Grandpa back up. In those times stomach cancer was a death sentence and morphine its only consolation. It took only six weeks for Grandpa to die.

After Dad brought those jars home, I never took a second look at the dark, scary contents. He, however, strained glassfuls of the concoction and gulped them each morning through a bitter expression. The family and all the neighbors waited to see if herbs from a Chinaman could cure Dad's pain.

Eventually, Dad ran out of herbs and the town doctor cut off two-thirds of his stomach. His ailment had been only ulcers, not cancer, and in no time Dad was back to eating two plates of food for dinner. He would die by his own hand decades later, diagnosed with a brain tumor.

Suddenly, I felt a nudge at my elbow. The mysterious white-haired manager motioned me back to the meat counter. The turtle butcher had returned from the rest room. Again I chose one, another karmic stain on my soul. I turned my back before the sound of the first chop and for the second time wandered the aisles again. When I returned, the bag was atop the counter. The butcher apologized for a misunderstanding that I still did not understand.

That night, along with ginger and white wine, I filled my slow cooker with the bloody meat, brown shell, and green paws still with toenails. By morning, a sweet, vile smell permeated the house, and the turtle had become meat and broth. The shell and paws were still too recognizable. Over the next few days, I ate the meat, a little at a time.

I returned to Dr. Chang's office for more herbs and with good news. Lab results showed my T cells had climbed back into the three hundreds. However, Dr. Chang was more interested in my tongue, which he examined visually. He announced proudly I had become more moist, which he attributed to the turtle. Suddenly it dawned on me: he expected me to continue eating them.

If nothing else, Dr. Chang has given me an alternative to toxic antivirals. Herbs and turtles are at least something to try as I live with the time bomb, its fuse shortening year by year. And to try something gives me hope, however fragile or ill-founded. After all, evidence has shown hope to be an immune booster.

I hope to live.

BY LAKE LUZERN

Tom Bezzi

The October sun is bright but not warm. It glares off the water. The water that is shallow by the edge of the lake. The water through which they can see the stony bottom. A large goose waddles in after crumbs a tourist has tossed. The glare fragments and dances.

They stand with their backs to the lake, posing for a snapshot. They have their arms around each other: he, his arm around her shoulder; she, her arm around his waist. His is forty-one; she, thirty-six. He is wearing a beret. On the side of it is a wooden commemorative pin found in an antique store near the Landesmuseum: a bare cross with equidistant arms on a red rectangular field. His sage-green jacket and aviator glasses, which he has taken off for the photo, as well as his features, make you think American military. But the black-and-white ACT UP button belies that. The khaki Girbaud paratrooper's pants continue the theme of military drag rerendered. He is wearing waffle-tread, lace-up shoes of undyed leather that he bought the day before.

Twenty years before, when they traveled around the Continent together, their shoes marked them as Americans. And their backpacks and down jackets. Now they don't stand out. They have been discussing whether it is that Europeans have become more Americanized or they themselves more cosmopolitan, further removed from their Kansas roots. The Louisville-slugger jacket she is wearing, for example, is very much in fashion. The details now that set her apart are the oversize men's rugby sweater and the ornate, diamond dinner ring in its platinum setting. It had been their mother's and grandmother's. He was surprised that she brought stuff to clean her diamonds every morning. In a big brother's eyes, a little sister is always young, so details like jewelry cleaner are surprising.

She has come with him because he has AIDS and she didn't want him to have to travel to Switzerland for treatment alone. He began the treatment two days before; it was her birthday. How is it that a disease that can separate him from her has brought them closer together? How can they enjoy each other so much, even more than ever? Why is the Swiss woman taking so long to frame the photo? He feels the sun on the back of his neck. He feels his sister's arm around his waist. She is pinching him and saying, "Smile, Buhbuh." The light, dancing on the water, freezes. . . .

Snow is falling on the gray waters of the River Reuss. The flakes disappear into the rushing water. The water that copies the pewter sky. The water that races under the Spreuerbruecke, draining from Lake Luzern.

It is a cold, indistinct dawn as the two men cross the bridge. One looks like a retired astronaut; the other, like Sioux Center's finest. The vegetable vendors are only just setting up their stalls on the river's cobblestone promenade. The two men are leaving at first light so they can be at Roka's clinic by eight, before the waiting room fills with other American PWAs. After the treatment, the two will drive their rental car to Austria to go skiing.

The bald one is wearing the same beret as in the photo from six months before. He has on a heavier coat, a Pendleton with a vivid, geometric Navajo design. He's never been wild about the beige background, but he values it because his sister liked it enough to buy it for him shortly after he had PCP. His boyfriend doesn't have a hat on over his freshly blown-dry white-blond hair. Snowflakes land in it.

They're calling it their honeymoon. They've been inseparable since they met two months before. It's costing a lot of money—

the flights, the treatment, then the trip to Lech—but the elder has learned to spend money on what brings him happiness. He's never been happier. Who would have thought it would finally happen now?

Because he speaks excellent German, he has helped out the last two mornings at Roka's clinic, translating. As thanks, Roka gave his boyfriend the treatment gratis, saying it would be good if they could stop the infection early. Roka speaks of them paternally, in the third person, using the German expression that means "the boys."

As they cross the river, the elder worries aloud about the snow and the drive to Austria. Maybe the younger is anxious, too. But everything is okay. The snow will make them pay extra attention to their driving. The snow is like the virus. The virus that can end life can also make them live life. The bell in the Jesuitkirche begins to clang seven. The snow disappears into the rushing water. They feel like the two luckiest boys in the world.

HOW TO SMART OFF TO BORDER GUARDS

Juan Candelario

"*Su pasaporte, por favor?*" asked the INS agent at the San Ysidro border station.

"Excuse me, but I didn't think that I would need a passport to come home. Here's my birth certificate and driver's license."

After a day of running around Tijuana trying to find enough Zentel (which the doctor told me would deal with the microsporidium), the last thing I wanted was to deal with this border guard who was acting as if he were God.

"Well," quizzed the guard gruffly, "what's your native language."

"What language do you feel comfortable in? *Español? Parla Italiano? Gavariti porusski? Specs-du Nederlandse?*" I replied. "Excuse me, Officer Jamison, I thought my California driver's license and a copy of my New York birth certificate would be enough proof to show that I am a U.S. citizen."

"Well," the border agent muttered, "we've been getting a lot of phony documents down here." All through this tirade, I was getting angrier. Here was this person telling me that I don't even belong in my own country.

"Look, buddy," I responded testily, "do you feel the imprint in the birth certificate? Hold it up to the light. Do you see the New York State seal in the watermark? *Are you trying to tell me that New York is no longer a part of the United States?*"

After a few minutes studying the birth certificate, the agent said no and asked me to follow him to another table. Great, I thought. This guy must think I'm a terrorist with loads of drugs. (I had all my meds for the day and was carrying extra Marinol in case I got nauseous.) Well, I thought, go ahead and lock me up. At the table were two other INS agents, one male and one female with big hair. Great, I thought, Joe and Susie Six Pack.

Joe spoke first. "What was the purpose of your trip?" More and more tired and just wanting to go home, I said I went to Tijuana to search out a medication that my doctor advised was unavailable in the United States. Joe asked if the address on my license was current. I said yes.

Then Joe asked about the medication. I replied, "It's for a medical condition called microsporidiosis, as I am a person with AIDS." Joe went on, "What are the symptoms of microsporidiosis?" What? I thought. Here's this GS-9 probably with barely a high school education and he's asking for a description of symptoms of an illness that I don't understand? Joe repeated, "What are the symptoms?"

Yes! I was going to give this clown a taste of his own medicine. I stated mockingly, meekly, "Well, sir, the symptoms are myriad: from diarrhea, constipation, incontinence, microbacterial avium complex"—through this litany, Joe's face was turning green—"cytomegalovirus, PID, myocardial infarctive distress . . ." Joe quickly excused himself and ran into the men's room.

Big Hair Susie, a little more controlled, quickly chimed in, "Why are there two last names on your birth certificate?"

"Well," I calmly responded, "the reason that there are two last names is merely a Latin convention to list the maternal last name along with the paternal last name. I simply use my paternal last name, which is the first name. And," I continued, directing Susie to the race section on the document, "if you look at the box marked RACE, it states Puerto Rican, which would make me a U.S. native."

Susie studied the box on the document, returned it, and then asked if I was taking the trolley.

"Yes," I replied. Susie said, "Welcome home." Yeah, I thought as I went through the glass door and boarded the red tram car to return to San Diego. Welcome home.

(FRAGMENT)

Steve Smith

Panic. Awake-at-4-A.M., hairs-raised-on-your-arms, can't-catch-your-breath, heart-beating-like-a-maniacal-timpani, want-to-run-naked-from-the-house kind of panic.

Xanax doesn't help—just postpones the symptoms.

Hot milk, hot baths, hot sex—all just palliatives.

Try to breathe—deeper, slower.

Close your eyes.

Think of fern grottoes with gentle waterfalls.

Of Japanese pagodas with tinkling bells.

Of immersion in a steel bubble twenty leagues beneath the sea, with eels and manta rays floating eerily, peacefully past your periscope.

PILGRIM

Brent Bellon

An esophagus is not meant to be burned. A breast is not meant to be sliced off. A lung is not meant to be butchered. An esophagus is designed for swallowing. Easily. To facilitate the smooth transition of nutrition from mouth to gut. But we are all the same here. Pilgrims to the shrine of life. The shrine of life at the hands of death. Killing. Killing. Killing. Killing tumors. And healthy cells. And healthy esophagi. The shrine of life sees it all. There is no shame among us. No. We all share a similar story, different only in the retelling. We accept. We have no other choice. Choosing is no longer an option. I have cancer. So does she. And she. And she. And he. And he. She doesn't look sick. He doesn't appear to be dying.

No one can see my charred esophagus after the twenty treatments that have fried it crisp—crisp as the beautiful food being fried to shit by a surly cook behind the counter in a greasy diner, then being softened up by an overload of grease. We don't get softening, any of us. How do you soften a fearful heart? a weary soul? a pained body? By more radiation, day after endless day?

She has breast cancer. Most of the women in my time period seem to be here for the same reason, while many of the men seem to be battling lung cancer. No explanations. Resignation. Ruth Barrus taught me the meaning of resignation at Rick's College many years ago. Grand old lady, an organist with artificial hips, who also taught humanities. I was smitten, taken in, awe-struck. Ruth taught the organ to Judy Johnson. Judy Johnson taught me piano and has agreed to play the adagio from Beethoven's *Pathétique* Sonata at my funeral in Roosevelt, Utah, a town where the public swimming pool is in the shape of the letter *T* in honor of the town's namesake, Teddy Roosevelt. AIDS-related non-Hodgkin's lymphoma. My resignation. Ruth insisted it was beautiful to be resigned to the inevitable.

Cancer is inevitable for my companions and me. It is now. We all sit around in our treatment gowns, curious, three-sleeved, unisex gowns in lovely surgical scrub green. Only we who are here for treatment are admitted to the exclusive club of knowing how to don the bizarre gown. One of the perks here—exclusivity.

We visit. Or sit shyly and with reserve. Or chatter nervously about peanut-butter cookies recipes, as if we'll be around for ages to cook them for our grandchildren. Swapping stories and treatments. Are any of us on the brink of death? It doesn't appear so. Not at all. We are alive, vital, going strong. I often scowl and sit with my head in my hands, unwilling to chat about fluff as I await my allotted thirty seconds of killer rays. And then, we are individually ushered in at our appointed time to the shrine. A shrine staffed with cold, Stepford-like technicians whose only priority is to get us zapped and out of there in less than ten minutes. Cold room, table, and staff. No warmth for cancer anywhere in this environment. I'm not a person in here—simply an object to be treated and moved. Outside of here, cancer-free people shake their heads and think I am crazy for undergoing treatment. I want to slap them. Let's see their choices when it's their turns. Curiously, I don't remember asking for an opinion.

Inside of here, I find acceptance. And approval. We all approve, we who inhabit the cancer chamber. Perhaps a death chamber. Possibly a life chamber. This is a group of lovers. Lovers of life. Life haters don't willingly submit to a burned throat and suffer for many long months the agony of swallowing hard foods and pills that create searing pain as each swallow takes the culprits down the damaged passageway.

A breast isn't meant to be removed. It is a body part of nurturing, of life-giving, of pleasure, of aesthetics. A lung is meant to last a lifetime, aiding the respiratory process, not to be sickly and taken from the chest. And still, the pilgrimage continues, the masses before and the masses still to come. Two machines in operation, eight hours a day, treating at tight, ten-minute intervals. I see just a few of the many.

And I do see, increasingly failing with an eye that is meant to give vision, not to be eaten away. I *still* see. And hear. And feel. And observe. I've lost no breast or lung. I'm the youngest one at the shrine, with "only" a fist-size tumor in my chest and a burned esophagus. That's all. What an odd comfort.

CHOSEN FAMILY
(ACT 2, SCENE 3)

Philip Justin Smith

*C*hosen *Family* is a play with three characters who are three great friends. Tory is in his early thirties. He is attractive but not too attractive. His charm is in his style, humor, and the attention he gives to Lolly and Teo. Tory gets AIDS. Teo is handsome in a Brooks Brothers way. You would never assume he was gay. The calm head in the storm. Lolly, a Japanese-American woman is vivacious, charming, and *tough*. She is the most outspoken of the three.

(Scene opens later the same evening. There is a loud banging on the door. Tory comes out of his bedroom.)

TORY

Who is it?

LOLLY

It's me, Lolly.

TORY

What are you doing here?

LOLLY

I just talked to Teo. He's a mess. I need to talk to you. Please just let me in.

TORY

Go home.

LOLLY

Please just open the door for a minute.

TORY

No, Lolly. Tonight is not the night. Just go home.

LOLLY

Tory, that's not fair.
(*nothing*)
Open this door!
(*again nothing*)
Let me in this minute or I'll start screaming and I won't stop until every one of your gooddamn neighbors is up!
(*The door opens; Lolly walks in and takes a swing at Tory he easily dodges. Then she takes another more serious swing; this time it's a "face-off."*)

LOLLY

Fuck you. What do you mean telling Teo you're going to kill yourself and not telling me. I'm your friend, too. I've got some rights, don't I? Don't I? Tory, talk to me.

TORY

Okay. But one thing. I was not ready to tell you. And I am completely exhausted so no big scenes. Deal?

LOLLY

Deal. Will you tell me why you want to kill yourself?

TORY

What are you saying? You have been through this with me. You have seen my dropping counts, no energy, the weight loss. Who held me every time I got my blood work back while I cried. And every time I said it didn't matter. It matters. Think about Mike and Todd. They died long, ugly deaths. "Todd, just hang on. There has go to be a cure coming, you can't give up. You've got to have hope."

Lolly, we all said it and we meant it. Well, he hung on all-right. He ended up dying choking on his own black vomit. And Mike, just skin and bones. He weighed eighty pounds in the hospital. He was so afraid of dying, he tried everything. Thank God you and Teo are well. But I'm not. I've got about two T cells and their names are Fred and Joe. Not a lot of hope for reproduction. Even my T cells are queer.

My doctor says in the next three months I have a seventy percent chance of developing Pneumocystis. And after that? KS, MAC, or PML or whatever the flavor of the month is. I respect the people who are fighting to live "no matter what." But I'm not doing that. For now I'm going to live and do everything I want while I can. But in my heart I'll know when it's time to check out. It's not going to be easy. Fuck, honey, I'm scared shitless. But that's the way I want it. And you are either with me or out of my life. They'll be no last-minute back-from-the-grave dancing to yet another swan song. My swan song begins now and it's going to be beautiful. Including the ending. I'm taking that right. And no one, I repeat, no one is going to fuck with it.

LOLLY
(She just stares at him, she has begun to cry.)
Stop talking like that. You are not going to die! You are not, you are not, you are . . . *(sobbing)*

TORY
(Embracing her, he begins to cry, too.)
You are my best friend. And it's breaking my heart to hurt you like this. But you have got to hang on. You don't have to agree with me, just don't try to stop me.

LOLLY
You can't ask me this, you son of a bitch. Why am I the only one fighting for your life? You can't give up hope.

TORY
I have hope. Maybe I'm just trying to spook the spirits. Maybe I'm just trying to avoid death by being ready for it. I don't know.

LOLLY
You're lost if you give up.

TORY
I'm not giving up, I'm just drawing the line.

LOLLY

I'll do the best I can. But I'm afraid. Very afraid.
(They hold each other.)

LOLLY

Can I stay over?

TORY

I'd love that.
(Tory heads for the kitchen to take out something to eat while Lolly heads for the bedroom.)

LOLLY

(slyly, knowing she's asking a big favor)
Can I wear the cowboy pajamas?

LOLLY

(from the bedroom)
Darling, did I interrupt something?
(Tory looks toward the door. Realizes, but too late. Lolly walks out of the bedroom with a big, black dildo.)

LOLLY

Why, I don't believe we've been introduced.

TORY

Lolly, you probably shouldn't touch that. At least not until it's been washed.

LOLLY

Ugh! I wish this thing could talk. We could do an interview show. "Inside Tory Hunt."

TORY

Great idea, too bad most of the people we'd need to talk to are dead.
(Lolly is heading for the bedroom with the "friend." She stops to give Tory a "look.")

LOLLY

Hey, you.

TORY

What?

LOLLY

Can I sleep with you in your bed?

TORY

I might have sweats.

LOLLY

I'll help you change the sheets.

(Lights fade.)

(FRAGMENT)

Michael Martin

No, I didn't call anyone. It happened real quick. My doctor called Tuesday saying that he wanted to see me. He had been talking about getting me in for this procedure for a couple of weeks. He said call this number.

A Dr. Miles. No, Holland's the eye guy. . . .

. . . Believe me, they make me feel as if they want to make me a poster boy for "Chemotherapy and You" campaign.

Dr. Miles comes back to say I qualify for the stem-cell transplant. I want to rush right home and watch all those sci-fi movies on transplants, starting with *Frankenstein*. . . .

Well, good news! I'll be switching from one chemo to another. . . . This new chemo will probably start the week of February 7. . . . The real upsetting part is at the end of March when it's time to give me back my harvested white cells. I have this vision of Asian farmers toiling away upon flooded rice-paddy-type floors at UCLA harvesting those cells. Of course we need to throw in a water buffalo or two.

I need to be in the hospital for about four weeks. They explained to me all the terrible things that can happen.

Yeah, they were very supportive. They'll call this week with more definite dates. They said they never lost anyone to the transplant. It's the tumors that get us.

OKAY, SO I'M IN THIS BED

Tony Gramaglia

Okay, so I'm in this bed. Hospital bed. Egg-crate cushion. Soft. Clean sheets. Inviting. I don't need to be in the bed, but I stay there. The TV keeps me there. The doctors keep me there. I keep me there. AIDS keeps me there. There are three chairs and even a sofa in the room, but I stay in the bed. My controls are there. Bed controls, TV controls. Nurse controls. Phone controls. Disease controls. I am the good patient in the bed. I can make doctors laugh. I can make nurses love me; I can welcome friends from this bed. This hospital bed.

At night I turn the TV on before I go to sleep. I put it on a nothing station that has only static and turn it up as loud as the remote will allow. I need the white noise to drown out the sound of AIDS. No people. I don't want to know that there are people. Down the hall. In that room next door or across the way. But the white noise of the TV still does not drown out the sounds of the hospital at night. The flushing of a toilet. That hacking cough. A pulling back of someone's curtain. A voice on the intercom. A faucet next door. My own breath.

You don't have to be awake to hear the screams of the man next door. You can't pretend it is just a sound. He is screaming, "No, no. Please don't. Please don't. Wait. Not now." And when the screaming stops and the coughing starts, I know they have stuck the tube down his throat to drain the fluid.

I know there are many scared eyes like mine opened now at

196

3:46 A.M. Eyes that are listening. There is a set in room 416. Another set in room 412. Another set of opened, scared eyes that should be shut and dreaming in room 411. But all of the eyes, those that can open if there is not too much morphine or Demerol in them, all those sets of eyes in the hospital beds are listening to this, to him. Or were.

You can close them now, your eyes. You wish you were someplace else so you could call the front desk and ask someone to please stop the man next door from dying so loudly. To stop injecting you with the fear of pain. To stop your eyes from listening to the death down the hall. In that room. In this room. In my room.

So close your eyes now. Listen to the white noise of the TV. Try to drown out the sounds. Drown out the fear. But the eyelids closed offer little peace. You can still see the empty room across the way where the black man used to be. You can't forget what you saw in another room, legs too skinny to be legs. You can see through the crack in the door the tangle of tubes that poke through another's chest. You can see her skin, too tight, too gray to be skin. You can see the fright.

At daybreak, I turn off the white noise. I am back in control. In this bed. I can make it go up or down. Call for a Coke. Turn a station. Open a blind. Flip on a light. Make a call. I keep feeling around for a switch to turn off the nights. Turn off the screams. Turn off the disease. But there is none. Not here. Not in this bed.

Dave Knight

I told you
when the nurses came
started marching in like that
the room fires red in combat

In clicks the identical shoe heels
more pairs than one
click! click! click!
"Where is Hitler?"
you are going to ask

You will check . . . yes
your tired but still mindful eyes
will search the arms, certain
there is
some kind of number

Something happened
during your sleep
you're not sure how long it was
when it started
only
that you're waking now
sort of

The nurses marching
tap! tap! tap!
everything is red
you fear red must be
the final color,
morphine
kept you from the violet
and blue stages

You are waiting for the white
but it's only a sheet
over you
translucent enough
to admit the battle zone
into your tired
but still mindful eyes

With the nurses marching
everything clicks
shoes, rollers,
floor, clamps

You keep looking for that tattoo
they burned one on you
you're sure of it

And of this you are certain, too
they will march you away soon
click! click! wheel!
into much more red
than you have ever seen

(FRAGMENT)

Christopher Gorman

The sound of bells ringing in the hospital reminded him of the bells that rang in the department stores of his youth. Slipping in and out of consciousness, he visited Abercrombie and Fitch, B. Altman's, and Best & Company. The last sound he heard was the rosary beads as they slipped from his hand and hit the floor of his hospital room.

Then there was silence.

Later, his friend sat beside the body. Spread before him were the contents of a wallet he had found between the phone and a half-empty can of ginger ale on a table next to the body.

AT and T calling card.

California driver's license number C3309445. Expires on birthday in 1995. Frank S. Zolin, Director, Department of Motor Vehicles.

Prescription Drug Identification Card. Group # CBS3000. Member # 104505650.

The dead man's sister sits in with her back to the body. Outside the window rain falls in the afternoon. She thinks the rain hides her tears from her brother's friend.

A punch card from Santa Palm Car Wash, 8787 Santa Monica Boulevard, West Hollywood, California 90069. After 10 washes are punched on the same line bearer entitled to free regular wash. (The card has been punched nine times.)

Frequent Shipper Coupon Mayflower Box and Ship, 7304 Beverly Boulevard, Los Angeles, California 90036. Ship 10 times and receive $10.00 credit toward shipping on your next visit. (The card has been punched three times.) Two days before he coughed himself into the hospital he mailed Christmas presents to Pennsylvania and St. Louis. To his cousin with Down's syndrome in Tappan, New York, he sent a woolen sweater. Inside the Brooks Brothers box was a card with Snoopy on the cover wearing a pair of sunglasses. "What do you call a relative like you?" Inside, the answer: "Totally awesome. Happy birthday." They had a connection, these two cousins.

East Side Sauna. A club for gentlemen. Member # 6906732. Out-of-town membership. The dead man's friend stares at this unfamiliar card for a long time.

Mileage Plus Mastercard. # 4086 3076 0407 2200. Valid dates Dec 1 94–11/97. If this card is found, cut in half and mail to Box 11830, Wilmington, Delaware 19850. (His friend remembered seeing the card in restaurants in New York and Los Angeles, London and Rome, Seattle and Chicago. His friend with wasting syndrome ate very well, he thought.)

The phone rang once disturbing the sadness in the room the three of them shared. One loud ring, then silence. A relief for the friend and the sister. Before the day was done, they would have to tell the story again and again. But not yet. The phone rang once and then no more. They waited for someone to tell them what to do next.

6

ENSEMBLE

Things I didn't know I loved [after Nazim Hizmet]

- fresh, cold spring water (or apple cider)
- fighting quietly w/ my mother (who's out here taking care of me)
- the inexplicable love of certain friends (Suzie, Colleen, David)
- the snow-peaked fresh mts. that surround Mammoth
- the smile of Zoe as she crisscrossed the entire playground to give me a hug (I kept thinking, "This can't be for me, it must be for her mother," but it was for me)

—*Scott Riklin*

How strange it is in the hospital with people pouring in to visit. There's a pleasure, a shadow pleasure, at the end of a day with fifty thousand visitors serving lunches and cackling—it's the salon I've always dreamed of. Then afterward, when everyone leaves, the sorrow is the most intense, the biggest. I think it's about imagining the loss, not being here where I feel the love on this earth—the separation is overwhelming.

—*Philip Justin Smith*

TODAY 12/4/93

Leonard Mosqueda

Feeling good, sunny day, delicious coffee, Escobar's dead, long live Michael Jackson, Chris looks like he has AIDS, the Chinese man on bus was very happy, the heroin addict looked like he dyed his hair black, Blessed Sacrosanct had seven homeless today in foyer, the buses were empty, Latin Mormons shouldn't wear latex, the Japanese gay shouldn't try to love so, APLA is huge, Winchell's is dirty, the coffee there is bad, Starbucks is better, the waitresses at Crest are desperate for TIPS, the new porno for December had no Santas, what happened? Vine is a tawdry street and there was a man in front of the Cinerama Dome last week who lost his pants. He was wearing an oily rag around him. Tonight is Las Posadas. Lots of memories and lots of cruising. What color should I wear? Better take a coat though. I should avoid heavy-duty Christians tonight. Should be home by 7 P.M. Xmas is coming. Should I buy cards? Rats! That elevator makes a hell of a lot of noise and that squeal got to go.

DISHES

Doug Bender

They are piled there on the counter like a ceramic sculpture, remnants of previous attempts at feeding. They are not terribly dirty: bread crumbs, and spots of apple juice dull now against the shiny black surface, spaghetti sauce brown and crusted from a night in the air.

This is my last year.

It takes so little time to wash them but it gives me great pleasure to see them clean once again, dripping on the white, waffled dishcloth that rests on the counter. Like applying paint to an old seedy wall or alphabetizing a stack of index cards, there is finally order and calm in a chaotic, frenetic world.

You take control where you can.

You find joy where you can.

You allow respite when you can.

This is my last year.

I do these things every morning. I wash the plates and set them to drip on the cloth. I wash my hands and set the medicine to drip through the tube, each drop marking time like sand through the hourglass, so many drops per second, so many seconds per hour. How many hours are left?

I rinse the soap residue from the bowl. I think this year will be the last one. Across the street I can see my friend's kitchen window. This was his last year. We used to do dishes at the same time each day, facing each other, smiling and waving hello. Perhaps he ate more, or more often, or worked more slowly, because I always finished the ritual before he did.

He got sick one week and died the next.

I tried to tell a friend that this would be my last year. He got angry. He was upset. He told me not to think about it or it would become a self-fulfilled prophecy, that somehow I would talk myself into it, into dying, that I would cause it. "Do not go gentle into that good night," he said.

I do not understand what causal relationship rage has to living. Many who fought the dying of the light are dead. And many ornery, ungrateful "life is bad" types still live on.

I remind myself that I am allowed, no, required to figure this out for myself. It is my right, my privilege, my responsibility. I cannot color my thinking about illness and death with someone else's paints.

What should I do if this is my last year? A month on a tropical island? Lavish presents for loved ones bought with never-to-be-paid-off credit cards? Find a lover who will hold my hand, caress my cheek, and pull the blanket up close so I won't be so cold and lonely in those very last moments?

I rinse the glasses and put them on the cloth. I remember washing dishes with my lover, that once-upon-a-time guy. He would stand at the sink, his back to the door. I would come from behind and hold him, my arms around his chest like ribbon on a lovely gift. He would make a contented sound, and we would stand there quietly, my head sideways, cheek on his back. Sometimes I turned him around and said, "Dance with me," and we would dance there in the kitchen on the caramel-colored tile to the sound of the water running off the plates, shuffling our feet on the tile, our faces touching softly, our bodies intertwined like sophomores at the prom.

I'll make a deal, as if there's someone to deal with, as if that bogus wizard behind the curtain has something in his bag for me. Just a little longer, let me find someone and go a little longer. But I cannot come up with my part of the bargain. There is nothing I can do, nothing I'm willing to give up. I've worked too hard for what I have, those precious wisps of people and things that have been collected over the years. Trade those for a lover for a too short length of time and then die? It isn't worth it. Or is it?

What is the price of time?

I wipe my hands with the towel on the refrigerator door and feel my belly stir. I can't remember the clinical term. Is it *void,* or *vacate?* I only know I must negotiate the pole from which the drugs hang through the living room into the bathroom, manipulate the buttons and zipper to take off my pants, and I must do it quickly. I have hours ago removed the special plasticized garment I wear at night to protect against an incontinent incident. "Get back into life," says the aging but perky former film star.

There is nothing I would rather do.

I am lucky this time. There is no accident. The brown water gushes from my body like the falls at Niagara. I am amazed that the vacuum created by the last episode of this harrowing drama has been filled, that the water continues to invade and dominate.

I am dying, dying slowly, not by inches, but by pints.

I am not ready, I think, with or without a boyfriend. I know I am not ready, yet there is a certain calm that settles around me like a lovely, quiet snowfall. No more fighting. No more feeling. No more bolstering the spirits of those who love me, a task I take on because in most ways I assume all of this is harder on them than on me. After all, I am inside my body. I know precisely what it's like, how monstrous and how manageable. I know the exact level of pain. They can only peek into the unknown, without fact and without light, which, as any horror-movie buff will tell you, is the most terrifying.

I have been this sick once before, two years ago, a five-month incident of wasting and miraculous rebuilding. I did not think I would die then. My biggest fear was that I would live and be sick, not be able to go and do. I got back into life by making sure I had an outing each day, to the video store, or to the grocery for something small that I could carry. If it was a really good day, I went to a movie. But I did not think I would die.

I wonder what the difference is now.

I clean myself with the special medicated pads. They feel cool and wet, soothing against my battered skin. My face is also wet, and I realize I am crying.

I return to the living room. The shades are open, and the room is light. It is a lovely day. I can see the blue sky and the fluffy white clouds above the trees with the new growth of green buds. The dishes are done. The rest of the day stretches before me like a highway in the desert, mile after mile of the same view, no sharp contrasts to provide moments of interest.

There are things I could do. There are things to be done. I could try to make sense of the many piles of mail and other papers that have accumulated past due since my last spurt of energy. I could practice the piano and get some return on the investment of money spent on lessons. There are floors to be vacuumed, bathrooms to be cleaned, books to be read, walks to be taken, letters to be written, computers to be mastered.

I sit in the chair. The room is silent except for the birds outside, and the hum of the refrigerator. I cannot bring myself to do anything on the list. Nothing is strong enough to break the tedium. Nothing is engaging enough to deserve my limited enthusiasm.

I am caught. I worry that when I am dying, I will feel as if I didn't do enough; yet here I have this perfectly good day ahead of me, and there is nothing I want to do. I have no more appetite for life than I do for food, as if my desire for excitement got flushed down the toilet with the rest of my waste.

I can hear the cars on the busy street behind my building. The world is maintaining its pace, rushing around and past me like a river buffeting a small branch. I have such a tentative hold. I am becoming smaller and slower and more insignificant as the world stays fast and big. I want to scream, "Stop! Wait for me." But I do not think this is possible.

I look at my clasped hands resting calmly in my lap. There is something on my right hand, a small spot I haven't noticed before, a small purple spot. It is the size of a small peppercorn, slightly raised. How long have I had it? I remember seeing it last week. I thought it was a blood blister. But now it dawns on me that blood blisters usually occur when the skin gets pinched hard, and I can recall no such injury. The reddish bump sits to the left of the knuckle next to my thumb.

A quiet panic slowly comes over me like hemlock. This is Kaposi's sarcoma. I have Kaposi's sarcoma. This is a lesion, not a mole or a blister. This is not a birthmark. This is a lesion, a KS lesion. I have a KS lesion. I have KS.

I rip off all my clothes. They fall haphazardly on the floor. I am searching for more lesions, plague markers from which I have escaped until now. I scan my thighs and calves and the bottoms of my feet. I see nothing. My arms are clear. My chest and stomach are spot free. I twist to see my butt, stretching my neck over my shoulder, but the attempt is futile. I curse the lack of a full-length mirror. The inspection of my back will have to wait.

I can see no more lesions. The damage seems to be limited to the one little speck on my right hand. I try to calm down, but my pulse and mind continue to race.

I call the doctor. He has an opening in his schedule if I come right away. I dress, and go.

I have been seeing this doctor for more than three years. The staff and I know each other well. The nurse comments that I don't seem my normal cheerful self.

The doctor comes in. He is very handsome and has become a wealthy man treating people with AIDS. He has a big house in the hills, with a pool and a view. He is an outstanding health-care provider, but I resent the disparity in our lives.

The spot on my hand is not KS. It is a blood blister.

I apologize to the doctor for making such a big deal out of nothing. He reassures me that I did the right thing. "There's no reason to live in fear," he says.

I feel like an idiot for conjuring up the worst possible scenario. I have been sick for more than five years; I should know better than to spook myself into panic. I am such a fool. I thought I had rejected that strategy long ago. I am embarrassed.

I leave the building. The air blows gently through my hair, cool and fresh against my sun-starved face. It is a lovely day. The houses on the hill glisten in the light.

I could have had a house on the hill, with a pool and a view, like my doctor. I made a different career choice, but that life could have been mine. Any life could have been mine. I am smart enough to have become a physician, ambitious enough for a lucrative corporate career. But I didn't care about making money. I wanted to be a performer, an artist. Success was uncertain, especially since all my teachers told me that I was not good enough, would not be competitive, could not have a career.

I am amazed that I was able to make any decision at all, that I was not completely paralyzed by the fear that I would make the wrong choice. I only knew I didn't want to become an old man and regret spending my precious time chasing after money and lifestyle instead of pursuing my dreams. I didn't want to look back and say, "I never did it, never gave it a shot."

I found enough nerve to become a dancer. I lived in New York and trained as an actor and singer. I started getting work. My teachers were wrong: I was going to have a career. Then I got sick.

I look at the houses once again and feel the sun on my face. I am relieved that I do not have KS. It occurs to me that I have had a good life, a rich life, a life that still interests and delights me. It is not the life I once envisioned. There is no house on the hill with a view. I am not a Broadway star. But I have many moments of pleasure and tranquillity, flashes of sweetness and joy. I have a place to sing, and friends who laugh at most of my jokes. I have people I can call in the middle of the night when I'm scared.

For the first time in months, it occurs to me, at least for the moment, that I may live.

GROUP PHOTO

Jeffrey Marcus

We should have taken a photograph at the start of the class.
You know, like a team shot—all of us arranged by height, stretching
    our spines to get as much of our faces into the camera's eye,
    straining from behind someone just a hair shorter.

We should have taken a photograph.
Then we could take a black marker—put a big indelible x through
    the latest victim.

The last death was sudden—like a heartbeat.
Here yesterday, gone for all tomorrows.
For months he breathed the same air, and poured out his wild mind
    into our ears.
Now he is gone—those leaky Southern eyes turned to ash.

We should have taken the group photo.
Nine Little Indians—who will it take next?
This specter lurks among us, taking just one day for the kill,
The grim reaper leaves no fingerprints, save for the shock of those
    around the beloved.

"One down, one more to go."
"Almost done with that little group."
"They were easy game, they went too fast."
"Not terribly satisfying, that little group."

Just a whole bunch of terrified faggots trying to keep their heads
    from dropping in exhaustion.
Straining to straighten their spines—not knowing when it might
    strike.

We should have taken that damn photograph—so that I could
    remember how many are left besides me.

J.

Doug Bender

J. died this week. He is the third person in my group to pass away, but I barely met the first two. J. and I were not friends; we never had lunch or saw a movie. We had no common past other than our sexuality, and an interest in writing. He was, I thought, already ill when I first joined the group and showed up using a cane for a while. I couldn't tell what was wrong with him. His speech was halting when he read his work, and even sometimes when he spoke in conversation. He would always preface reading with an excuse or two, usually something about how short the piece was, and how he couldn't get a handle on it. His work was good, not brilliant, but good, often an interesting snapshot of life as a gay Latino man with AIDS. When he finished reading, he would look at the leader with the big innocent eyes of an eight-year-old, as if to say, "How was that? Did I do okay?"

I always wonder when someone dies: what is the difference between death and distance? What if J. had said, "I am going to live in the Himalayas with the lamas, and we will never see each other again." Is that different from death? Or even if one of us had decided not to attend the group any longer? We would probably still not have lunch or see a movie. Clearly death is different because it precludes any possibility of lunch or a movie, but if we would never have done it anyway, what does it matter? And, of course, they don't have lunch or movies in the Himalayas.

He died from a seizure. He was on his way to a restaurant,

alone, and evidently just dropped dead, although I'm not sure it's fair to say he just dropped dead after being as ill as he was, for as long as he was. I never think of people dropping dead anymore. I always think of long, drawn-out Camille-like trage-dies, with plenty of time to make lists of who should be con-tacted, and what music should be played at the service, and what to do with the last day's mail. That's how Michael died. He died in New York three weeks after two years of conversations that began with "Guess which part of my life I had to let go of this week?" His illness whittled his life down and smaller, each bit of shavings swept away in an attempt to clean up his days, his pres-ent time, until, in the end, he had to let go of every part of his life.

MEMORIAL

(A WILD WRITE, WRITTEN AFTER HEARING OF THE DEATH OF A DEAR WORKSHOP FRIEND)

Donald Colby

A friend dies and you want to call the lover, face him at the memorial, shake his hand, place your other hand on top of that, say something to comfort. To ease. To make it all easier. For both of you. Nothing is enough.

Sit at your desk later, alone, dog at your feet. You won't play, won't play with him, play fetch. You sit and stare, slumped. Stare at the notebook open to a fresh page, dim, you don't even want to turn on the light. You have to say something, tell a story, his story perhaps, but nothing will come. Everything's in place. Nothing will come. What are you hiding from?

It will never be enough. Not enough words or sentiment or not good enough. Bad, perhaps, or inadequate. Even now, imagining, something sticks in the mind, lodges there, won't come out for fear of being seen. Tucks its head back behind a plank, a wall, something thick and solid, built to last.

What are you hiding from?

Too abstract. You're getting too abstract. He was your friend. He could have been your lover. In another place and time, before any of us got sick, that was a possibility. You could've flown together, Icarus wings touching the sun, that's what he did and you hated him for thinking that. Thinking he was reaching for something when all he was, was scared. Scared to death.

Do not look at this. Break through.

Life was unfair, he told you. This was just the capper, he said,

216

aids was just the capper on the whole thing: no father, no mother. There are at least two ways to abandon your child: Leave town, never come back. And tell him you hate him for being queer. Tell him that to his face in front of a friend or a relative, someone who will remember. A witness. We are all witnesses for one another. What I am hiding is what I have seen: him lying there in that bed, propped up, hooked up, beeping, dripping, bleeding, trying to heal, trying to keep anything from showing.

(FRAGMENT)

Philip Justin Smith

October 12, 1991: Elaine is dead. I'm so fucking sick of losing people, of people dying, of feeling sad, of crying. It feels as if I were marble and great fractures are running down me. Blast, and one runs from the corner of my mouth like a line being drawn with a marker down my neck onto my chest. Blast, one appears at the back of my head following the indentation of my spine down to the top of my ass. Blast, an arm falls off. The marble statue, me, retains its genuine compassionate but elusive smile, retains its distance, its coolness, as pieces fall to the floor.

I want to die, not because of the handicap to my body but because the steady stream of sorrow drowns me. I can't get a breath in the midst of its swirling rapids. If the stream, the pain, presses forward, I want a shield—some protection—some distance.

Elaine is dead and she died like thousands have before. Pain, suffering, withdrawal. She put her least attractive face forward as a means to disengage. But I remember an Elaine who held the power in her soul. Elaine who could laugh or gesture and stop a room. Elaine who could tell you a story on two levels at once. David Greer, Robert, Dan, Michael, Rory, Byron, Elaine, and what about those out of touch? Keith? Robert MacP? Tightness, tightness, chest contracting, shoulders cramped—it's uncomfortable being marble.

Tired, tired, tired. I just want to go to sleep. Shut down. Shut out shut off shut up. Shuttle. What do I care. I don't care. It doesn't matter to me.

Bam! Now the cracks fill with blood and the pieces wash away like glaciers exploding and rearranging themselves to flow downstream. And what is left? Nothing. Just space. Air. Breezes pass through and a small imprint where someone once stood.

THE FIRST DAY

(EXCERPT)

Tony Gramaglia

I am sitting here, at this fake-wood-grain table, wondering what a dying man would write about. What are these other men, who are probably dying, going to write about? . . . Why are we here? Why am I here?

To write stories. To tell stories. To be voices that are heard.

As we read from our pages, things change. I change. The lights become softer . . . the shaky hands of one thin man steady as he reads. I watch him become a fourteen-year-old boy at the lake. The other man who could only whisper is suddenly speaking with the strong Southern voice of his father. Another man makes me hungry for the delicious French meal he describes. Another stirs my fantasies with his tales of passionate lovemaking. . . .

I don't see the actual faces or bodies or shapes or diseases sitting around this table anymore. Instead I see what they write about. Their fascination, their humor, their pain, their homes, their childhoods, their lovers, their children, their mothers and fathers. I see what they tell me. I hear their voices.

And I tell my story. One of many I have held for years. One of the many stories I will tell here in this room and even in bookstores and at auditoriums, in publications and on the radio . . .

Our camaraderie in this room transcends this disease. We are connected by our willingness to create stories and our need to be heard. That is why we come here and sit around this table.

I have found a voice here. A voice to be heard. The others and I are not writing the words and hearing the words of dying men. These are stories from the heart and soul of truly living men. Stories that will always breathe life as long as there is someone who will listen, someone who will breathe in our words.

(FRAGMENT, 10/12/91)

Marc Wagenheim

It's been leading to a certain madness of late—the fevers, the bleeding, the malaise. (What a nice way to say like feeling like shit.) A logic and a world seem to be forming that aren't attached to me. The other night [going] to sleep it was all about the annual day when you picked something of yours and gave it. No idea where or to whom or what variety. And some of my illness feels so detached from me now—that fever isn't Marc's—it's a background fever. What was that Lewis Carroll summation—my, but aren't things getting odder and odder? I don't think that that is right, but I don't want to dwell on this anymore. My heart's in New England now, or wherever there's fall foliage. God, how I want to be there looking at rolling hills aflame with reds, and yellows, and oranges. So intense. So real. So magnificent. And I suppose that it is trite but true, but they're dying—this is their last stand—soon they will crunch underfoot, then they will be smothered and melted by winter's snows. I talked to my friend Suzie in Boston yesterday. She's a photographer and she told me how, partially for business, partially for pleasure, she and her fiancé, Peter, took a few days and clocked two hundred miles all over the upper Northeast. She told me about a photograph she took. Peter was wearing a black sweater and had picked some dazzling red apples off a tree. His arms were full of them and the contrast with the black and the light from the trees and the changing sky . . . I see that picture and I feel that moment. I can smell those apples. I sense the chill in the air. I feel the awe of autumn.

(FRAGMENT)

Robbie Hilyard

[*A list he made of the subjects he wrote about in the Writers Workshop*]

Inner critic, inner guide, invoking the inner spirit, opening the heart, lighting the third eye, rekindling my pilot lights, recovering my soul, confronting barriers, speaking the unspeakable, what is in my heart, fear, anger, self-control, self-denial, commitment, belonging, community and exclusion, group identity and self-identity, talking in sleep, internal melodies, Planet X, Giuseppe Verdi, home, healing, happiness, the tears of a formerly cynical queen, my place in the world, Tinkerbell, firemen, the infant heart, Peggy Lee impersonators, Aurora Borealis, little boy in a fireman's cap, lists, childhood, love, memory, parents and other monsters, earth time, shame, Europe, the playground of Eternity, what keeps me alive, tradition, identity, soapboxes, mirrors, blindness, medical miracles, warrior queens, pilgrims, hope and the future, littleness, reserve, the pink and the blue, powerlessness, silence, postcards, what I know, tap-dancing on peanut butter, grief, fear and ill health, getting and forgetting, abandon and abandonment, NOT testing HIV+, the lived and the unlived, true or disguised selves, secrets, time, painted face beneath the mask, the forbidden, inner life of the one-eyed clown, the seen and the unseen, the sung and the unsung, the hung and the unhurried, resignation, desire, reckless leaps into the void, worldliness, alienation and alliteration, aversion, subversion, perversion and diversion, sharing and not sharing, the involuntary and the willed, personal disarmament, the lungs from hell, chemical men, anything headless, Medusa, angel of death, snakes and hairnets, dangerous companions, barriers, the guilty secrets, white sofa, gossip, favorite poisons, favorite prison, the way you smile at a mother you don't like, the cuddly and the dangerous, dancing, daily acts of kindness, fishnet stockings, the nice and the not nice, four hors d'oeuvres of the apocalypse, the black and the blue, family legacy of failure, poetic injustice.

THE FRAGILITY OF PAPER

Nathan Clum

"I have a memory," I said to Gene two months before he died. We were sitting on his small balcony, talking about nothing in particular the way friends do. "I believe," I said, "that when I was a little kid, I could see through my eyelids." We were both wearing just our undershorts, T-shirts, and no socks because the snow was finally gone and the afternoon sun felt warm and good on our legs. It had been his idea to strip down. You could smell fresh dirt in the air and it was nearly time for the first crocuses to poke up in the planter box Gene kept in front of the railing. It was a good time, nothing remarkably special, just nice. Gene laughed, that high peal of laughter that made him sound so girlish.

"I wonder if it's spring yet," he said, trying to ignore me. "When does that happen?" He had his arms crossed and his feet spread on the railing.

"It's true," I continued. "I remember one time sitting in our den with that movie on, the one with the huge treelike plants that ate people and everyone went blind."

"*Day of the Triffids,*" he interrupted. "It was called the *Day of the Triffids.*" Gene had a gift for names.

"That's the one. I remember watching it with my hands covering my face and my eyes closed. I couldn't have been more than five. But even with my eyes closed, I remember seeing everything that happened. I saw the whole movie right through my eyelids."

Gene blew a puff of air through his teeth as he did if he was going to tease me. Then he laughed again. "Sure," he said. "That's right. Bet you could."

He crossed his ankles up on the iron railing and leaned the back of his chair against the wall behind us. It took what seemed an enormous effort, and I reached out to help him, but he shrugged me away. His bare legs were so thin it looked as if I could have put both my fists end to end in the space between his thighs, and I felt my chest catch. It was the kind of thing I thought I'd gotten used to, one of the details I thought I'd stopped noticing. But I hadn't. I never did. These reminders were always present. He was out of breath and I thought about going inside to get a blanket. It might have been too early in the year for us to be sitting out there in just cotton underwear. A cool breeze still blew and it raised goose bumps on our arms and legs. I was afraid someone might see us, and every once in a while I shivered, but Gene looked as I imagined he would have twenty years ago—a scrawny ten-year-old too innocent to be aware of appearances or the wind.

Gene pretended nothing was wrong and gave me another of his still-dazzling smiles.

"My parents thought I was lying," I told him. "I suppose they're right, but that's not how I remember it. I think I could see through my eyelids. Maybe they were thin since I was so young or something. What do you think?"

He just said, "Well?" then dropped his hand down on the edge of the planter box. "They'll be up soon. That's when we'll be sure it's spring."

I want to say that I can easily remember each small detail of Gene, that I can quickly recall the way his hands looked when he ate a pear and how the juice dripped off his elbows, or that I can see just how his lip pulled up to one side when he was em-barrassed by something he'd said, or that his face was asymmet-rical.

"It's off," he'd say, looking in the mirror. "I wish I could have it done." Then he'd pull the corner of his right eyebrow up with a long finger and frown so that his whole face evened out.

"It's perfect just the way it is," I'd say back, gently taking his hand away. "It gives you character you might not otherwise have." He'd laugh at that and turn to punch me on the shoulder.

I wish I could say the small details of all these things were easy, but there are moments I have forgotten and remembering takes effort. I am afraid that Gene is leaving me, bit by bit, the failure of memory taking from me the feel of his warm hand against my cheek, the press of his shoulders in my arms.

What I do remember clearly is the very first time I noticed a difference in Gene. It was the last Sunday in January; we were eating breakfast together and we sat in the Polish diner at the end of our block. The difference was in his fingers, just there, nowhere else. They were thin and suddenly so very fragile looking, like an old man's fingers, the skin soft and shiny. He'd picked up a piece of fruit, keeping his fingers straight, as though it were painful for him to touch something even as tender as an apple. He chewed very slowly while the snow blew horizontally past the front window and it seemed the weather would never change.

"Here's something I never told you," Gene said. This was a game we played to learn about each other: we took turns telling stories from our past. It sped things up between us. As he talked, he broke off pieces of a twig and threw them into the planter box.

"My grandmother was schizophrenic," he said. "On my mother's side. Really nuts. Couldn't even hold a conversation. By the time I knew her, she'd spent about ten years in an institution. She died when I was twelve." He paused and flicked a piece of twig over the railing with his thumb. We watched it fall out of sight. "When I was sixteen I thought I'd inherited it. Thought I was going crazy, too. It can come down that way. From your grandmother. I wish I could ask her how you knew, what it felt like. I used to get up every morning and look in the mirror to see if I could tell. I was afraid I'd see something changed, something different in my eyes. But nothing ever was." He sighed. "Still, that's what I'm afraid of, you know. Losing my mind."

The twig was gone and he drummed his fingers slowly on his

leg. Then he said, "I don't suppose it matters now anyway." I closed my eyes and listened to the faint sound of his fingertips against the parchment skin of his thigh.

For an uncountable number of times since we'd first met, I tried to memorize Gene's every gesture, commit to memory the way he used his hands to emphasize a point, or the way his left cheek twitched just as he drifted off to sleep. I replayed these movements a second time as soon as they happened in the hopes that years from now these same hand movements and facial expressions would appear suddenly and with stunning clarity. And each remember gesture would bring with it a story, the words creating a portrait of Gene to remember him by. But I realized then that there were too many stories he would not have time to tell, so many gestures I would not see, and this made me very sad, to think that no matter how hard I tried, there would always be pieces missing.

I wanted to say to him, Tell me, tell me everything now.

Instead, I asked, "Did you get those papers back from Michael?"

One early-winter day, Gene had rung my doorbell and said, "I made an appointment for us it's with Michael he's a lawyer I want you to have my power of attorney do you think you can do that?" just like that, one long sentence without a breath. I remember that there had been just enough wind outside to make the tiny snowflakes hang delicately in the air. They sparkled around his head. And I could smell the clean out-of-doors on his clothes. But what I wished I remembered, and could not, were important details such as whether he'd been smiling when he asked me this or how his eyes had looked, if he was scared. He'd stood up straight and stretched his back while he waited for my answer, and I'd wanted to ask him if he'd lost weight, because even though I tried not to, I was always looking. I still looked. I believed I should be able to detect the changes in Gene's health, but I was afraid I would miss them if they were gradual, just as I was afraid I would see them if they were not.

"Oh, that," he said. "Those forms are with the rest of the important stuff in my desk. Do you want them?" He took his legs down from the railing as if to get up. He had to cup his hands under each knee to move them, one by one. He was not strong enough.

I touched his shoulder, the bones sharp against my palm. "No, you keep them. It's okay. I'd probably just lose them anyway." We sat for a moment and listened while a car moving too fast for the neighborhood rattled over the speed bump in front of the building. Tires squealed and the car roared off. My heart was pounding.

It had been nearly two years since I'd met Gene, but I could still be amazed at how casually we talked about this, his death. We arranged his memorial over dinners and spent our Sundays choosing the music to play during the service. We discussed the business of his dying in the same spirit as planning a vacation: timetables to meet and checklists to complete. It was an adventure. I would forget. But then some small, sudden thing—a dog barking or tires squealing—would trigger in me the revelation that this was real, that it was final, and the horror would flood through my chest like ice water all over again.

I looked closely at Gene to see if he'd noticed, but he wasn't paying attention to me anymore. He'd squirmed around and was looking at the plastic straps of his chair. "Chair's too hard," he said. "Hurts."

I had known about Gene's illness from our very first conversation. I believed at one time that this knowledge would make me treasure the moments I had with him more, give them a certain intensity. But as I watched him next to me trying to get comfortable, I wondered if that was true or at all possible.

Suddenly it seemed that no matter how much time I was given, whether it was months or years, knowing with certainty that our relationship would finally end stole it from me before I had the chance to make it fully mine. I did not believe I could hold Gene inside of me as solidly and indefinitely as I would have had I not known of his illness. It seemed he was already fading, had started leaving the instant he'd told me of it. It was not at all true that the knowledge of death gave life more intensity, rendered life with its imperfections and beauty somehow more profound. That knowledge only outlined the beauty with a slow and constant pain, a dull ache that rested permanently in a hollow space between my shoulder blades.

"Remember our trip to the canyon?" Gene's voice was thin and small, from somewhere far off. "We should do that again. We should go back there." The year before, we had driven to the Grand Canyon on a whim, just the two of us, and camped at the North Rim. There were patches of snow still in the woods and ditches, and we'd slept curled together in his old goosedown sleeping bag. He'd said that the campground there in the pines was his favorite place of anywhere he'd ever been, and that he wanted to share it with me as soon as he could. The world spun faster than it should have had to; there was never time.

"Remember the hide down?" He leaned his chair back softly against the wall again. "You told me it was impossible to fall off a mountain, that you had to work at it. But I couldn't shake that feeling. Like I was floating." He reached over and put his hand around my wrist and squeezed.

"At the bottom," he went on, "it wasn't so far at all. And so clear. Tiny people were up there, I could see them standing at the top. Then you pointed at the cliffs and said to me, 'You can't fall up, Gene. Once you're at the bottom, you just can't.' And I couldn't think why I'd been scared." He turned to face me. "We should go back. That was good." He squeezed my wrist again and smiled, remembering.

Gene had told this story before, recounted it to his other friends even. But I didn't think it happened that way at all, since I am the one afraid of heights, not him. And in my version, he was the one who pointed at the cliffs and said, 'You can't fall from up there. You can see now, you just can't.' But I didn't know how to tell him the truth of it or if it was important that I did at all. Instead, I concentrated on the feel of his hand encircling my wrist, the pressure there no more than a whisper. I stared into the planter box, looking for new green shoots. I wanted to say, Yes, I see them, Gene. There they are.

A cloud passed overhead and Gene shivered. The movement

started in his shoulders and intensified, running trough his body right to his feet. He yawned.

"Want to go in?" I asked. I was getting colder, too. If it had been possible, I would have stayed hours longer right where we were, with the sun warming our legs. I did not want the afternoon to end. But the courtyard below was being swallowed by a sharp line of shadow that had gradually moved toward us.

"I guess. Time for a nap." He put a hand on my shoulder to steady himself and with a rush of breath stood up.

"It could happen," he said as he lay back on his pillows. I'd put them end to end the length of the bed. The mattress wasn't soft enough for him anymore. He seemed to sink down in; white cotton enveloped his face and thin yellow hair, absorbed the edges of his underwear.

"What could?" I didn't understand. I had to lean over him to hear, his voice was that soft. It was as if the bed were soaking him up. I wanted to reach my arms underneath him, cradle him, and separate him from the blankets and pillows, rescue him back into the room.

"Your eyelids," he said as he drifted off to sleep. "That story. I can believe you. You were right."

"Oh." I did not want to disturb him. "I think so, too." I tucked the quilt under his hip and left the room.

Gene died not long after one final snow of that winter season, and after the crocuses did come up and bloomed yellow and blue in his little redwood planter box.

The legal documents we signed together sit in a plain white envelope I have never opened. If I take the pressed envelope out from under the glass on my dresser top and lift it up to the light, I can see the spidery, curved lines of Gene's signature there, glowing through the nearly transparent paper. And if I close my eyes and concentrate, I can see a picture of Gene sitting on his balcony, waiting for the flowers. It is like the image you see after staring at something painfully bright, a photographic negative, the edges blurred. I keep my eyes closed very tight, and as the picture begins to fade, I practice with every detail, naming them over and over, remembering.

NEIGHBOR

Stephen Jerrom

I walked daily
near the window of the house
which framed the dying man.

Saw his silhouette
sometimes seated, usually reclined
always thinner
as the sounds of television,
muted talk of visiting friends
made shadows around his bed.
Once I caught the outline
of a nurse hovered over
his extended arm
heard a twisted groaning
as I hurried, late to work.

In the morning, light
from uncurtained windows
on the far side of his house
would shine across the hardwood floor
stopping at the bed
a whisper-reach from where I passed;
I saw highlights on the blankets,
his young man's sleeping head

cheeks hollow, mouth agape
propped up on pillows—
later, on a rolling bed
with railings high
that bound his wrists.

I hoped my routine footsteps,
the gate lock turning
would not wake him
as I went about my day
a little guilty of my health
my freedom, my mobility
speeding past the sports car
sunken, now, and dust-brown
with four flat tires.

I was glad to see a cute new tenant
when Rick moved into the house next door
another artist on the hill
would be a welcome neighbor;
saw his photographs through an open window
large color prints of high-style women
but he never asked me in.

Recently I saw him at a local bar
he kissed someone, it caught my eye
but he brushed past me for the door.
Was I mistaken? Did he not see me?
Was there something
I was not supposed to know?

Now I watched while passing by
shadows of an ominous play,
nurses, buddies, twelve-hour shifts,
hospital smells in the morning air
Meals on Wheels each afternoon;
sullen, narrow shoulders

of an oxygen tank
beside the profile of an IV bag
dangling high like a hanged man,
lights ablaze at four A.M.
as I wake up to take a pee;
the rushing, flushing
commotions of a private war.

I said little.
Went to work.
Came home.
Entertained.
Made the motions
of the walking well.

His friend said in the last few days
he clung to a life
which had become unsustainable.
"Why are you holding on?"
he asked his dying friend.
They were all exhausted
aiding, comforting,
at last facilitating
an uncontestable passage;
there were no more breaths
for euphemism;
the buttress of manners
redundant as scaffold
on a finished building;
so the dying man was asked
Why do you linger?
"It must have helped," the friend concluded.
"Rick died the next day."

After that the house went dark
possessions carted off and scattered
his friends all thanked me—

but what did I do?
Took out the trash on Tuesday night
swept the path and kept my distance.
They thanked me, hugged me—why?
I didn't go to say hello
didn't want to say good-bye,
pretending we were friends
'cause we were not.
We were only neighbors.

COURT

John Mulkeen

Arles was pretty. Not as pretty as Paris, but pretty enough. Court and I checked into a hotel that used to be a convent. If I remember right, it was the only four-star hotel in Arles with, supposedly, a four-star restaurant. That was a major selling point for both of us. I wasn't crazy about French food as far as main courses went, but if a four-star pastry chef was attached to the place, then I was happy. Court would eat anything.

I really don't remember how the *tarte fraise* was, or even if there was one to be had.

May 1984. My first trip to France with my first boyfriend who ever told me he loved me without a lot of prodding. Sometimes it just came out of him spontaneously and I decided to believe him. Paris had been great. Even though he was tired a lot of the time, we still did the Eiffel Tower, the Rodin Museum, the Jeu de Paume. The weather was beautiful. Our room looked out over the Seine. It was just what I'd hoped for.

Going to the south of France was Court's idea. He had already been to the Loire Valley and really wanted to see Arles, Aix-en-Provence, and Avignon this time. He had gone to the Riviera with his ex-wife in '78, so we decided to go only to places that were new to him. He had a thing about van Gogh. Always wanted to play him onstage or in a movie. Actually, Court was a good painter. When he was in the hospital, he painted a picture of two irises that actually looked like two irises. I told him he was perfect to play Vincent. He loved those tortured souls.

On our third day in Arles, Court said to me, "Johnny, I'm not walking so good today."

"What?" I really hadn't noticed.

"I just feel like I'm going to fall over sometimes."

I remember that he had mentioned this to me before. Two weeks earlier, in New York, he had the same complaint. "I think I'm going to fall down," he said as we walked up Ninth Avenue.

"Just put your arm around me," I said. He did. We walked up Ninth Avenue for about six blocks with Court having his arm over my shoulder and me with my arm around his waist. I'd never been happier in my life. I didn't want the walk to ever end.

"Do you want me to call Dr. Starrett?" I asked. "She said that she'd be available in case you needed her."

"What do you think?" he asked.

"Couldn't hurt. Do you want to talk to her?"

"Not really. Just let me know what she says."

The pay phone I used was in a town square. There were people walking around. Court sat on a park bench. Alone. Looking to the sky, I think.

"Hi, Barbara, it's John. Court's having more trouble walking." I almost had to shout into the receiver. The connection was terrible.

"Does he have a fever?" she asked.

"No, I don't think so. He sweat a little bit last night, but he says it's just a problem with his balance. Anything serious?"

"John," she said.

"Yeah?"

"John, he's dying. You might want to come home soon. I think the virus is in his central nervous system and it's going to be very difficult to slow down."

I really didn't know what to say.

"Maybe it's just toxo again. Or maybe it's an inner-ear infection. Is that possible?" I yelled.

"Try to enjoy your trip. Come home if it gets any worse."

"What should I tell him?"

"See if he feels like praying." She hung up.

I walked over to Court and noticed that his green eyes seemed a bit bigger than usual.

"How ya doin'?" I asked.

"What'd she say?"

"She said that maybe it was time to start praying."

"There's got to be a church around here somewhere," he said.

We walked about a block and found this Catholic church just sitting there waiting for us. I'd never been to a church with Court. I hadn't been in a church since the previous Christmas, and I don't think Court had been to one in ten years. We walked in. Of course it was very quiet inside. A few people prayed. A couple of tourists looked at the stained-glass windows. An old lady lit a candle. Just a usual church. Except it smelled very, very old. Court picked a pew and we both knelt down. I started to ask for help in getting him back on track. I looked over at him and he held his face in his hands and shook his head just slightly. After about ten minutes, I nudged him and told him I was going outside and that he should take his time.

I hadn't noticed how bright and sunny it was that day, but as I left the church, the contrast between the dark interior and the spring sunshine was startling. I walked over to a bench and sat down to wait for Court. I started to cry a little bit and then I couldn't control myself. I started to bawl. He was dying. Dr. Starrett said so. We were in France and he was dying. I remembered that when my brother Daniel died, my sister, Margaret, kept saying, "It's just so sad." This was, too.

This was just so sad.

Court stayed about twenty minutes in the church. By the time he came out, I had pulled myself together. He stood at the doorway and looked out. His eyes adjusted to the light. I whistled my family's whistle to get his attention. He half-smiled and I walked over to meet him.

"How ya doin'?" I asked.

"Fine," he said.

"You were in there awhile."

"It's weird," he said. "I must have been in there for at least half an hour, and you know what? I just don't get it. I didn't feel a thing."

"Nothing?" I asked.

"Nope. Not a thing. I really tried, too. I don't know who to talk to, or about what. I just went blank."

"But I saw you with your head in your hands," I said.

"Yeah," he said. "I thought maybe if I looked like I was praying, something would happen. You hungry?"

"Always," I said. "Let's eat."

LAURENT

Steve Maher

Warm me from the cold, damp, charcoal pallor
*   you hot, frightened, amorous thunderbolt man*
I say: you tower over your enemies
So don't turn your face from me
I still want to receive you there
*   in that hollow wounded boy place*
*   in my embrace*

1995

I know this place better than any place I have ever lived. It must be the repetition, the sheer number of times I saw it, the quantity of hours I spent there over the years, and its intimate size that helped embed Laurent's apartment in my mind, his apartment at 65 rue de Seine where the rue Jacob dead-ends in Paris's Sixth Arrondissement. It must also have been how distinct it was from the "custom-built" ranch-style house where I was raised in Texas. Laurent's apartment was old, about 350 years old, and solid like I'd never seen. If you banged on the wall, you would hear the thud of your hand against the thick stone and plaster, no hollow echo as I had known, never a peep from a neighbor, except perhaps the sound of the blond woman's door closing in the winding stairwell where sound reverberated loudly against all the hard surfaces. I know the sounds even now, the click of the street

240

entry door as it opened, at first accompanied by the jangle of the old tarnished brass key, and later without, when keys were made obsolete by the modern digital entry. The door would close with a clean, finely assured click, and I would reach for the button that would turn on the lights down a short, narrow hallway, and all the way up the stairs, a minute of light for my ascension. The stairs were old gray, unpainted wood; hundreds of years of foot traffic had worn them down, a noticeable round indentation in each one. Up I would climb to the fourth floor, *le troisième étage*.

Laurent's door was the larger one of two on his level. It was painted that dark mallard green, high-gloss enamel, very French. It had two locks to discourage thieves and a round brass handle in the middle to pull it closed.

Inside, there was a small entry corridor, and just on the left, the tiniest excuse for a kitchen. It had all the essentials, barely, except an oven, and sitting in the corner of the ceramic-tile floor of this not quite square room was a proportionately tiny waste can, the first thing I had ever bought for him. Laurent did his share of entertaining from here, multicourse dinner parties for six or even eight, cooked from this windowless little cell of a kitchen.

The apartment was small and glorious to my young eyes. The ceilings were low and white and lined irregularly with old rough-hewn dark-wood beams. The wall just to the left was covered in moss green linen. It was tailored to accommodate bookshelves and an inset cupboard, which was filled with glassware and china. Even today I remember where everything was.

The furnishings were a blend of antique and modern, sleek Italian modern. There were four organically curved, fully uphol-stered rolling chairs, and a black, square table that doubled in size for dinner parties. There was a daybed on the far wall where I slept in the beginning, many years ago.

Everything else was antique and grand. There was a French commode with elaborate inlaid wood. On top was a slab of rust-colored marble with white veins. Accenting the bowed contours were gold, carved metallic pieces that matched the ornate drawer pulls. Over the commode hung the most beautiful mirror I've ever seen, the lavishly sculpted frame covered in gold leaf.

I admit with some embarrassment that I don't know the proper period style names of these pieces, though I have attempted to learn the basic French and English terms from a picture book I bought off a sale table years ago. Often I would ask Laurent to identify pieces when we shopped the antique stands at the Clignancourt flea market, but I would forget. I couldn't say for sure that Laurent's treasures are even French, but I would swear that they aren't English. I do know they were glorious, and I admired them countless times, often while I was alone waiting for Laurent to return from his job at the chic Italian-furniture showroom that he managed. I imagine that most of the valuable pieces were gifts from Jacques, his wealthy ex-lover who had been showering him with presents since Laurent was a young bathing beauty on his yacht deck in Cannes. By the time I entered the picture, Jacques was over fifty and becoming a priest, something neither I nor Laurent ever understood.

The sleep alcove was a separate room, though it had no door. When Laurent and I met, he slept on a twin bed, but that gave way to the *grand lit,* roughly a queen-size bed, that Laurent surprised me with, covered sumptuously in gray velvet. Over the bed hung a magnificent, unframed nineteenth-century oil painting that covered the entire wall. Probably a mythological scene of some sort (a more educated man would know), it showed an imprisoned woman, a nude Rubenesque Venus, at least life-size, lying in her prison bed in a dark cell. Her translucent, alabaster skin was illuminated by a heavenly light from above, where a cherub poured coins down to her. This painting was the last thing I saw at night and the first thing in the morning. Even in her naked imprisonment, a heavenly light shone down on all of us. The painting was museum quality, and Laurent told me he had been offered a handsome sum for it. This was my favorite of all his possessions.

Apart from the acquisition of the big bed, the only significant additions to his apartment in the ten years that I knew him were the purchases of a large, beautiful portrait of an aristocratic adolescent boy that we found together on a Sunday stroll in the countryside, and the prized shower curtain, purchased for me. Shower curtains are a novelty in France. Laurent could hold the spray nozzle in his hand and easily direct the water into the tiled wall. Despite my best efforts, I always managed to spray all the bathroom surfaces, making for a slippery hazard. Laurent, ever patient with me, his *bébé,* never said a word.

I forgot to say that the floors were covered in brown commercial carpet. I can feel it against my back, hard but not abrasive. It was there that we first had sex, hungrily, in front of the antique commode.

1979

I saw him through the mirrors at the Vitatop health club in Paris. What I really saw, stared at through the panes of reflective glass, was his chest, exposed intentionally by the way he'd pulled his T-shirt down, showing sinewy definition. He contracted his chest muscles as he heaved the weighted pulleys. He was swarthy in a way that I liked, olive skinned, with thick, black, curly hair, and beady, sinister eyes. He looked a bit old for me. But his chest was a seduction. I stared. And kept my distance.

About a week later:

There was a swimming pool, floating magically right there in the river Seine, enclosed by wooden walls from the view of passersby.

After paying the twelve-franc *prix d'entrée,* I entered. It was a spectacle of lipstick-red, glossy deck, a large crystalline pool, and scantily clad bodies, silhouetted on patterned beach towels against all that red, their tiny bathing suits like primary-colored polka dots; a visual kaleidoscope begging to be secretly photographed from the *passerelle* above. But I never did, wasn't bold enough.

And there was skin. Lots of skin. French men wore tiny spandex suits. The women were topless. Just outside on the streets, the Parisians wouldn't be caught dead in a pair of shorts, even on sultry summer days. But once inside the walls of the Piscine Deligny, virtual nudity was de rigueur.

After being assigned a private changing *cabine,* and trying diligently not to expose my limited French by asking any questions, I changed into my bathing suit and joined the masses.

I'd taken something to read but I was distracted. It was a weekday afternoon and most of the men were gay. I was looking for sex and hoping for love. I was twenty-three.

A couple of hours later, when I was preparing to leave, I spotted him, that man from the Vitatop. We seemed to be headed toward our *cabines* simultaneously. In a tiny white suit, his bronzed stomach muscles rippled, his eyes not quite meeting mine. It became apparent that he was timing his exit to coincide with my own.

After dressing, he pushed through the turnstile just ahead of me. He turned and introduced himself, as if exiting had given him permission to speak. He spoke French to me and said his name was Laurent.

First moments always made me nervous. Though I was soaking up the language like a dry sponge, I was a novice, and I hated revealing just how little I knew. In English I considered myself charming, occasionally clever. In French I was like an awkward, tongue-tied four-year-old. I told him my name without incident. The he asked me if I'd like to get something to drink. I understood that. "Oui." Where would I like to go? I used what I thought was just the right colloquialism to say, "Anyplace is fine with me." Instead I said more like, "I don't really care about it." Within thirty seconds of our meeting, he corrected me, as the French reliably do. "Oh, you meant to say . . . ," he began. It was a promising start.

Once we'd introduced ourselves, once I knew that our desire was mutual, my restlessness gave way to intrigue and excitement. Soon we would quench our lusts.

First, Laurent led me to Café Mabillon on the boulevard St-Germain, a place I would later learn was his regular stop amongst the plethora of cafés jammed together there.

Our time at the café is blurred to me. I remember it was

late afternoon and hot. We sat outside on the sidewalk. Laurent ordered for both of us. Though I can't remember what was said, I know the conversation was limited.

His home was just around the corner. He led me up the dark, winding wooden stairs into his small, though charming and eminently French, apartment.

Seconds later we were coiled together naked on the carpet. His energy was electric. I feasted my eyes and hands and tongue on his smooth, muscular, oiled body.

I don't want to go further here. I don't want to say that I stared hungrily at his beautiful torso, that I used him like an object to satisfy my sexual desire. But he liked that, liked hooking me to himself through desire.

But now, years later, now that he's gone, I want to show the romance, that sacred element between us, the part that better honors the dead.

But it isn't so simple, is it? It did begin with a sinewy chest; our lust, his penchant for young American men, my romance with all things French, my need to be taken care of, his desire and ability to do so.

So we launched our relationship. He gave me his phone number. I gave him mine. I can't remember who called first, just that it was, and still is, awkward for me speaking French on the phone.

We made a date to go to dinner. Not making a large investment, he picked a touristy restaurant *dans le quartier* with tacky lime green, palm-printed wallpaper and white lattice-wood trim, very seventies, the kind with the prix fixe menu standing outside to lure tourists.

We worked our way through dinner making primitive conversation. He was good-natured and patient as I asked him to explain and occasionally reexplain something he'd said. Speaking English was not an option. His only words of English seemed to be "hello, boy." Listening to Piaf years later, I found out where he'd learned them. In one song she plays a prostitute, seducing foreign sailors on the wharf, each in his native tongue. To the American she says, of course, "Hello, boy."

For my part, I explained that I was a flight steward for *la Braniff*, as the French referred to my Texas-based airline, and that I adored Paris and was living here for six weeks, sharing an apartment in Montparnasse. When I spoke French to him, I created the illusion that I understood the language, so he would chatter back to me full speed. *"Comment?"* was my general reply. "Say that again, more slowly please." Loneliness, bicultural intrigue, and sexual desire got us through that first dinner.

Almost immediately I stopped all other amorous adventuring and settled in. Within a week he had given me keys to his apartment. I had a French boyfriend who couldn't get enough of me.

He became my unofficial French professor. With Laurent as my model, I learned body parts first, and a few coarse colloquialisms. My desire to be intimate fueled my language acquisition. A pocket-size *carnet* and pen were never far away:

belle poitrine, cuisses, cul, affiches, gitanes, clochard, grosse bise, pneu, ours, antiquaires, peinture, roter, immeuble . . .

After work, Laurent would bound into the apartment, change out of his chic, daringly colored designer suits and into his street attire: tight jeans and T-shirt, black boots and leather jacket, his uniform for many years. I would be there waiting for him, after my day of touring museums and gardens, or sitting in cafés, translating the French equivalent of *People* magazine, *Paris Match*. Having a camera in Paris satisfied an almost spiritual need: I discovered a link between beauty and God. Simple things seemed profound: a curlicue iron chair casting its shadow against an ancient stone wall, a garden worker raking fallen leaves in dappled sunlight, the impassioned young violinist playing in the Buci street market, eyes closed. And the ubiquitous lovers.

Soon he began introducing me to his friends: Gerard, Claude, William, Jean-Claude, Marie-France, and Jacques his ex-lover of fifteen years, who inspected me like a toy. Jacques was older than Laurent, wealthy, polite, and snobbish. I was warmly received.

Several weeks later I returned home to Boston and resumed

my flight-attendant duties, which mercifully included at least two trips with layovers in Paris each month. After flying all night, I would take the briefest nap, then race over to the Tecno showroom to see Laurent. We would sneak down to the basement level and make out.

He was the consummate tour guide. He adored his city and loved showing me things, all of which had a history: Place des Vosges, Palais Royale, les Invalides, even the Bateaux Mouches, that *très touristique* river tour on the Seine, and Simone Signoret's apartment. After dinners in restaurants, or more often in the apartments of friends, we'd walk home, half-drunk, back across the river to the Left Bank. Entering his building, we'd chase one another up the stairs, pinching asses and laughing as we climbed.

Back in Boston, I continued to date as usual, Felix the Italian, Larry the Pol. I was interviewing all ethnicities. I fantasized living in France, but knew I would be miserable not working, and I had no plan. Within a year my airline was teetering on the verge of financial collapse, and my flight-attendant career ended. I moved to L.A. soon after and met my boyfriends of the next period: Patrick, then Bruce, then Manuel. Each of them warily accepted the existence of Laurent, who came to visit me two times in L.A. Each boyfriend found his sweetness undeniable. And Laurent, for his part, considered all my boyfriends valuable caretakers when he wasn't there to take care of me.

I made an annual two-week pilgrimage to visit him. He would usually take a week's vacation and we would take a lovely trip: Cannes, the tour of the Loire Valley châteaus, and finally, Italy, where I embarrassed him by forcing him into a gondola with me in Venice. An old-style gay man in that way, public displays of affection embarrassed him. Nevertheless, we were serenaded on the canals.

From afar, Laurent wrote me sweet, simple letters. We talked often by phone. I would call him just before bedtime, waking him up, already the next morning in Paris. During our longest absence from one another, we discovered the joys of sex *au téléphone*.

1989

He hadn't wanted me to come so soon. "Wait till I'm feeling better." Until he looked better, he was thinking. Laurent was twenty years older than I and had always been self-conscious about aging. Now he was afraid to let me see his shrinking, sick body. Did he think I wouldn't love him if I didn't desire him sexually? Did he think so little of me, of himself?

He kept thinking he would get himself together, if he could just get a little rest at Jacques apartment in Cannes, his *maison de repos.*

When I arrived in Paris from L.A. in May, Laurent was still working almost full-time. Though he was thinner, I think I was relieved he didn't look worse. But he felt horrible and had a relentless fever. His mood was brittle and irritable. I thought it was crazy that he was working and told him so. For the first time in ten years he barked at me angrily when I asked too many questions about a medicine I would try to find for him in the pharmacy down the street. I lacked the vocabulary to distinguish between things like *tablet* and *capsule,* and all the French packaging that was familiar to him was foreign to me. Laurent had always treated me gingerly. I had been the moody one.

The flight down from Paris was tense. I carried his bags, flagged down the taxis, helped him as much as I could. Laurent couldn't talk to me about what he was feeling. He could hardly accept my help. And he couldn't accept what was happening, at least not in my presence.

He got into a terrible argument with the cabdriver in Cannes, accusing him of taking the wrong route to get a larger fare. By the time we arrived at the Rocher St-Georges, the poor driver, too upset to notice, banged his head on the all-glass entrance door while carrying our bags.

Laurent's fever never went away that week, and he almost never got out of bed. When the sun shone, I tried to get him to go out on the terrace. He was too sick to care. A man of hearty appetite, he was never hungry. I tried to pry him open to tell me what he could bear to eat. Being no cook, I'd walk to the market to shop for thinly sheared ham, bread, canned pea and tomato soups, inflicting my culinary incompetence on my dear, sick French boyfriend.

I was uncomfortable all week. I had been hoping for a dose of vacation myself. Not only was Laurent not getting better, he was on edge and incapable of being with me in a way that I recognized. And he couldn't open up. It was intolerable.

So I went out. It was Cannes during the film festival of 1989. The town buzzed. I tried not to stay out more than a couple of hours at a time. I would stroll down the Croisette oceanfront walk, watch Brigitte Bardot wanna-bes pose for hordes of hungry paparazzi. And I found the two local gay bars.

By midweek I had run into an American guy, a Hollywood type, who offered me a ticket to one of the premieres. Not fully understanding what kind of scene it was, I showed up wearing a smart, but casual, summer linen ensemble. As I approached, I saw a red carpet extending as far as the eye could see, and a parade of men and women in tuxes and sequined evening gowns. There were cameras and lights everywhere. I hoped I could sneak through unnoticed, but everyone had to pass a bottleneck checkpoint. The security man began screaming at me as I approached. *"Vous ne portez pas un smoking!"* I pretended I didn't speak French. He gestured wildly at my outfit. No one without a tuxedo would ever pass him. Humiliated, I bolted out of line and into the streets. Muttering through my rage, I declared that something would happen that evening to make me glad that I had been refused entrance. I entered the gay bar *au coin* to lick my wounds and have a cocktail and began chatting it up with a small group of men, eyeing one whose eyes sparkled when he smiled. Would he be an answer to my pain? No. But soon I was introduced to an American, living in Cannes, who offered to take me through some mountain villages that he loved. That is what we did each of my remaining days. He was my angel of diversion.

Except that Laurent, who had told me to go out, was home alone and miserable. I had deserted him.

Finally our trip was over. We flew back to Paris where Laurent could get the care he needed. His doctor put him in the hospital. The nuns greeted him warmly. He had charmed them during his previous stay. I visited every day, but was no comfort to him. I just reminded him of duty unfulfilled. He was supposed to take care of me, amuse me, gratify me sexually, and he couldn't do any of these things. So when I visited, after fifteen minutes of strained interaction, he would tell me to go, to go have "fun." Both of us were feeling guilty and neither of us could say a thing.

I had planned a very different trip. I had wanted his dying to be a spiritual process. Laurent didn't know what I was talking about when I would try my New Age philosophy out on him; dying could be a "process," a "letting go," a "learning experience." My French, which generally served me well with Laurent, seemed useless. I had no way to make him well, not even a way to make him feel better. I couldn't admit it then, but I couldn't bear the stark discomfort and pain of watching a man I adored die a miserable death, silently, and against his will.

Laurent had lost faith in God early. He and his brother were bastard children of a man who was forbidden to marry their mother, judged to be beneath her by an authoritarian father she never dared defy. During mass all those years ago in a small Basque village, Laurent and his brother were banished to the back row of the church, unworthy to sit in the family pews. His cousins would shout at them, *"Bâtards!"* He never knew his father, who died in the French Army during the war. He had no use for God.

The day of my departure, I came to see him in the hospital one last time. The morning was gray and cool. A light drizzle began as I walked inside the gates and crossed the old stone courtyard through the entrance doors and past one of the elderly nuns, who greeted me. Did she know who I was to Laurent? I wondered. I didn't admit to myself that this might be the last time I would see him. I sat for a few minutes holding his feverish hand, staring out at the sad morning. We were quiet, neither of us wanting to say good-bye. Finally, as I stood to leave, I kissed him. He patted my hand to say he wanted me to go quickly, to minimize the pain. I looked back at him. He had turned his face away.

I never saw him again.

It was a bright, sunny L.A. morning when we spoke the last time. I was folding the laundry when the phone rang. *"Steve, c'est Laurent,"* he said weakly. I gushed a guilty apology for letting a week go by without calling. He comforted me, said he could have called, too. Then, "God how I've suffered." I moaned and, after a moment, told him how sorry I was. Our silent wall had broken. It was, perhaps, the most intimate moment we shared. All pretense gone, Laurent allowed me, this one time only, to share his enormous, unfathomable suffering.

He sounded tired. We didn't talk long, except to say *"Je t'aime"* one last passionate time. This was our good-bye. It's this last conversation that helps me to forgive myself for not staying with him in the apartment all those long days that week in Cannes, for not being able just to be with him in his misery.

Laurent died in July. I don't know what day. I didn't go to his funeral, couldn't imagine myself there without him, stumbling through my grief in French among his friends. I didn't even have the right words to say in English.

I asked Jacques to send flowers from me, something beautiful. He asked how much I wanted to spend, and when I offered four hundred francs, he said that wouldn't buy anything nice. He wouldn't tell me what I needed to spend, just left me floundering on the phone, wondering what would be considered generous. He was punishing me for not coming to the funeral.

Today I wish I had gone.

1990

The next winter, in February, while in Paris on business, I stole some time for myself to go by Laurent's apartment. Since my last visit, a tiny park had been installed in the vacant space just across the street. It was composed of one bench, some greenery, and a dramatic lattice trompe-l'oeil arch on the rear wall. Beauty materializes in Paris all the time.

I sat on the bench to have my reckoning, knowing that the impact of his death had waited for my return. As the grief surfaced, I dared to look up at his building and counted the floors to find the right window. The apartment was vacant, the window curtainless. I was struck by how narrow the building was. Hadn't there been two windows across? Had it thinned, impossibly? After a time, I got up and walked away down the rue Jacob, pausing to look back at Laurent's window three or four times. His world—and mine—had been removed.

THE KERN BROTHERS

Droze Kern

I don't remember when we left Galveston Beach. I just remember how good it felt to be leaving. Was the sun setting or was that how it felt about our lives together? We squeezed into Michael's new mint green Honda Civic (he said, "I shudda got a four-door") and waved Thank-you's and Love-you's and See-ya-soon's to our hosts, George and Claudine. I don't remember much except feeling that there was something awfully final about the See-ya-soon's.

I don't remember when we left Galveston Beach, but I remember how close I felt to Michael. Michael and I had felt close for years, but this was different. A profound reverence, even a sacredness, had emerged between us. It was the same type of feeling that I had once felt as a boy of ten when I walked this same stretch of beach while on family vacation and felt God's presence suddenly breathing in my soul. I felt something wonderful and terrible had happened between Michael and me that March weekend on Galveston Island in 1991.

After arriving on Saturday morning, Michael asked if I would like to walk with him along the beach. The day was warm and clear. The wind and waves seemed to drown out all noise except the sound of children playing far off in the distance. The air was filled with the smell of oyster. Our feet sank in the sand as we walked.

We noticed all of the pretty brown-skinned Texas boys in wet cutoff jeans. Whenever my brother saw a red-haired boy, he would look him over, stare at his crotch, and whisper to me in his soft Cajun drawl, "Girrlll! There's fire down below!" That was Michael's way of describing red pubes.

As we walked along the beach, we told stories. I had not seen Michael for a few months (he lived in Houston and I lived in New York), so we spent time catching up. Our conversation moved from stories of friends to the stories Michael and I always told each other again and again: stories about our family, stories about coming out, and stories about being gay. Our stories were always embellished and rarely philosophical. They wove our lives together. Telling stories was the way Michael and I broke bread. They were our Eucharist. God, I remember how much I laughed with Michael that afternoon.

Having a gay brother meant the world to me. We were friends, allies, comrades-in-arms. Our friends called us The Kern Brothers. We were often inseparable. When life kept us apart, our frequent late-night phone calls kept us laughing at life and loving each other.

Having a gay brother changed my life. He came out to me after I was painfully outed during my senior year in high school. He grew angry as he watched many family members and friends turn away in disgust as they heard about my "turning queer." One Sunday afternoon in the middle of a family barbecue—after completing his second six-pack of Pabst Blue Ribbon beer and a pint of Johnnie Walker Red—my father decided to bring up the subject of my homosexuality for family discussion. My mother yelled, "Oh, shut up! You're drunk!" and buried her stone face in a cast-iron pot of simmering pork and beans. Michael became enraged and stood up in the middle of the kitchen and shouted, "Well, I'm gay, too! Droze is not your only gay son, so if you're gonna pick on him, you'd better pick on me, too!" We became soul mates that day.

Twenty years later, that afternoon on Galveston Beach, we walked and looked at brown-skinned boys and told stories. We talked about the time we shot up some weird medication used to combat epileptic seizures and wrote HONKY in three-foot letters in salt across my aunt Mavis's front lawn. After the grass died, HONKY was spelled out across her yard for weeks. We innocently said it was probably the KKK. She snarled and spit in our direction, "Those letters are too perfectly formed. Looks like the work of two smart-ass nephews." Her suspicion was confirmed when my mother went to see her a few days later to borrow a box of salt.

Walking along the beach, we talked about our drug and alcohol years and our years of shared sobriety. We talked about partying at the two gay bars "in the old days" in Lafayette, Louisiana, where quaaludes and Black Mollies were everywhere to be found, where we danced slow dances together and the bouncer locked the doors to the bar after you came in. We went to lots of drag shows together and talked about the year we went to Mardi Gras in New Orleans as "sisters." I went as Yvette the Girl-Whore and he went as Helen and Her Gurgling Hernias. I looked like a drunken, recently fucked Jayne Mansfield in stiletto heels, capri pants, and mink pelts stolen from my grandmother's closet, and he looked like Julia Child on Thorazine. We told story after story and talked about how wonderful our lives together had been.

And we talked about our family. Michael was my link to them. He was the one to whom I felt connected. He made me laugh. He made all visits and holidays tolerable. By then, he had found great humor in our family dysfunction and taught me how to laugh at it, too. Michael became the Kern family to me.

We walked for over three hours that afternoon. Our stories and laughter eventually gave way to silence. Michael was tired. We listened to the great yawning of the ocean. The silence was ominous. The stories had been told. They were the great myths that held us firm as Kern Brothers. They were what we knew. What lay before us was unknown and frightening and terrible.

Say it, Michael. Say it! You're dying!

But he wouldn't say it. We walked. There was such obvious silence. We both knew he was very ill. We had to stop ever so often for him to sit and rest. But we looked at the brown-skinned boys. I helped him up. We walked along farther. I held his arm and supported him as we walked. We were the Kern Brothers. Friends. Allies. Comrades-in-arms. And I was losing him.

From the moment Michael and I came out to each other, it was as though we had made a secret agreement never to hold anything back in our relationship with each other. This unspoken arrangement seemed to be the backbone of being a Kern Brother.

∞

Through the years, we told each other boyfriend secrets, shared our drugs with each other, talked about our fetishes (he showed me his collection of tit clamps, anal beads, and Mary Kay cosmetics, and I showed him my collection of bondage pornography, erotic photos of the hot, young Irish priest I seduced when I was a seminarian, and my colorful collection of size-13, women's four-inch-spiked high-heel shoes with pointy toes). We dressed in drag together, wore each other's clothes, and danced slow dances together to jukebox music at the local gay bar. He and I even had a three-way once with some straight trick we picked up one drunken night at the bus station.

When either of us was afraid or needed advice or needed to hear a good story, we went to each other before anyone else. We did everything together. We talked about everything with each other. No secret was unspeakable between us.

Except one. Michael never said to me, "Droze, I am dying." We never talked about it. I never asked Michael if he was dying. And I never told him that I knew he was. The unspeakable had finally happened. For the first time in twenty years, we shared an unspoken secret: Michael was dying from AIDS.

It was not that we couldn't talk about the disease. We did so quite freely when just one month prior to our trip to Galveston, Michael was diagnosed with acquired immune deficiency syndrome when cancerous lesions were discovered throughout much of his digestive and intestinal tract. We talked openly and often about his health while he was being burned alive by chemotherapy. But we never talked about his dying.

Michael and I experienced so much together. We loved each

other with extraordinary passion. Together we lived life ruth-
lessly. But the thought of his life ending so quickly was just unbearable. We could not go there in life together. I have often
longed for just one more chance to redo that walk with Michael
where we might have said the whole truth to each other. Because
we were so afraid to talk about his dying, his sudden death two
months later became the loneliest, saddest day of my life.

As we walked slowly back to the beachhouse together, we
were enveloped in brotherly silence and the overwhelming smell
of oyster. I felt as though he was being pulled out into a great
ocean with such a velocity that I couldn't do anything except
stand on the shore and watch. We walked for hours together that
day. We'd instinctively come back to the playground of our youth
to be together. I wanted this walk to last forever.

We stopped for diet Cokes. We always stopped for diet Cokes
when we traveled together. I paid. He let me. He usually never
let me pay. The least I could do was buy him a diet Coke.

We walked back in silence, with an occasional comment
about some hot young thing walking on by. I didn't know that
this would be our last time together. Ever. Alone. I had hoped
for more time.

Just two days before his death, we laughed out loud as we
spoke on the phone. He said how much better he was beginning
to feel after his second cycle of chemotherapy. We made plans to
go to Las Vegas. I told him how happy I felt that he was feeling
better and said that I'd speak with him soon. We ended our
phone call, as always, with, "Girrlll! I love you, girl!" "I love you,
too, girl!"

That was the last time I spoke to my brother. He died suddenly and alone two days later on Mother's Day.

I don't remember when we left Galveston Beach. But I remember the sun was setting. I remember how close I felt to Michael. And how much it meant to me to have a gay brother. A
Kern Brother.

(FRAGMENT)

William M. Franklin

. . . We have more time. A reprieve. And then the frantic search. A search for ways to stay alive. Experimental treatments. We consult fanatics, spiritual healers, and simple quacks. One doctor wears a huge diamond pinkie ring and a toupee, which slides down his forehead every time he lights a cigarette, and has a clock on the wall decorated with the twelve sexual signs of the zodiac. Another doctor who speaks only French assures us he has all the answers thanks to a microscope he smuggled out of Nazi Germany. They all take our money. You meditate, pray, and sleep with crystals. You will yourself a reprieve. You will us more time. . . .

. . . Our world keeps getting smaller and smaller, shrinking back until we're on a small raft floating in a sea full of medications, meals, and bodily functions. We laugh a little and I'm grateful we still can. We tease each other, hold each other, sometimes cry in each other's arms. We confess our fears, we make promises and speak about the unspeakable. We communicate in our own private language, our secret little signals and gestures full of nuance and history perfected over years.

JOHNNY APPLESEED

Robert C. Murphy

He told me he wished he could be like Johnny Appleseed and sleep for twenty years.

I corrected him, "You mean Rip Van Winkle."

"Oh, yeah. I wish I could be like Rip Van Winkle and sleep for twenty years."

I didn't know what to say.

I sat down on the edge of the bed next to him and gently placed my hands on his shoulder.

"I'm so tired," he told me, "my body feels like it's on fire from within."

"Maybe your time is approaching."

He mumbled in agreement.

He told me often of his childhood, growing up in poverty. He helped his father build their house. His mother would have another baby and they'd build another room. He was the first. His mother was thirteen when he was born. They lived in a small, dusty desert town in the Southwest.

He told me he always had to be strong. They boiled water to wash the clothes. Dogs and cats were not allowed in the house. He worked all summer for $5 a week so he could buy clothes for each new school year. His parents were thrifty with their money. They were not into rewarding. He told me he wasn't allowed to get sick. His parents closed themselves off from his pain. He told them his stomach hurt. They told him he couldn't be sick. He finally collapsed from a bleeding ulcer. They sat next to his hospital bed and cried.

He told me he loved his grandmother. She lived next door to him when he was growing up and she always called him over for treats she'd cooked. Fresh tortillas with cheese and mouthwatering, warm cookies. She had a garden and tended it lovingly.

He told me I was devious and manipulative and untrustworthy. He told me I caused him a lot of pain. He told me he wished he'd ended the relationship years ago before we became irrevocably connected. He told me he loved me. I told him I was sorry. I would try not to cause him any more pain. I told him I wanted him to die in peace. I had other motives. I also want peace for myself.

He told me he wished he could be like Johnny Appleseed and sleep for twenty years.

"You mean Rip Van Winkle," I corrected him again.

This time he said, "I wish I could be like Rip Van Winkle and sleep for twenty years."

I told him he had my permission to leave, but that I would miss him. I asked him to forgive me.

I kissed him on the forehead and left the room. He closed his eyes and tried to sleep.

(FRAGMENT)
[The last writing in his notebook]

Robert C. Murphy

. . . Fruit is not afraid. An apple has no fear or so we assume. . . . Sometimes I wish there was no fear. No time to worry or wonder. Can I exist just as a simple apple? Can I exist in the orchard without thought? To be a simple apple. To be a luscious, sweet orange . . . My entire existence leads to the point where I will be eaten even on a sunny, brilliant day. . . . I sit in a cherry orchard, the world around me spinning. The day bakes with heat. The luscious cherries are ready for consumption. Their time is coming. So is mine. I feel it now and I can't shake the reality. I always thought I'd live to old age. I used to want to live to be one hundred. . . .

I often long for death now. Is that a bad thing to say? Do I have to continue living for myself and others and so that I can go to the movies and munch on salty popcorn? I'm afraid of being eaten and ravaged. There must be a lesson here. . . .

Recently, I lay in a hospital and watched a full moon rise in the sky. A gift to fall asleep by. The brilliance of the light pulled me in and took me to a place of peace. I wondered how can it all be.

THE DOORKNOB

Rodney Rauch

Your terrible eyes,
  blue-green smears just underneath,
lengthen my breathing to counts of six,
have me picking at a scab
in the fleshy valley
on the inside of my thumb.

You catch my folding
  and rush in with
nonsensical flows,
stories of two summers ago
when you met an older man
whose talk got you tested.

The anonymous sex
  you had with three strangers
the time we drove to Las Vegas
to visit your father,
felt to you
like the plug-in.

Your folded, bony hands
  (almost a lovely, china white)
toss haunted cathedrals into my head,

and a holiness
glows round you—
I watch your silvery sickness turn golden.

Then spit up some trite wit
  straight from "The Small-Talk Manual,"
my eyes darting from slow-drip
to red light,
past lacy drapes to outside,
return and rest on the doorknob.

I fumble for reasons to leave
  when your eyes go hard
and dark,
the gleam of your transgressions
washing away as I bend
to kiss your parched, peeling lips
good-bye.

HOSPITAL

Brian Sturtevant

The room is dark but for the muted fluorescence coming through the half-open door. Your room—your home is located next to the nurses' station. The singsong of the Filipino nurses speaking in Tagalog adds to the surrealism. The large display digital clock I bought for your bedside tells me in glowing red that it is 2:14 A.M. I cannot leave you, I want to stay. I check to make sure everything is positioned within your reach: water, phone, call button, Kleenex, washcloth. I ingratiate myself with the nurses to the extent my charm will carry me. I don't want your needs ignored in my absence because I failed to smile at Teresita or forgot to say good-night to Clarita. I think of everything, but it amounts to nothing. I am arranging furniture in a burning house, because I don't know what else to do.

You have lived in room 717 at St. Vincent's Hospital for almost a month now—a space half the size of our bedroom at home has become your world. I have tried to make it comfortable without making it cluttered. You have your teddy bear, which I think you appreciate. There are always flowers on the shelves. I bought you a portable CD player with speakers and various CDs. One contains sounds from nature. There is a track of ocean waves crashing against the shore. I have put up large, colorful posters of relaxing scenes: a white sand beach in the Bahamas, a Vermont maple forest in the fall, a view of the Manhattan skyline at night. They cover the blank walls and create places for you to escape to—or so I imagine. You would probably prefer a tasteful pen-and-ink drawing rather than these jarring, mismatched images of color. But, I brought them in for you and put them up with the excitement of a little boy bringing his mother flowers, or a puppy fetching a stick. Wanting so desperately to please that you wouldn't say anything negative for fear of hurting my feelings.

I lie in bed with you sometimes. It is a stingy mattress on a narrow bed, with electric controls to adjust the height and angle for the patient's comfort. But how comfortable can a bed with tubular-steel side rails be? Antiseptic, utilitarian, made for easy cleanup. Beauty is not even an afterthought. Our bed at home has massive oak posts and headboard and a soft, king-size mattress. It has Laura Ashley printed cotton sheets that you picked to match the room. It doesn't adjust, but it is oak, it is real. Real, like you.

I lie in bed with you sometimes. It is incredibly comforting; like coffee in the morning or a warm blanket on a cold night. Lying in bed with the person you love is a mundane event—not dramatic or heroic. There is no crescendo in this simple act, no diminuendo, yet it is so deeply life-affirming and sustaining. The subtle touches and glances of an old love that runs deep is difficult to convey by word or cinema because it is so epic, so cosmic in scale.

I lie in bed with you sometimes. You have become incredibly fragile. I think of a different time when I would chase and tackle you in some rough-and-tumble game of dominance. Now I must handle you like some fractured baby bird that has fallen from its nest. I want to pull you tightly to my chest, but I could kill you with my love. The chest catheter under your left scapula leads directly to your heart. I dare not risk contamination. You cannot put your arms around me because you have multiple tubes in your right arm whose purpose I have long since forgotten, and the veins in your left arm are embolated from so many sticks and ruptures. I can kiss you on the lips—not passionately because your mouth is dry and your lips are chapped. So I press harder—

reduced to expressing the depth of my love as pounds per square inch, because I don't know what else to do.

I cannot leave you, I want to stay. I hover in the doorway. I have already kissed you good-bye for the evening. You are in a restless Demerol/Ativan sleep. I can make my getaway now while you are sleeping. I cannot bear to leave you while you are awake and conscious of my absence. I notice the single chair in the room is menacingly close to the bed. It could trip you if you made the drugged decision to get up in the middle of the night. I push it back into the corner before I leave. I am arranging furniture, because I don't know what else to do.

(FRAGMENT)

Christopher Gorman

"Our story isn't over," I tell him as the Filipino nurse checks the IV medication dripping from a small plastic bag attached to a pole that follows me from bed to toilet, up one hospital hallway and down another. My mother was never without her little black purse—is this IV bag my version of that coveted accessory?

"I'm not afraid of losing you," I say to him. He is sitting in the corner of the hospital room reading a magazine with Mel Gibson on the cover. "I just can't seem to accept the notion of my death. Even now with everything diminished and diminishing—my hair, my weight, my ass, T cells, hemoglobin, hematocrit, platelets, testosterone—I can't imagine not being here anymore. With you. I mean, broken chairs and old radios and rusty sleds don't go away—they go up to the attic. That's what death will be for me. I'll be up in the attic next to the box filled with my tax returns and Playbills. If they can stay, so can I." My friend answers by reading aloud from the Mel Gibson interview. Something about how Mel's favorite TV show is *Circus of the Stars*. He watches it with his wife and his twenty-four children. Blah blah blah . . . I hate Mel Gibson and my friend knows this will shut me up. He doesn't like when I talk about my death.

"Our story is the very first one I'm going to tell," I say as he helps lift me out of the bathtub in my hospital room. "Oh, yes, I'm going to sit with Eugene O'Neill and Siobhan McKenna. We're going to do shots of Bushmill's and smoke Luckys until our fingertips turn yellow. They're going to hear about our long journey. I'll start slowly, leaving the really good stuff until last—that's how it happened anyway. I don't want to overwhelm Gene—he's been through so much. What if O'Neill and Mc-Kenna are Catholic homophobes and after too many shots of Bushmill's they both turn on me with the venom that only the Irish can muster? Fuck them. If that happens, I'll find Noël Coward and Michael Bennett and sit at their table. I'll tell Bennett how we saw *A Chorus Line* together during Christmas week in 1989. He'll *love* that. I won't tell him how shabby the show was, it might piss him off. Anyway, honey, this is all the long version of a simple fact. I'm going to tell our story forever—to anyone who will listen to me. It's a wonderful story and I like telling it."

7

VANISHING

I feel like the last days of Pompeii.

—Robbie Hilyard

I have found a voice here. A voice to be heard. The others and I are not writing the words and hearing the words of dying men. These are stories from the heart and soul of truly living men. Stories that will always breathe life as long as there is someone who will listen, someone who will breathe in our words.

—Tony Gramaglia

MONOLOGUE FROM
CHOSEN FAMILY

Philip Justin Smith

Act 1, Scene 3

TORY

David had sat me down "to talk." I imagined that once again he was going to tell me "it" wasn't working. That our relationship wasn't working. That he needed to be alone. And once again I was going to have to fight to save the relationship. Fuck him! Fuck him and his constant running, his hiding, his walls. Maybe this time I would let it go—let him go. "David, what's going on?"

David sat there in his green corduroy armchair, in that room that was so like him: manly, quiet, and classic. Variegated light from the blinds falling across him. Little swirls of dust in the opaque light of a San Francisco sunset. "That spot on my cock, it's KS." Time stopped. It felt as if some giant hand was squeezing my whole body so hard I would explode.

David stopped me with a look. His eyes begged me not to cry, to be strong so he could be strong. I shook so violently inside. I was losing him. And I didn't know what to do except honor his silent plea. I stood strong.

One month after David was diagnosed with KS, PCP. One month after the PCP, toxo.

David couldn't speak or walk. The man who had been so

powerful—had run the *Western Journal of Medicine,* had held to-gether an alcoholic family, and had been lover to me when most men would have fled—was helpless.

He sat through the most humiliating situations with eyes that begged for understanding and release.

I had been this man's lover for years. I had watched his moves and probed his heart that was so hidden.

I understood his every wish. There would not be another spinal tap so painful he wailed like a wounded animal. No. There would be no more blood drawn. Yes, Mrs. Greer, we are leaving the hospital and going home. I am taking your son home to die. Your son and your hope are now "no code." No reviving. Just releasing. The battle waged and over.

I awoke that morning having slept for maybe two hours. I heard that sound. David was lying in bed with his mouth open and his eyes rolled back. The sound rose out of him like a dried gourd slowly shaking. I knew today I was saying good-bye. I checked the condom catheter we used because he couldn't walk to the bathroom. It was full of blood. It had backlogged, and when I tried to remove it, both David and I were covered in blood. Baptized.

I held him in my lap, cradled him. That man who meant everything to me. And I sang, "Hush, little baby, don't you cry . . ." And I prayed. Time passed without being noticed. The room became thick with bands of silver and gold light. It was as if all the people who had passed before had come to help my lover die. Breath like a cry and all the world adjusted itself to life without David Greer.

The American Indians have a saying that there is one moment you are born for. One instant . . .

(Lights go down for a four count)

The day after David died his parents tore up the will. Paid the lawyer off to shut up, changed the locks on the house. All I really wanted was some of my clothes and a picture of David taken when he was the editor of his college newspaper.

All my friends said I should just walk out gracefully. That it wasn't about "things." So I wrote his parents a letter asking for a copy of the photo, nothing else, no property, nothing. And they never wrote back.

(*Lights down*)

RED

Leonard Mosqueda

It was beautiful and balmy that late afternoon as I hurried across Hillhurst to reach our apartment. My thoughts retraced old ground in my mind. What was happening to you? All that constant fatigue, all those tests. Epstein-Barr, Reiter's syndrome, MS. What the hell was happening? I was getting so frustrated by the uncertainty. When I reached the door, I had a premonition something had gone wrong. No music. No TV. No radio. No telephone chitchat. I entered and called your name. Nothing.

So stubborn. So independent. You didn't want any "buddy" from that new organization. You said he would probably steal or sell drugs. I walked down the corridor looking. The kitchen. The den. The bedroom. The bathroom door was closed.

I knocked. I nudged it. I couldn't open it, yet there was no way to lock it. I pushed. Then I saw your wrist by the doorjamb. I realized you had fallen and blocked the door. I pushed. Is this hurting you? I wondered. No sound. Finally, I squeezed into the bathroom. It was so hot. Like a steam room. The heater was on. Then I saw it. A bloody black strip of meat where your back lay against the red-hot grill of the wall heater. In your dementia, you noticed nothing.

My jaw dropped in horror. I dragged you to the bedroom and called our MD friend for help. My hands, shirt, pants . . . covered with a redness I would never see again without the sensation of pain. I was losing you and finally knew it.

Our friends advised ice, so I packed you in ice. Neighbors helped. You were sedated. We all agreed to keep you at home. In an emergency room they would have left you alone to die.

A respite of a few more months while I watched you stare at the static of the TV. Sometimes you remembered me, mostly you mumbled about your first lover. You kept repeating his telephone number. Did I exist for you then?

I love red now. I placed the Rothko print by the bed. I know what it means to me now. It's you.

THREE NIGHT SCENES

Kenneth Bartmess

One

There was a carnival set up in the parking lot behind the auditorium. We had been there earlier in the evening. They put down sawdust so deep there were still flakes of it sticking to my socks when I pulled them off for bed. I could see the lights from my bedroom window, just an arc of the Ferris wheel and the occasional flung arm of the Octopus. I could hear fragments of music, splinters of carnival glass. My older cousin, Donald, stayed over in the room next to mine. He called to me, said I could see the lights better from in there. I sat on the edge of his bed. It was summer; he was just covered by a sheet. We looked out the window together, and he put my hand on his hard-on.

Two

I worked nights in the hospital as an attendant. The patients usually settled down on that shift, and often my crepe-soled shoes made the only sound away from the quiet gossip at the nurse's station. I helped give out evening medications, and when a male patient couldn't urinate after abdominal surgery, I would hold his penis in my hand and slip a sterile tube down inside to tap the bladder. His night would be easier then. When the floor was at its quietest, I took the bodies of those who had died during the day down to the morgue. They were never moved when there were patients or visitors in the halls. They were kept in their beds, stiff and heavy under the white sheets, waiting for me to come for them.

Three

When my lover decided it was time to die, we had tea and toast together, and I had a dab of that sticky English plum spread I'm never sure I like. He pulled a rubber band off a rolled-up envelope and spilled the capsules out on the glass top of the bedside table. They rolled about until we cornered them in little piles of ten. I felt that something had to be done in an allotted time— some kind of timed test with death the good grade. Get ten down with a swig of Scotch and then another ten, and again, six times ten. We looked at each other without speaking as the clock of our world stopped. I slipped under the sheet next to his ruined body. I rubbed his back, and we talked quietly, laughing, like we used to do after sex. I stayed when he fell asleep, rubbing, rubbing until he was gone, and then until his skin was pale and cool.

THE PACT

Steve Smith

We are killing Donald.

The six of us—friends for so long now that we disagree on when we met—have discussed it endlessly. The method, the timetable, the possible legal repercussions. We have strategized and agonized and plotted and vacillated and conspired.

But finally there is consensus. We will murder our best friend.

I suppose it softens the act that we won't resort to blunt force, strangulation, or stabbing. We are gentlemen, after all, and there are more refined techniques. Still, the result is the same. His blood will be on our hands.

Donald has always wanted things "just so." The product of a hardscrabble, lower-middle-class upbringing—"Long Island deli money," he used to say—he has cultivated manners and worldliness well above his station, with a style simultaneously grand and restrained; never vulgar, but with a touch of drama. You see it in his decor, the way he entertains. And how he has planned his death.

He issued the summons in late July, not an invitation so much as a command. We, Donald's dearest friends, his "sisters,"

were instructed to be at his apartment one Saturday morning at
9 A.M. Sharp.

We found fresh coffee, a full tea service, muffins and scones
laid out on the sideboard. His tiny salon-cum-tenement seemed
even smaller—crammed that morning not only with fussy, mismatched divans and ottomans, but with almost a dozen large,
sober-faced men, each somewhere between youth and middle
age.

"Kirk Anne, there's a Tommy Tippy cup and a bib for you in
the kitchen. I don't want you spilling all over someone's inheri-
tance."

"I'll be careful, Mother."

"Humor me, Kirk. Sit on the floor. We all know your history."

"I won't spill."

"Yeah, that's what he always used to say when we lived together. Nine goblets and five champagne flutes later . . ."

"At least get a napkin."

"Oh, for Christ's sake . . . I'm not a child."

"That's readily apparent, especially in this light."

"Honey, you are workin' my last T cell!"

That morning, the familiar banter felt rote and forced. We
knew what to expect. Donald had discussed his intentions with
us individually for months, testing our reactions, steeling his
own resolve. Though we might still be sketchy on the details, we
knew the outline of his plan. Certainly, we knew this was more
than a social call. Six of us were to seal a pact. The others would
bear witness.

With a sterling teaspoon against Limoges, he gaveled the
meeting to order.

Donald was tired. After more than a half decade on the HIV
treadmill, he was tired of hospitals and specialists and waiting
rooms and visiting nurses and food banks and caseworkers. He
was tired of being biopsied and dilated and infused and trans-
fused and refused. He was tired of insurance forms, disability
forms, Social Security forms, doctor bills, hospital bills, phar-

macy bills. He was tired of Hickmans and needles and pills and swabs. He was tired of neuropathy and bony shoulder blades and stomach cramps and lesions and warts and encroaching blindness and the smell of his own shit. Most of all, he was tired of loss. The loss of independence, of privacy, of meaningful work. And, of course, the loss of most of his friends.

Donald was sick, and he was tired.

So it came as no surprise when he laid out his scheme. Starting immediately, he explained over a cup of Earl Grey, he would be discontinuing all medication except painkillers. No more ganciclovir, Neupogen, Bactrim, Zovirax, or any of the other polysyllabic toxins he has ingested or injected for so long now.

Then, he continued, in one week's time—sooner if the progression of the disease warranted—his doctor would approve a low-level morphine drip for "pain management." Exhibit A: the murder weapon.

The plan was straightforward. Each evening, when the lone insurance-approved twelve-hour duty nurse finished his shift, one or two of Donald's six chosen accomplices would arrive to watch him through the night. Nothing suspicious in that—we had been sleeping over for so many months, it had become routine. No need anymore to check the photocopied calendar and emergency phone list we each carry to see who's scheduled when.

But now, our dull, familiar vigil would acquire new urgency. Instead of helping him to the bathroom or reassuring him when he became disoriented, we would slowly, methodically, deliberately be cranking up Donald's morphine dosage.

Within a few hours, he explained, he would lose consciousness; within a few days, his organ function would slow and then stop. Finally, his lungs will come to a rasping, wheezing, rattling halt, and it will all be over.

Ghoulish, certainly. Yet it sounded relatively simple. And, he added, it would be painless. But for whom?

I said, we all said, "Of course, Donald. Whatever you want."

And so we return on the following Saturday, exactly one week later to the minute, to say good-bye. There is no tea this morning—only grape juice and consecrated wafers.

An intelligent, thoughtful, young Episcopal priest has been called in to administer Communion and perform the Anglican version of last rites. She handles herself with such grace, I am almost able to choke down my resentment against the Church along with my wafer.

She reminds us that Communion commemorates the Last Supper, during which Christ said good-bye to his twelve disciples. There are twelve of us here today, not counting Donald. A shiver runs through me.

It is late now. Each of us agreed to busy himself during the day and meet again at Donald's at nightfall—just like in a Chandler novel. I don't know how I've spent the last eight hours. Only that the phrase "Why hast thou forsaken me?" has reverberated since morning.

As I trudge up the stairs to his apartment, the hallway seems even more tatty and depressing than usual; frayed carpet, chipped paint, harsh fluorescent bulbs—the few that still burn. Such a step down from the comfortable house he shared with his lover—the one who deserted him, fleeing to Atlanta so he wouldn't have to watch. In that moment, near the top of the stairs, I am struck by the sudden recognition that poverty has weakened Donald as much as disease. A wave of nausea runs over me at the thought that he may be choosing death over destitution.

Outside his door, I pause and breathe deeply, then again. It seems a melodramatic gesture, but I know I must compose myself for what I will find. Donald will be unconscious. He has been dripping since morning. I visualize the scene in order to soften its impact. Then I fish out my key ring and slip his into the lock—like Ray Milland in the Hitchcock classic. I turn the knob and let myself in.

Music plays on the stereo. I am surprised to see the guys all sitting at the dining room table. I'd imagined them in a hushed vigil around the bed.

Then I see Donald. Sitting at the head of the table in his bathrobe and slippers, hair slightly mussed but otherwise impeccable, he has just taken a huge bite out of a grilled cheese sandwich and is about to wash it down with a gulp of diet Coke. He looks up, arches an eyebrow, and swallows. "You better sit down, hon. You look like you've seen a ghost."

The others rush to explain. The doctor has set the initial dosage too low—lower than he and Donald had discussed. He is out of town and can't be reached until Monday. The nursing supervisor is powerless to override the doctor's orders. And we, the collaborators, are stymied, too. Although we've received instructions on how to adjust the dosage, the drip regulator is computerized and programmed to the doctor's specifications. We can only increase the dose 1.5 mg at a time, and then only up to the maximum allowed in the doctor's prescribed parameters.

I sink into the sofa, realizing this ordeal is going to be longer and more complicated than we'd bargained.

"Isn't there a 'no snacking' rule after last rites?" I manage weakly.

Three nights later, Donald is still alert, ambulatory, and eating. There is an undeniably dreamy quality about him, and he tends to drift off immediately after an increase in the dosage. But he is nowhere near death, at least not as near as he'd hoped.

We have all become slightly anxious, wondering how long this will take. And we are racked with unspoken guilt about wishing him dead.

When I arrive for my shift, he is rifling through a stack of CDs, looking for Clint Black.

"I miss two-stepping. When was the last time we went to Oil Can's?"

"Not long enough. Hey, why don't you come over here and sit on the sofa, Donna Mae? Let me look through those."

"I feel like movin' around. I'm not dead yet."

"I noticed."

Donald's doctor is still missing in action. Since Monday, we have been leaving increasingly urgent messages at his office, but he doesn't return the calls. One friend, the lawyer, even identified himself as Donald's medical power of attorney and left the name and number of his law firm for a return call. Still nothing.

Meanwhile, Donald is only up to 12.5 mg, a moderately high dosage for pain, but far from lethal.

A new nurse has been assigned, who seems more sympathetic to our cause. The last was deliberately obtuse, ignoring our hints and subtle entreaties about Donald's "pain." Cold bastard. This new one has taught me how to administer a "bolus," a single 1-mg burst of morphine, in addition to what the computer is pumping. If delivered conscientiously, on the hour, these boluses allow us to exceed the doctor's prescribed parameter. Slightly.

It's a Pyrrhic victory. Each time I deliver one, I feel as if I'm pricking Donald with a pin, when what he wants is the knife.

On the seventh day, Donald is still up and around in a loopy, happy haze. At times, he seems self-conscious, struggling to remain lucid and coherent. We have begun to envy him his pharmacologic euphoria. Unlike Donald, we are tense and short-tempered and scared. With each passing day, our own culpability, legal and moral, is harder to deny. Worse, our mission has changed. Instead of helping an anguished and suffering friend to a peaceful end, we seem to be strangling a playful, dopey puppy.

Desperate, we resort to alarmist tactics. Patiently waiting until Donald is at his most disoriented and pathetic, we dial the doctor's office and put Donald himself on the line. The receptionist, alarmed by his incoherence, places an emergency page to the doctor. Forty minutes later and a full week into the crisis, Donald's doctor of seventeen years finally returns a call. Angry, defensive, and clearly more concerned about possible legal consequences than about his patient's best interests, he grudgingly agrees to increase his prescription. When this ordeal is over and my first murder is under my belt, I know who my second victim will be.

"Time for your poison, my pretty." My pathetic attempt at humor is reflexive, not so much for his benefit as mine.

I punch the numbers on the computer dial, waiting for the digital readout to confirm my selections. It is a complicated process, with a series of checks and double checks intended to discourage amateur meddlers like us. I must refer to my notes each time, even the twentieth and the fiftieth. I wonder absently whether the routine is truly so complicated or whether I simply refuse to learn it. After all, this is not a skill I hope to market. Yet, like any competent contract killer, I fear I may be called upon again to demonstrate my proficiency.

As I complete the sequence, the computer bleats its final report and the rush of opiate fills his veins. Donald's mouth hangs slack and his eyes roll back in their sockets. He is up to 20.5 mg, supposedly within the lethal range for most people. Our friend is not most people.

Two days later, we have upped him an additional six milligrams, with no appreciable deterioration. Donald is making very little sense. He trails off midsentence. Yet he still insists on staring blankly from his chair at the table, trying valiantly to follow our conversations. We are all exhausted.

For several days now, he has been hallucinating. At first his visions amused him as much as they did us, and he would describe in detail the vivid patterns and colors in his dull beige carpet, or the jolly, stout black lady who beckons from outside his second-story window. But now, he seems oblivious as he drifts back and forth from his world to ours. He scolds an imaginary child, who he fears will disturb one of his precious objects as she twirls through the living room in her long, lacy skirts.

We, the accomplices, are nearly hysterical. We bicker and snap at each other. Our resolve has begun to waver. Yet we have taken Donald too far to turn back. He is addicted now and would never survive withdrawals. One of us suggests injecting air bubbles into his veins. Another wants to add bleach to the IV drip. Our silent, panicked entreaties are so urgent now, they are almost audible. "Die. Die!"

⁂

Finally, on the fourteenth day, Donald loses consciousness. Occasionally, he tosses violently in a near-seizure, moaning and keening in a voice I don't recognize. Mostly he lies motionless in a diaper.

The routine is familiar to me now—I have done this part before. We turn his limp body hourly and keep a toothbrush at the bedside to clean away the ugly brown mucus that dries hard on his teeth and gums. We rub his feet gently but firmly, the only stimulus that still elicits a response—a weak moan, signifying either pleasure or discomfort. Occasionally, his eyes snap open and stare up fiercely at one or the other of us, but there is no sign of recognition, or even intelligence. I am struck that an act merely reflexive can seem so imploring.

I wash his face with a cool cloth and try futilely to part his thin, oily hair with a brush. The regular, measured rasp of his labored breath is oddly comforting, its rhythm so primal and insistent.

For the fifth or sixth time today, I apply lip balm to his cracked, chapped lips. The act seems resonant of some ancient burial ritual, an anointment, Blistex instead of myrrh. Together with his thin, swollen-knuckled fingers, skin stretched over bone, nails flat and gray, these bloodless, desiccated lips are the body's first concession to his coming death.

I shudder involuntarily as I lean over slowly and place my lips against the dry plane of his chalky forehead, feeling my warmth against his cooling. I move my lips to his ear, unsure of what to say, needy for my victim's absolution. In the long silence, I listen to his breath rattle and wheeze.

"I love you," I whisper softly. "Please forgive me."

⁂

Next to the bed, a skirted table is crowded with smartly framed snapshots. In one, taken several years ago, Donald and we six stand grinning in front of palm trees, hands clasped or arms draped over backs. We are handsome and strong and buoyant.

Today I see more than the sunny camaraderie I've noticed before. There is a tension in the grips, a strength in the embraces, even a wistfulness on a few faces, that belies the cheery holiday mood.

From my vantage point on Donald's deathbed, the men in the photograph seem to be forming a human wall, as if we mean to obstruct fate by our sheer physical solidarity. In some of those defiant smiles I detect a dawning awareness of what is to come, a tacit commitment to hang together, no matter what.

I stare for a long while at the photograph, at this fragile human barricade of caring and anguish and mutual devotion. There must be an engineering formula that applies. How many stresses over what period of time at what intensity can be absorbed and withstood? How many bricks can be lost before structural integrity is so compromised that a wall crumbles and collapses? Without Donald, our mortar and cornerstone, we are irrevocably weakened.

I close my eyes against the photograph and, setting aside my stubborn agnosticism, form a selfish but fervent prayer:

"May the wall hold long enough to shelter me."

No sign. No divine intervention. Only silence, and an occasional rasping wheeze, like wind through ruins, from the shell that was once my best friend.

COYOTE

Jan Olof Olsson

The day you died was the first time we saw a coyote. He was standing in the dust, halfway hidden under a small bush, along one of the roads in Griffith Park. The color of his coat blended with the sun that filtered through the dusty leaves, and we only noticed him as he stepped out from under the bush and his head became fully visible. We stared in excited silence, each pondering the nearness of the other. The magical appearance of the coyote broke the spell that had been cast the day you told me you had decided it was time for you to die. You told me you had imagined death riding through the air like a melody played on a cello, or like the scent of vanilla in the air, sweet and suffocating, but never as a coyote in the hills. The coyote suddenly turned and disappeared into the shadows between the trees and became an image forever burned into my eyes. I wanted to follow, to see where he went, to learn where a coyote goes when he has seen a man the day the man is going to die.

The first two days we took care of details. Made sure all the papers were signed. Talked to the mortuary, picked out an urn. Since it was going to be shipped to your family, we decided to go with a more expensive one made out of brass. At night we lay awake. Talking. Remembering. Forgiving. Silently holding each other. We read letters and poems, we read about angels: you promised to be mine. We talked about death. About what happens when one dies. We didn't cry much, just lay still staring

287

into each other's eyes; as we two days later stared into those of
the coyote, trying to figure out, hoping to find strength in the
other. Before dawn we would hear the coyotes hunting down
from the hills. Their frantic, furious yelps whipped into a frenzy.
Then a sudden silence—heavy, still, forever.

We saw a coyote for the first time the day you died. We had
only heard their chilling howls as they hunted down from the
hills at night. That last night you went and closed the back door,
then we lay and listened to the silence after their kill. On the
third and final day we decided to visit places we had enjoyed.
We drove around the reservoir, slowly, paying attention to every
detail. Every house climbing the hillsides, every tree growing
along the water. We watched the dogs run loose in the park and
the young men play basketball on the hot asphalt court. We went
to La Conversation for croissants—we split a smoked salmon
and cream cheese, and a ham and cheese. Before returning home
we drove through the park. We stopped at the observatory for a
walk. The hazy air concealed most of the city, and we could only
make out the different areas where we had lived from memory.
On the way down the coyote appeared, illuminated by the dusty
sun, standing by the road, lost, and looking as out of place in the
sunlight as we felt driving home for the final time. Face-to-face
he didn't look forbidding but curious, almost brave, trying to
decide who we were, as he stood in the dusty heat; still, as still
as you lay in my arms, so close our heartbeats reverberated
through the flesh of our bodies, bouncing back and forth, giving
us both courage to go on. Gradually the signals I received back
grew weaker and further apart, and my heart pounded faster and
stronger, as if by mere strength and intensity it could keep yours
alive, until no more signals were returned and each of my heart's
beats died without resonance and you, reaching for your last
breath of air, stretched your arms out, clenching your fists as if
to grab hold on the air itself and pull yourself back into life,
before turning and looking into my eyes curiously, wondering,
then bravely letting go and falling back into my arms. In that
final moment of terrifying clarity I wanted to follow you, to find

out where a man goes who has seen a coyote the day he is going to die.

I lay still holding you. Quietly kissing the soft baby hair that grew back after the chemotherapy, touching your lips, your eyebrows, your nose, your ears, running my fingers across your face, feeling the stubble of the beard you had been growing, thinking, "I'm so happy your hair grew back." You said it so often: "I hope I have some hair when I die." I held you so tight, so close, hoping that the warmth of my body would bring you life, that my lungs would keep yours breathing, that my heart would pump life through your veins. I kissed my tears off your face wishing they were yours. I lay still holding you, not wanting to let go, not wanting to say good-bye, holding you as they came to take you away. Before I let them touch your body, I put on your best shoes, put money in your pocket, a photograph of us, and a letter saying thank-you. I watched as they put on rubber gloves, put a tag around your ankle, put you in a bag, as they closed it over your face. I watched them wheel your body out of our house, and like the coyote, you became an image forever burned into my eyes.

HOSPICE CHRONICLE

Jerry Terranova

December 23

He's lying over there on the bed, his hands crossed over his heart, dying, I guess.

I'm over here in this chair, hand over my heart, living, I guess. I'm here to be with him. He is my friend.

I'd only met him three months ago, here at the hospice, but I knew right away that he would be one that I would walk all the way with because he had touched my heart so swiftly with his elegance and grace—a princely manner. He was always clear and lucid, always told the truth. So it was easy to love him so quickly. Though his condition was called "terminal," I, as always, expected him to live forever. And one day, all at once, he said to me, "God is letting me live just long enough to see how life should be lived." But now it seems at last he is dying, and I am here dying with him.

The atmosphere in this room is awesome.

He's been given two morphine shots today, and they say he's hallucinating, but he makes sense to me.

He awoke, for the first time, and I got up from my chair to see to him. He said there was a woman in the room, her back to him. I thought she might have some loving message for him, so I asked him what she was saying. He said, "She's saying that the cops are stealing all the cars." Then he went back to sleep. I went back to my chair, dozing slightly. I felt myself beginning to melt—a dream come true—old boundaries dissolving.

He awakened again, and I went over to him, and he said, "I better go get them quick; they're leaving." I said, "Who?" and he said, "The hula dancers." He fell off again, and I went back to my chair. He awoke a third time with a start. He thought I had left. He was so glad I was still there. I don't think I've ever seen anyone happier than right then. He and I. As I sat on the edge of the bed, holding that spot on his neck with my hand as I usually did, I looked at him, and he looked like a little boy. And at that precise moment he said to me, "You look like a little boy." We had both been stripped down and we had both been lit up. There was a long pause, then we both beamed, and I've never seen anyone more peaceful than he looked in that instant. We both just beamed in love until he said out of nowhere, "I will never forget this moment," and I cried then because I knew he said it for me, too. We were one in an instant, one in an instant of love.

He dozed off again, and I went downstairs, leaving the concentrated energy and silence of his room. In the living room, life was going on full blast. So full and happy and noisy. Johnny Mathis singing, his Christmas record on the turntable, and laughter. I laughed, too. And everyone was making Christmas cookies. Stars and hearts and reindeer and Santas. All together. The staff and the patients, the residents and visitors, the living and the dying.

December 23, later

He's sleeping a lot, saying little. I'm here, keeping vigil again. Two times his eyes opened wide, his voice strong and coherent.

Once while I was trying to feed him and he couldn't eat, he said, so strongly, "We have more important things to talk about." And I said, "I'm game," and I was eager, but he fell off again.

Later, even more startling and direct, he said, "You know what's happening here, don't you?" and I said softly, "Yes, I think I do."

His friend on the stairs told me, "He knows what's happening and he's not afraid to die. He just doesn't want the pain to get any worse."

To be "conscious" that you're dying . . . that's something to ponder.

His eyes opened again. I asked him what he was thinking about and he said. "Electrodines." And I said, "I don't know what that is." And he said, rather sharply, "I don't know either."

He awoke at five-thirty in the morning, making sounds. I got up and went over to the bed, sat beside him, held his hand. He said, "Pull some plugs for me, please." I said, "There are no plugs to pull." He smiled, almost laughed. He thought he saw a woman in the room and tried to get up to talk to her. "Madam . . . ," he said, but she wouldn't tell him her name. I said, "She's here to help you. They're all here to help you." Then he fell back to sleep and I went back to my bed.

We both got up around 7:30 A.M. He asked for some water, and for some help in urinating.

Frail, frail body.

I tried to help move him, to shift his weight, because of the bedsores, and together we did it. Some more medication, then he fell off for a few moments. He later woke up saying, "I want to change faster," and I knew just what he meant.

December 24

He's suffering now.

Grimaces of pain on his face, punctured by a beatific smile of peaceful surrender.

"Give me the strength" was his cry. He said it four times.

Then later he said, "I don't care anymore, it's not important." And I mumbled some mumbo jumbo about letting go—intolerably superficial—but anything I'd say under these circumstances would sound that way.

I'm here now more fully with him. I feel my heart opening, and it hurts; my whole chest area burns and I keep crying and I don't know why anymore, not for me, not for him, maybe just for the passing.

Tears by his bed, helpless prayers.
Please don't let him suffer.

Christmas morning

He awoke at 3 A.M. to pee. He sat up and then he stood up for
the first time in days, and it was awesome. I saw his whole body,
that racked body full length, exposed and so frail. That he had
the strength to stand up at all was a miracle.

Then he called out for Jesus several times.

But his death still seems so far away, though it's right here in
the room. But you can only see it when you back away, and you
say, "Oh, yes. He's dying." But up close, it's not that simple. He's
just here, living, suspended—you can't see his approach to
death. You only see the living. All the sleeping, hallucinations,
spitting, and the sighing, and the grimacing and the radiant,
childlike smiles . . . it's all life. And you want to look behind his
eyes and say, "What's going on in there? How long do you think
this will take? Are you close? What's it like?"

December 26

His breathing is so sporadic, and fluid-filled, so much mucus.
His coughing is his breathing, with long gaps between in which
you could swear he had stopped breathing.

I'm mad now, and I don't know why. Because of his suffering
and I'm trying to remember now to release.

Like the stench in the room when they changed his diaper,
and how much I love him, and how I'll never be able to express
what kind of love and how deep and what makes me stick
around for a full week. That look in his eyes so distant, and the
grimacing pain when they had to move him and how much I
love him and how I just keep holding his hand and telling him
it's all right and how all the platitudes about death don't get you
anywhere.

And how it's just me and him and his halo in a dimly lit
room, just the night-light that I bought for him, and his fitful

breathing and my helplessness. And how the door keeps flying open spontaneously at will bringing in another staff member, bringing in the bright fluorescent light from the hall, that artificial light of the rest of the world, penetrating your whole world with this person you tend to. The little things become so precious. You wipe the crust from his lips, tenderly, you wipe his forehead—clean, white, wet washcloth against his black, withering skin (the corrupt body, he called it once). And you feed him water through a syringe and you talk from time to time, say anything to pierce the awesome, horrible silence. Your skin saying "I love you" with a helplessness and terror and force that you didn't think was in you. And you know in time when everything settles, it will be all right, and you'll be all right, too, and that calmness fills the air for a moment, and then the turbulent mind storms begin again, "planning" the moment of his death, how you'll react—how ludicrous, as if you have any control—will it be fitful, peaceful, when it actually comes, what will you do next, planning the rest of your life when you haven't yet fully met this moment. And you cry and cry and you don't know why you're crying, no simple judgment or loss, just the awful magnitude of what's happening, and how you're supposed to play a role in it, and you can't for the life of you figure out how to play it.

Then they barged into the room, and thank God they did because the unearthly sound of his gasping seemed interminable—till I finally saw a clock and it had been two hours. It reminded me of when he had more consciousness—was it tonight or two days ago?—when he awoke, he always asked what time it was, like something to grip. They swept into the room and said they were going to make him the A#1 priority of everyone there, and that brought real relief because I thought I was totally alone in this, but I was only so alone; there were actual things they could do to ease his pain, and that helped ease my helplessness. They said they were going to suction out his lungs and put him on oxygen to help his breathing. The knowledge that these people really cared for him comforted me, and I knew then, by extension, that they really cared for me, too. I knew then, too, it was all right for me to leave the room. I went to the living room and ate a lot and I couldn't believe I was doing that. But I wanted that tuna fish sandwich someone had offered me earlier now *so bad*, right now, as if it were denied me, and I reclaimed it. I love tuna fish; it always reminds me of summer and happiness and boyhood and Good Fridays. I ate it hungrily. As I sat downstairs while they tended to him, I saw the guy who administers the morphine and asked him if this might be my friend's last night. I didn't want to ask in the room because it seemed so immodest, disrespectful, to talk about someone's death in their presence—no matter how near they were to it, or how far away they were from the sound of your voice—to talk about it in front of them is like sealing their fate. So, I told him about the breathing and he told me what to make of it. Then he wiped the tear from my eye, tending to me in that instant so gently.

Then I went back to the room and got in my roll-away bed, never thinking I'd sleep. I rolled the bed close to his, and I just held his hand while we both were in our beds. But I did sleep for a while and I awoke to the presence of someone else in the room. It was one of the staff. He said some feeling told him to check in on my friend at that moment and he did. He told me that this was probably his last few breaths, and then he left the room. I just stood next to him stroking his cheek, doing what I normally do.

Oh, those eyes of his—open, glaring, gazing far off, unreachable, unimpeachable—he was on his left side, and I was hyperaware of witnessing someone's last few breaths on earth. I stood there, frozen, just watching. And then, sure enough, he just did it; the time came, and he took his last breath and he was done; all done with all of it. He looked no different the moment after, felt no different, yet everything was supposed to be different because now he was supposed to be "dead."

I went back to the living room, sat there, dazed. A hospice worker had a few "next-of-kin" type questions for me. Then I went home, climbed into bed, asked for comfort, and I do believe my friend came to me—to comfort me at my bedside—to tell me he was all right. He touched my left side with some kind of wand, and that dissolved my tears in light, and I fell asleep.

THE WESTBOUND TRAIN

Jimmy Drinkovich

When someone dies, Hobos say, "They took the Westbound."

Now these two men are Homos and meet on a train platform. They make introductions of names, but then it's not

"What do you do?" it's

"When were you diagnosed?" It's not

"Where do you work?" it's

"Who is your doctor?"

They exchange stories of their most recent battles, relishing the victory that they are still alive. They talk of lovers and friends who have boarded before them. Only one train comes to this station, no local, no express, and the destination is the same for everyone.

They notice the others who are waiting. Some are dressed and ready to go, anticipating the Westbound's arrival. Perhaps a lover or dear friend is waiting for them. They stand very close to the edge listening for the first timbre in the rails.

Others are very nervous, pace back and forth, check their watches, volleying from fear to calm.

Some are freaked that they might have forgotten something. Like Pharaohs they insist on bringing some things along.

Others desperately try to exit the turn rail, to go back to the street. The rail refuses to turn and they are too weak.

Many, many more line the wall, brace themselves, cover their faces, not wanting to see where they are.

Some are quiet and serene. Patients who have been waiting a long time.

Not everyone boards the same train. The station is the last wait. When the train arrives, the porters will come off and escort those whose tickets are ready. Newcomers don't know this and almost always have a difficult time.

Some will take matters into their own hands and steal aboard. Others plead for more time, but there are no reprieves if your ticket is ready.

Some fight bitterly and give the porters a hard time. But there is no shortage as more porters arrive.

The two men turn silent as the first rumbling of the rails begins.

Progressing louder, the whistle screams like the ambulance. As the train grinds to halt, hissing steam, the one man grabs the other.

"I'm afraid, are you?" He puts his arm around him.

"Sometimes. Maybe we'll ride together."

"Yes, perhaps we can share a berth."

The doors open and the angels begin the selection.

THE PHOTOGRAPH

Tony Gramaglia

Here is his picture. Go ahead. Hold it. When you touch it and look at his eyes in the photo and see that wide-open smile, his head thrown back a little, you can hear him laugh. Just by holding his picture you can hear him laugh that way. Even if you never heard him before. That's how I met him, laughing. I want you to know him this way.

I am still waiting for the minister to say something about AIDS at this service. Some acknowledgment of what killed my friend. But there is none. He only mentions that he has never met the deceased, but his parents are fine people who have attended his services for years.

I'm sure they are fine people. I think they are brave, his mother and father. They took turns staying with their son in the hospital in New York. I don't think that they had ever been out of Ohio. But they are scared, too. They haven't told anyone. Never mentioned the fact that their son died of AIDS.

His mother is standing next to the open casket. Some shiny metal tomb. I am sure not to look at the body of my friend. She keeps mentioning that she is not sure she picked out the right outfit for him. She is still wet from crying and she wants me to look over at him. To tell her it is okay. What he is wearing here. How she has dressed him. I pretend to look. My eye catches the wig. I feel in my pocket for the photo. I can feel it against my chest.

I begin to think of a mother dressing her son for his first day of school. Tying his shoes. Buttoning his new shirt collar. Pushing back his hair with her moist palm. That is what mothers do.

I am angry now, though, that she has dressed him for this occasion. This funeral. I am angry that he is displayed. Draped like a mannequin for some cheap sale at a department store. But she is his mother. That is her son. Who am I to say? I can tell she wants to push back his hair with her moist palm. But she knows it is not his hair.

Here. Hold this picture. I tell his younger brother. You can hear him laugh. He wants to know if his brother had AIDS. I know he already knows. He is sixteen. Yes, I say. I am not able to lie about this. I don't want to. I want to tell everyone here that he died of AIDS. I want to slam the lid of the coffin shut. Not to hide the disease or the death, but to hide the body that is not the man in this picture.

I want to hear people tell stories about him. Like the time he was modeling a pair of platform shoes he designed when he was in the seventh grade and the heels fell apart and he broke both of his ankles. Or the time in college when he and his black lover ran across campus naked with whipped cream and chocolate syrup poured all over their bodies to demonstrate their interracial love. Or the time he came to my college fraternity house dressed like Twiggy.

I can't stand the quiet. I want them all to hold this picture. I want them all to hear him laugh.

I say I will meet them later at the house. I cannot stand the thought of lunchmeat and cookies and the quiet murmurs of distant cousins of his who barely knew him. But I will go, so they don't forget the man I knew.

Look, I say, to the woman who is sitting next to me on the couch as she eats a piece of cake. Hold this picture. You can hear him laugh. You can hear him laugh, even if you've never heard him laugh before.

She is slow to put down her cake and hold the photo. But

when she does, she smiles. She can hear him laugh. We both begin to laugh. Me and this stranger with this photograph of him.

This is where he lives. Here in this laugh.

Here. Go ahead. Hold it.

JANESVILLE'S OWN

Arthur Shafer

It was terribly cruel, and not one of us could really believe what we were seeing. The flight from New York City to Janesville was quick enough, Janesville is a mere forty-five minutes from La Guardia, but it spanned light-years in the difference of life that existed there.

To imagine this small, quiet, gray town as Joseph's place of birth, the place where he discovered the joys of musical comedy, the intoxication of fashion, the very essence of his rowdy sexuality, was "UN"-imaginable. To me.

He could have been sent to Janesville to observe life in the outer realms of New York City. He must surely have felt that way. There was no trace of this sleepy Janesville past when we met. Joseph was a party boy. That is how and where I met him . . . at a party.

Halloween in Manhattan is really no different from any other day. It merely gives license to indulge in one's fantasies without too much disapproval. "I don't want to know anyone you come with. Bring someone new." Those were the words Joseph added to the invitation for his costume party on Halloween, 1979.

"Someone new" was not an easy thing to be in New York City, but having just moved there, I qualified. That's how I got there. My roommate knew Joseph from the garment center, where Joseph was making a name for himself on Seventh Avenue.

I knew no one else at this party. Held in a SoHo loft owned

301

by Joseph's best friend, Bruce, whom he'd known from his days at RISD. The food and drink consisted of all things clear, white, and unable to stain Bruce's newly bleached floors, and ivory canvas slip-covered furniture. But Joseph dealt with these limitations. The vodka flowed, and baked potatoes provided a sponge to help ward off hangovers. The party with Joseph, for me, was just beginning.

Slight of build but with tremendous attitude, with his long, shoulder-length hair, jet-black and full, so ahead of the craze of ponytails and goatees that was to come in the nineties.

His success on Seventh Avenue gave him license to dress as he pleased; but only Joseph would be asked to use a service elevator when he would go to his office. Tank tops, hot pants, and Rollerblades were just too much for the other tenants in the building.

Never one to wait behind velvet ropes, Joseph's presence was instant admission to the trendiest and the newest of clubs and restaurants. I learned "never to leave home without him."

But today we weren't waiting to get into Studio 54. With the memories of those evenings, those outfits, in mind, we entered the church and confronted the sight of a young man lying in an open casket in the plainest of black suits, white shirt, and tie.

"It's a blessing he's dead," I said to my friends, "because this outfit would surely have killed him." His face was a mortician Max Factor–white. Not adorned as it had so often been with eyeliner and rouge. The lightning-bolt sideburns were gone. The massive head of to-die-for hair had been cut to an obscenely conservative length. This deadly black suit was the most frightening costume we could ever imagine Joseph wearing. Joseph, who paraded down the beaches of Fire Island in pink tutu and tights, giving impromptu ballet lessons to the boys of the Pines.

The priest began his eulogy, and we waited to hear the words that would bring us some closure, some verification of the event we were witnessing.

"Jodi," he spoke. "Jodi, the devoted son," "Jodi" this, and "Jodi" that. "Jodi"? We would never have dared call him Jodi. We turned to each other, hoping to find something in the proceedings that seemed slightly related to our friend, our Joseph.

" 'Jodi'?" we whispered. Where was the evidence? Who could this be?

We looked at the corpse, the coffin, the church, and each other.

The priest standing before the open casket looked like a magician preparing some sort of hocus-pocus.

Well, that explains it! There in front of us, performing for the last time, his most outrageous act. The disappearance of Joseph.

LOST

Steve Smith

I t shocks me, how quickly they have swooped down. Tad dead only six hours, still cooling really, and already his family is picking over the spoils.

"Got to beat the federal marshal," they explain. Back taxes. The whole place will be cordoned off by the IRS within hours. But their zeal belies their excuse.

Giddiness in the air. No other way to say it. Exhaustion and grief and an occasional crying jag, certainly. But an undeniable sense of exhilaration among the assembled relatives as they pillage and plunder.

"Oh, Mom, won't this painting look great in our family room?"

"Well, dear, your father and I want that one for the beach-house. Besides, you two got the Hockney."

The house looks fairly tidy—a far cry from the way I saw it last. Tad lying sprawled in the hallway, unconscious. Tubes pulled out, blood and shit everywhere. Dehydrated, incoherent even after I roused him. Must have been lying there for hours. Still stubborn though. After I'd cleaned him and gotten him dressed, he refused to be taken to the hospital until I promised not to alert his family—a promise I kept for ten days, until it was obvious he would die this time.

"Where's the tea service? I hope he didn't hock it. He knew I wanted it. It was mother's."

I stand silent on the perimeter of the room, dumbstruck, trying to make myself very small to avoid detection.

I fail.

"Oh, Steve, honey . . . Why don't you pick out a little something for yourself. You've been such a good friend. I'm sure Tad would have wanted you to have something."

Yes, I think—he intended that I get his wardrobe of Italian suits, the ones that will never fit your fat, squat son-in-law, who is nevertheless busy pack-ratting them into a steamer trunk. And the Waterford, which disappeared mysteriously before I even arrived, probably before Tad gasped his last. And the paintings.

It's all in his will, I believe. But then, since Tad never bothered to get it notarized, you've conveniently disregarded that document. Let's hope you do the same with his diary. For your sake.

But I say only, "No thanks. His memory is all I need."

Very noble. Hopefully just a little bitchy. But I know I'm lying. There is something of Tad's that I truly want right now. His goosedown pillow, in order to cheerfully smother every one of these craven hypocrites.

❦

I am dreaming of Donald. We are lying together on a beach. It must be someplace local, because his big, dumb, loyal blond Lab is lying at the foot of the blanket, panting and drooling.

I am distractedly flipping through the pages of a glossy magazine—registering ads more than reading articles. Donald has on headphones, humming tunelessly.

I cast an affectionate glance in his direction—just checking in—and am startled that I can't see his face. Not that it's covered or obstructed from view—it's just blank, a featureless expanse of skin, where there should be that familiar arrangement of nose, eyes, freckles, mouth.

I panic for a moment, until I remember that I'm only dreaming. My friend is not really faceless—I simply can't recall what he looked like.

I wake up and I'm crying.

They've got to be here someplace. I know I haven't loaned them out and I haven't worn them since Robert's memorial. It seemed somehow appropriate at the time.

They're really not my style—all that chunky gold, so flashy and conspicuous. Always feel as if I should leave my shirt unbuttoned and sport a zodiac medallion nestled in my chest hair. Besides, the only time I wear French cuffs is with my tuxedo, and then I prefer the matched sets, studs and links all perfectly identical, simple and elegant, nothing subversive.

But some odd urge compelled me to look for Robert's cuff links today—those gaudy gold clusters of nuggets. I remember the weekend he gave them to me—a wild, heady, early-eighties New York whirlwind of excess and consumption, one long cab ride from Barneys to Saks to the Saint to the Anvil, Robert swathed in chinchilla or some other endangered species, a coke spoon buried deep up his nose.

And always those insistent cuff links glittering at his wrists. He took them off and stuffed them in my pocket as he poured me into the Town Car for the airport that last morning, both of us drunk and delirious.

"Think of me when you wear these, *cheri. Ciao, bello.*"

And now I've lost them, along with any memory of Robert more substantial than a camp pose and a deep, haughty laugh.

The sun filters down through the giant redwoods only in places, shooting brilliant shafts of light to the forest floor. The rays have a distinctly green cast, filtered through the dense foliage, and their planes are clearly delineated in the light mist—sharp lines of warm brightness against cool dark, illuminating verdant ferns and wildflowers and the soft bed of pine needles along the roadside.

As I wind along the highway, I recall that this is the last trip Ric took before he died—I still have that rhapsodic postcard, so florid and sentimental.

I pop in the chorus CD—the one we recorded together, standing side by side. I advance it to track eight, the gorgeous, lush "Agnus Dei." At full volume, the speakers near distortion, the car booms with a chorus of ecstatic angels chanting their sweet call and response. The sheer beauty of the moment raises the hair on my arms. A tiny pool of tears wells at the corners of my eyes as I feel Ric's presence, hear his clear, strong voice among the scores of others on the recording.

I concentrate on conjuring his image, seeing again the strength of his jaw, the mischief in his eyes.

When I fail, I pull to the shoulder and weep in earnest.

The candles twinkle silently across the expanse of the darkened stadium, thousands of mute points of light flickering in dim memory of lost souls.

The mood is appropriately somber and elegiac. The songs and prayers and polemics from the stage have left the assembled throng hushed and sniffling. And now the ritual turns to the obligatory recitation of names—a quiet personal accounting from each individual ledger of loss.

All around me I hear the names whispered.

"Antonio Ramirez."

"James Lockhart."

"Tom Pirelli."

I open my mouth to let the litany spill forth, to make my own contribution to this offertory of grief. But no names pass my lips.

I pause, trying not to panic. Think harder. Just four years ago at this same event, I recited over forty names without stopping to think. Surely I can call them up again, along with the dozens who've gone since.

I manage to choke out one or two, the most recent casualties, the horror and banality of their deaths still fresh. But then my mind goes truly blank.

And I am no longer panicked. I am enraged.

How dare my memory fail! I, who intended to bear witness, to serve as a living, breathing memorial to all those men, those vibrant, frivolous, talented, difficult, precious men, to chronicle their frailties and heroism and outrageousness. And now I can't even remember their fucking names?

Clearly, my subconscious has decided to tidy up the files, to wipe that database clean and avoid the risk of sensory overload from too much grief and pain and longing. But my conscious mind would sooner short-circuit, let the system fail, than face the future as a blank disk, only dimly aware of all that's been deleted.

I blow out my candle in disgust and bolt for the exit, roughly shoving aside all the pious mourners in my row, each one declaiming his list of lost loved ones in a steady, sure cadence.

�֍

The restraints bite into my hands and ankles. My fault—he asked if they were too tight. I didn't respond.

Haven't said a word, in fact, since the scene began. Not even a yelp or moan as he beat me with the strap. It disconcerted him, I think, and so he redoubled his efforts, which is why my back and buttocks are now a throbbing welter of pain.

No light permeates the tight leather hood, which started out claustrophobic but now feels snug and familiar and comforting. I listen to my breath as the white-hot pain of the candlewax sears me.

Breathe. Breathe. Breathe. Gasp.

Breathe. Breathe. Gasp.

I keep waiting for the epiphany I've come for, the moment when I'm lulled into oblivion, transported to another place— semiconscious, unthinking, mere sensation, no sensibility. Lost.

A place where I won't remember and won't agonize about forgetting.

CHRIS'S THINGS

John D'Amico

One Tiffany's crystal vase[1] with red roses.[2]

A drawing.[3]

One file cabinet with personal, not-so-personal items, papers, bills,[4] gas bills, phone bills, love notes, phone numbers,[5] doctors' bills,[6] camera instructions, an old shoelace,[7] tax files, and a box of rubbers.

One drafting table—dusty tools.

One tall oak table, two small lamps[8]—halogen.

One oak, six-drawer dresser.[9]

Two nightstands with lamps.

Closet full of clothing, boxes, shoes, boots, leather belts.

Ambient direct and indirect February-morning light.

Queen-size bed, white, 100 percent cotton sheets, and four white goosedown pillows.[10]

One dead thirty-three-year-old man,[11] matted, oily hair.

Two angry friends.[12]

One oak cabinet filled with medical supplies and one IV pole.

Bookshelf with books: *Huckleberry Finn, A Confederacy of Dunces, The Unbearable Lightness of Being,*[13] several books on healing the body with the mind, a large crystal collection, several candles and spiritual trinkets, a collection of poetry by Virginia Woolf, Rock Hudson's biography, *Citizen Cohen, As I Lay Dying,* Foucault's *Pendulum, The Shining, Roget's Thesaurus, Webster's Dictionary, The Complete Works of William Shakespeare,* Marcel Proust, and F. Scott Fitzgerald, and several Bibles including a copy of *The Word.* At the top of the bookshelf were two trophies,[14] and a photograph of Chris with his parents, Sony AM/FM digital clock radio, 11:18 A.M., cut crystal vase with red and white tulips.[15]

Wooden, six-panel door, screen, light breeze, and rustling trees.

Technics stereo with music playing[16] and Sony television with remote control.

"Just put the pillow over his face. Just put the pillow over his face. Put the pillow over his face," David said. He was trying to convince Mark that it was time.

Chris had said his good-byes, had said that he had made peace with God, and that he was ready. Chris had taken what he thought was enough sleeping pills to kill himself, but he didn't die. He had battled his battle and here was Mark with the pillow they had both fought over, slept with, held together and separately. Helping him die now was his choice.

Mark told me not to ever tell the story of how he and David had had to end Chris's life. But, Mark is dead now and so is David.

---

1. The vase came from Chris's first real lover, Robert. The two of them went together to Mednales, New Mexico, for a winter vacation. Robert had surprised Chris with a vase full of bright yellow daffodils. Chris's Christmas was made by those daffodils.

2. The roses were delivered on Monday morning by Chris's friend Charles. They were really quite beautiful.

   Charles and Chris met in 1982 in a disco along Santa Monica Boulevard. Chris followed Charles over the hill into the Valley to the apartment Charles lived in. Charles had lived rent free in this apartment for nineteen months because the landlord had filed for Chapter 13 protection and had died and the property was held up in probate. Charles eventually went to Europe for six months on the rent money he saved. The Coliseum postcard from Rome is still in the filing cabinet.

The two of them had sex that evening and tried over the next few weeks to get a relationship started. It didn't work out and they ended up becoming friends. Their friendship was the holiday-party, Sunday-breakfast type of friendship.

3. The David Hockney drawing was given to Chris by Scott. Scott died in 1989 of "heart disease." Scott was a big-deal Hollywood something-or-other, an art collector and part-time dealer. He had a million-dollar collection, and instead of giving his art to a museum or a foundation he gave it to his friends. He spent many hours those last few days deciding which piece would go to which person. The Johns went to the Salazars, the early Warhol *Flowers* went to Chikk, the later Warhols went to Robert and Dave, the whole photo collection, including the Stieglitz, the Adams, and the Shermans went to Paul, and so on and so on.

Chris ended up with the Hockney. He didn't really know what to make of it at first. For a long time it sat on his file cabinet. It just sat there. He had wondered sometimes what it might be like to own an important work of art. And when he got his drawing, it seemed nothing happened. Nothing changed. Occasionally a trick or a visitor from out of town would remark about the drawing, but mostly it went unnoticed.

4. One day Chris stopped paying his bills. He told me that he knew that day that it wasn't necessary to pretend anymore. It was just after Labor Day. "There really wasn't anything that could be done," he'd explained. He always got a kick out of shocking the bill collectors with flip comments about his illness.

5. Chris kept a box full of the phone numbers that he had been given over the years. There were 2,167 numbers from the men he had met in bars, discos, clubs, gyms, on the beach, at the baths, in shopping malls, airplanes, airports, hotel lobbies, ski-lift lines, movie theaters, restaurants, grocery stores, shoe shops, Laundromats, art galleries, post offices, rest areas in most of the Western states, several foreign countries, bicycle shops, clothing stores, among others.

Chris was really popular.

6. At last count his illness had cost his insurance company $278,964.97.

7. When Chris's father died, his mother had said, "Why don't you help yourself to whatever you want from your dad's closet." At first he was overwhelmed with the idea of having as his own the many fine things his father had once worn with pride, the cashmere coats, the blazers, the hats, the white shirts, the expensive leather coats. As he sat on the floor crying and aching from his stomach, all he took was an old shoelace.

8. These lamps had belonged to Kevin. Kevin died in 1986. He was really the first person whom Chris had known who had died. Kevin was never very open about his illness; he denied having AIDS right to the very end. Someone had said that Kevin lived in a lot of shame. Kevin came from a wealthy Chicago family, and during the memorial service everyone told his family what a terrific television producer he had been and how tragic they thought it was that someone his age would die of cancer. No one ever told his family that Kevin had been in love.

9. This dresser was the last piece of the bedroom set that Chris had bought, or rather had made. It was imported from France, made by the hands of a man whom Chris had spent the summer of his twenty-second year with. Audinet was a tall,

dark-haired Frenchman with lousy English. As Chris and Audinet grew older, they maintained contact and even managed to visit each other over the following years. Chris knew the dresser and all the bedroom furniture was made with the same careful hands that had once held his own body. On the inside of each drawer Audinet had scribbled the words to his favorite poems. It was corny but Chris loved the sentiment. Every morning Chris would see the final lines of Hugo's "Le Printemps":

> *A travers l'ombre immense et sous le ciel béni,*
> *Quelque chose d'heureux chanter dans l'infini.*

The dresser was neatly filled with the clothing of everyday life. Eighteen pairs of Calvin Klein midthigh briefs, twenty-nine and a half pairs of white, 100 percent cotton socks, white T-shirts and tank tops, neatly folded striped and solid polo shirts, dungarees, khakis, cotton sweaters and sweatshirts. A forgotten note from Davis.

10. Chris had ordered these pillows from the Home Shopping Network.

11. Chris.

12. Mark and David.
    David was Chris's oldest friend. They had met twenty years before in Euclid Junior High School in Littleton, Colorado. From the moment they became friends they were inseparable. They watched the same television shows, they went to the same movies, they skied together, rode bicycles, all the things best friends learn to do together. David and Chris both moved to Los Angeles to attend college. Although they went to rival schools, they managed to remain friends. As young adults they began pursuing different interests, and as they got older, their friendship was often strained. But there was always an underlying sense of safety.
    Mark and Chris were lovers, longtime companions, sigs, boyfriends, husbands. Mark and Chris met at the California Pizza Kitchen four and one-half years ago. They were both waiting for their dates to show up and struck up a conversation. As it turned out, the four of them ended up dining together that night and exchanged numbers. They never got together again as couples. About six months later Chris called Mark and asked him out. They were both single at the time, and slowly the two of them began to trust each other and managed to forge a relationship unlike one either of them had ever had.
    Chris used to say, "It was a simple case of being in the right place at the right time with our hearts open."

13. This was Chris's favorite book and favorite movie of the same title. He read parts of *The Unbearable Lightness of Being* over and over from the day the book was given to him by Jane, his actress friend whom he lost touch with before he met Mark.

14. These trophies came from Chris's high school football days. He had recently found them on a trip home to visit his mom. The "last supper" he called it when Mark and Chris had discussed what it was going to be like to be in his mom and stepfather's house for three days. He had decided to go alone. Although the two of them had visited Chris's parents before, it was decided that the air would be clearer and maybe eventually cleared if the "Gay lover" wasn't there.

15. Mark had kept this vase filled with tulips from the moment Chris had become bedridden in late October. Mark would stop at the flower mart and buy a bunch of tulips from Jorge. Jorge asked Mark several times who the lucky girl was, and one day Mark told him the story of how sick Chris was and how much it meant to Mark to be able to buy these flowers for Chris every week. On Christmas eve, Jorge gave

Mark a huge bouquet of red roses and said, "God bless you both, merry Christmas." They both started crying and Jorge sent him away with a pat on the back.

16. The Peggy Lee CD was on its third trip through. Chris's favorite song had always been "Is That All There Is to a Fire?" Through disco, punk, new wave, pop, techno, rap—through it all he loved to listen to and laugh when Peggy Lee would ask, "Is that all there is?"

THE VANISHING

Ricky Hoyt

He noticed, the first time, the vanishing, in a small spot on the back of his calf. Not a place on the body one usually notices, he supposed. He happened to catch a reflection in the white metal surface of the refrigerator one morning. He stopped to investigate. A place on his leg had become not a place, a blank spot, an emptiness, not a wound, nothing. A hair growing from the leg just above the vanished part lay across it. He brushed it aside. Tentatively, he felt the nothing. It felt like skin, like solid leg. "Curious," he thought. He pulled his sock up higher to cover it.

The next spot disappeared on his hip. Then another on the back of his thigh, then a fourth disappeared on the bottom of one foot. He contorted himself before the mirror each morning trying to count the latest vanishings as they disappeared over his body. They worried him. He wondered what they meant. Fortunately, no nothings yet on his face or hands, so he dressed himself as usual and went to work confident that no one would discover his absences. One afternoon, at lunch, he locked himself in a stall in the bathroom and rolled up his sleeves to look at an emptiness that had broken out on his arm. He found that if he pushed deeply into the vanished spot, the sight would flood back into the area and stay for a moment, then slowly vanish again when he took his finger away. He spent all lunch hour pushing at the gone place on his arm, making it visible. He so loved seeing his arm again where it hadn't been that he gave himself a bruise, a bruise only visible when he pushed on it.

At home it was more difficult to hide. He hadn't told his lover, and as the vanishings increased, it became very hard to keep them from him. He kept his clothes on all evening. He undressed and got into bed only after the lights were out. He rebuffed his lover's requests for lovemaking in the mornings and kept the covers pulled up to his chin. He didn't feel like making love anyway. He could have worn pajamas and socks to bed, but it was summer and he and his lover had always slept only in underwear. As he sat on the couch in the evenings in the warm apartment with his long pants and socks and long-sleeve shirt with the sleeves rolled down, the lover asked, "Aren't you hot like that?" And he answered, "No, I'm not hot. I feel fine this way."

The next day he walked to a drugstore near where he worked and bought a tube of makeup in a color he thought would match his skin. Locked again in the bathroom stall at his office, he rolled up his sleeve and spread the sticky paste on the part of his arm that wasn't there. The makeup stuck to the vanished spot but didn't match the rest of his arm. Nevertheless he rubbed the cream into all the nothings on his arm. His arm once more looked solid, but looked no better. It looked as though he had a skin disease that had produced lesions on his arm, a different disease, but just as horrible as what he really had. He wiped himself off with toilet paper, washed his arm in the sink, then rolled down his shirtsleeves and went back to his desk.

He wondered what was happening. He wondered why it was happening to him. The vanishings continued to increase. His lack of presence frightened him. He dreaded anyone discovering his secret. He prayed that the disappearing would stop and the parts of him he hadn't seen in weeks would return to where they had been. He dreaded especially telling his lover. How would his friend react? If the lover, too, was frightened, perhaps the lover would also leave, and then he felt his abandonment would be complete.

But when a spot disappeared on the back of one hand, and simultaneously on the side of his neck, he knew that the time had come to confront his friend with the truth. He skipped work that day and instead went to a movie theater. Hardly anyone was there to notice him, and he felt safe in the dark. During the fourth showing of the movie, at the time he would normally have got off from work, he left the theater and went home. His lover was there. His lover sat on the couch reading a magazine. His lover was wearing short pants, with bare feet and no shirt. His body looked strong and complete. As he stood in the doorway, the man couldn't help staring at his friend with sadness and envy. The lover greeted him. Then, as the lover noticed him staring, he asked, "What's wrong?"

"Nothing's wrong," the man answered sadly.

"Well, come on in and shut the door."

The man came in and sat beside his lover on the couch. He took his lover's hand and placed his own hand on top of his lover's. The lover looked down and saw the vanishing on the top of his friend's hand. The two men stared without speaking.

"What's happened to your hand?" the lover asked with a mixture of fear and concern.

"I don't know."

"How long has it been like this?"

"On my hand, just a day, and here on my neck, too." He pointed to the vanished spot. "But I'm gone all over my body. I've been leaving for weeks. I tried to hide it from you."

"Why didn't you tell me?"

"I was hoping I'd come back. Oh, I'm so scared!" He began to cry. He threw his arms about his lover's neck and sobbed. The lover hugged him back. The man leaned into his lover's chest and felt the comfort of his solid body.

After that they went into the bedroom and the man took off his clothes so the lover could examine him. The man was embarrassed but relieved at last to have his secret shared. The lover looked at him all around from every side. So much of his body had been removed now that he looked more air than man. He thought of his body as a sheet of metal from which a thousand plug nickels had been stamped. In some places the vanishings overlapped to the point where whole sections of his body had fallen away. He stood on a foot that he could not see. Only the weight of his body applying pressure to the sole of his foot brought back a thin glimpse of where his foot should be.

Eventually, he put his clothes back on and they had dinner. It felt good to have his clothes on again, it made him feel not so vacant. His lover asked him questions. It felt good to be able to speak about it. His lover's confidence even made him feel a little hopeful. They went to bed and they made love for the first time since the vanishings had begun. Afterward, and even as they fell asleep, the two men held each other tightly.

The next morning, vanishing had begun on his other hand and on his face as well. He called his office and told them he wouldn't be coming in. His lover asked, "Do you want to go to a doctor?" The man said, "I don't feel sick." The lover wanted to stay home from work also, but the man said not to. "I don't need caring for. I feel perfectly fine. I know I look horrible, but I feel okay. I'm just tired."

The lover kissed him good-bye and went to work. The man slept in. After a while he got up, got dressed, had breakfast, read the paper. He cleaned up around the house. He listened to the radio, he watched the TV. He took a nap. Later, he worked on making an extravagant dinner to share with his lover. He set the table with candles and a white tablecloth. He went into the hall closet and got out the china and the real silver silverware that had belonged to his grandmother. He took a shower and looked at himself in the mirror for a long time. He dressed in his nicest suit.

He was still dressing when the lover arrived home from work. The lover was worried about him, but pleased with the dinner. The lover took a shower and put on his best suit also. The dinner was lovely. They had champagne. The lover suggested they go for a drive, so they left the dirty dishes on the table and went out. They drove through the night up into the hills above the city and parked the car and looked at the city lights. They held hands and talked. They sat on the hood of the car and finished the bottle of champagne. The lover kissed the man lightly on his lips and said, "I can barely see you."

The man answered, "I'll be gone by morning."

When they were tired, they drove home. They took off their suits and hung them in the closet. They went to bed wearing only their underwear. The man saw in the bedroom mirror, before he turned off the light, that save for a few inches around one eye and a patch on his chest and another on his belly, he had completely vanished. Standing beside the bed, his lover hugged him tightly, and where he held him, the sight flooded back into the emptiness, and as long as he held him, where he held him, the man was whole.

IN MEMORIAM

Forty-four members of the Workshop have died.
We celebrate their courage in living their lives aloud.

George Anton
Steven Augustine
John Bell
Tom Bezzi
Juan Candelario
Panos Christi
Jimmy Drinkovich
William M. Franklin
James G.
Cary H.
Robbie Hilyard
Paul Holt
G. G. Hunt
Robert Lagersen
Byron MacDonald
Michael Martin
Leonard Mosqueda
Robert P. Murphy
Bill Pearson
Michael S.
Tom Sweeney
Marc Wagenheim

Antonio Apodaca
Andy Avalos
Brent Bellon
Robert B.
Joe Ceo
John C.
Alan Erenberg
Don Fusco
Tony Gramaglia
Victor Heineman
Elaine H.
Stephen Howard
Alex Kennedy
Ezra Litwak
Jeffrey Marcus
John Megna
Robert C. Murphy
John Olson
Ben Rubin
Philip Justin Smith
Darian Walker
F.W.

—January 12, 1996

319

CONTRIBUTORS' NOTES

*All contributors' notes have been written by the writers
themselves unless indicated in brackets.*

Kenneth Bartmess is a sixty-nine-year-old gay man, a California native and longtime Los Angeles resident with a background in theater and dance. He is proud of his seven years as a volunteer peer counselor at the Gay and Lesbian Community Services Center. He recently earned a degree from Santa Monica College and plans to pursue a psychology major. A craftsman, he has a custom lamp and lighting-fixture business and makes masks for artistic expression.

"Three Night Scenes" was written in the APLA caregivers writing group in response to the AIDS-related death in December 1991 of C. J. Meagher, Kenneth's lover of twenty-two years. It was read as a part of A Day Without Art at MOCA (L.A.) December 1992.

Jack Beard: I was born in 1949, in a small town in Pennsylvania, where I'm again residing. I left home when I was called to military service, as were so many during the conflict in Vietnam. I served as a medic with the Marines for a time, among other assignments. After the military I settled in Los Angeles. I've crewed a charter sailboat in the Caribbean, have flown airplanes, been a bartender, a salesman, and a paramedic. I always wanted to write but never felt I had anything to say. With much encouragement I'm trying to overcome my inhibition and hope others will find some interest in my words.

John Terry Bell, an actor, writer, director, and executive director of American Theatre Arts, died of AIDS on August 24, 1995. He was fifty-three years old. John began his career as one of the Siamese children in *The King and I.* He appeared in rep, with touring and light-opera companies, and at the Old Globe. Most notably he helped develop the playscript and created the role of Weller Martin in *The Gin Game,* which also went to Broadway with Hume Cronyn and Jessica Tandy and was awarded the Pulitzer Prize.

John received an MA in English/theatre and a Life Teaching Credential, was on staff at ABC for the first APLA Commitment to Life Awards in 1985, worked in Casting & New Talent at Universal, in development at Aaron Spelling, typed and edited two of the last books for late novelist Irving Wallace, and was once nearly fired by Cary Grant.

For almost a decade Mr. Bell was executive director of American Theatre Arts. He worked as a producer and a director in theater and appeared in numerous TV commercials, series, movies, and magazines. A crowning achievement was writing two seasons of blackout sketches for TV's *Love American Style.*

John is survived by his father, stepmother, brother, sister-in-law, three nieces, four grandnieces and grandnephews, an ex-wife, and wonderful loving friends, who miss his witty and loving presence. [Candace Howerton]

Brent Bellon was an extraordinary person. I can't say that he "loved" life, but he certainly "lived" life, with zest and exuberance. His creativity manifested itself in his music, his cooking, and his writing. He was a gentle man: generous, tenderhearted, amiable. At the same time he was full of fun: stimulating, spontaneous, a bit of a prankster. Brent had a delightful sense of humor and an infectious laugh. He had a rare ability to listen and to hold a confidence. He was a favorite of everyone. Not a day goes by that he is not missed. [Jan Bellon]

Doug Bender is a gay, Jewish man born and raised in southern California. He has been an administrator for the Boy Scouts, a flight attendant, a dancer/actor, a word-processing supervisor, and, since 1989, person with AIDS. He believes the world is an amazing and miraculous place, that all people are completely good, totally blameless, and deserve to be happy and have a good time.

Tom Bezzi was born in Oklahoma in 1950, and he grew up attending Catholic schools. He did his undergraduate work at Notre Dame and the University of Kansas, and his graduate work at the University of Bonn, Germany, and at San Francisco State University. He lived in San Francisco during the seventies, then moved to West Hollywood in 1981. Bezzi is a professional writer, having published a novel, a play, and approximately a thousand magazine articles. Until he went on medical disability in 1994, he was technical editor for *4-Wheel & Off-Road Magazine*. Bezzi has been HIV-positive since 1981 and sympto-matic since 1991. [Tom wrote this author's note. He died of AIDS on March 25, 1995.]

Stan Brodsky is a native of Los Angeles. He has had an active career in television production spanning twenty years that has provided op-portunities for domestic and world travel. He has taken Perry Como's annual Christmas special to such countries as Israel, France, Austria, Mexico, Canada, and the Bahamas.

After serving as both director and vice president of television pro-duction for Radio City Music Hall Productions in New York, Stan re-turned to Los Angeles to produce the Emmy Award–winning series *Adventures in Wonderland* for Disney.

Today Stan lives in Los Angeles with his life partner, Larry, and is enjoying being one of the newer members of the APLA Writers Work-shop. This forum is helping him learn the tools to develop the voice he's always felt within. The weekly sessions with other "positive" men, who have developed an eloquence and sense of craftsmanship, inspire him to grow and take risks in his own writing. The Workshop is a constant source of stimulation and encouragement to express himself without limitation or judgment. At a stage in life when time is generally measured between doctor visits and infusion schedules, the Workshop and its resulting purposefulness is a welcomed and much appreciated addition.

Juan Candelario

> *What you cannot as you would achieve,*
> *You must perforce accomplish as you may."*
> —*Titus Andronicus* (1593–94), Act 2, Scene 1, Line 106
>   William Shakespeare, 1564–1616

Born in 1955, the first of four sons of Juan and Maria Candelario, who migrated to the United States from Puerto Rico, Juan spent his early years in the small industrial town of Lorain, Ohio, thirty miles west of Cleveland. Lorain is also where Pulitzer- and Nobel-winner Toni Mor-rison was raised. After completing high school, Juan briefly toured Europe before settling in California. He attended the University of California at Los Angeles majoring in political science. He was employed at the law firm of Lord, Bissell & Brook in Los Angeles. He was an avid weight lifter, enjoyed writing and acting, and was active in local theater workshops. Juan died in 1994. [José Candelario]

Paul Canning, not unlike Donna Summer, was born in Dorchester, Massachusetts. In addition to looking for love, he has been an altar boy, paperboy, librarian, high school oratory champion, clerk, teenage poet, an actor in experimental theater, spokesperson in industrial films and bad cable-TV commercials, college dropout, college graduate, disco dance-contest winner, account executive, sales manager, aspiring Irish tenor, art student, homeowner, and recovering Catholic. He is currently engaged to an ex–Mormon missionary and living in Pasadena.

Michael Cedar is a pseudonym of a writer with other work in this book.

Panos Christi was born in Athens, Greece, and emigrated to America in 1966. He began Aghape Players and Agaphe Theatre in 1975 with his longtime friend Edna Glover Mishkin and produced and starred in countless stage and screen projects. He won an L.A. Theater Drama Critics Award for *Cabaret* and was a member of the Board of Directors for Shanti. He wrote many articles for *Heartspace* and *Being Alive.*

 Panos struggled through painful complications from AIDS with remarkable bravery. He always had a smile and an open ear for friends and family. He possessed a strong spiritual outlook on life and always told me to look out for "life's lessons" because every new day brought a chance to strengthen and nurture the soul. [Olga Chrysostomides]

Nathan Clum was born and raised in Belmont, Michigan. He was graduated from the University of Michigan at Ann Arbor with a degree in music. He lives and writes in San Francisco, California. He is currently working on a self-help manual for people living with HIV and AIDS.

This story arose from a singular image seared into my memory: the particular look of my brother's partner's fingers as he tried to eat a slice of apple in a Lower East Side deli. They were the fingers of a man decades older than his thirty-five years—long and thin, brittle nails, tissue-paper skin. His fingers were (I know now) devoid of feeling from neuropathy. He handled that apple slice with such gentle grace. It was the same gentle grace with which he lived his entire life. It is not fair that he is gone. It never will be. I owe a debt of gratitude to Irene and the Workshop for giving me the chance to meet so many incredible natural writers and the space to hone my own craft.

Jeff Cohen is a native of Los Angeles. He lived seven years in Barcelona, Spain, teaching at an international school, traveling the world, and loving a Spanish man. Since his return in 1992 he teaches at a public high school, facilitates an emotional-support group for people with AIDS, and lovingly tends his garden.

"Show Hard-on for Blow Job" was begun at the Workshop in October 1995. Irene asked us to pick a body part and place it at the center of the paper. Then we wrote a cluster of ideas, thoughts, and story fragments radiating from and surrounding the word at the center. The word at the center of my cluster was *penis*.

Donald Colby is a writer and illustrator living in California and Tennessee. He writes under a pseudonym here because of the frank, personal nature of some of his Workshop writing. He has lived with HIV, symptom free, for more than eleven years and is currently at work on his first novel.

Phil Curtis has worked at AIDS Project Los Angeles for seven years and is currently a benefits counselor. He moved to L.A. from New Mexico, with the idea of working with people with AIDS for a year or so.

I wrote "Skin Stuff" several years ago in Irene Borger's Thursday-night workshop at AIDS Project Los Angeles, just to have something to write. I wasn't crazy about it then and I'm still not. "Skin Stuff" was supposed to be a deadpan what-I-did-at-work-today piece, but it came out more red-ribbonish than I would have liked. Nothing much has changed. I still want to write a comedy about social work and the "helping" professions. And I still think about the gods having become diseases. About the only thing I never think anymore is that one day "the whole thing" will just be over.

❧

John D'Amico lives in Los Angeles and treasures every moment with his friends and family and especially his partner, Keith. He misses his many friends who have died.

"Magic Eye" was written in May of 1992. We did an exercise on disasters: minidisasters, personal disasters, and near disasters. My list of disasters included:

Rich Little
Hurricanes
Tornadoes
Plagues
Floods and
Extinction

"Chris's Things" came out of a direction to write about things we must not write about, in March 1993. We made a list of things we must not write about, a second list of reasons why we must not write about them. I wrote down a quote Irene read from Adrienne Rich about omitted things becoming unspeakable.

❧

Sioux de Nimes is not a drag name but a pseudonym. Another writer in the book, now deceased, wrote of him: "He always wanted to write his story, that of the entrusted gay son of a Southern patriarch who reigned over one of the largest family-owned farms in America. In the last year of his life, he overcame his fear, found his voice, and read publicly the fragments he had time to describe before his premature death. In the end he fought and won, neither of which he had ever imagined possible." Sioux de Nimes died in 1993.

❧

Bob Doyle was born on August 2, 1955. He is a native of Kennewick, Washington, and a graduate of Washington State University and Southwestern University School of Law. Kennewick, along with Richland and Pasco, are downriver and downwind from the Hanford Nuclear Reservation in southeastern Washington State. Hanford produced the plutonium used in the bomb dropped on Nagasaki and for thousands of bombs thereafter. The Tri-Cities (as these three towns are known) is home to some of the most outlandish stories ever told to justify the continued production of nuclear bombs and other nuclear boondoggles.

Bob joined the APLA Writers Workshop in the fall of 1994. With the help of Irene Borger and other members of the workshop, he began to piece together the stories he had heard. Bob found that the best way to tell the Hanford tale is to tell the stories he heard from his neighbors, his dad (a retired Hanford worker), his coworkers at Hanford, elected officials, and now, thanks to the Freedom of Information Act, from the records of the Department of Energy.

The stories had been swirling around in my head for several years, and the need to do something with them became greater as more information came out about the tragedy of environmental and social destruction at Hanford. During one session of the Workshop, Irene talked about the need to write the story within you whether or not it seemed to fit in with what was going on in your life at that particular time. What I needed to write about was the Hanford or, as they have come to be called, "The Plutonium Stories," those that I had heard and those I found out about once people began asking questions of the Department of Energy and the Hanford contractors, questions I had been asking all my life. Hanford is like so many of those morality bedtime stories I had heard as a child, especially "The Emperor's New Clothes." I have always thought that the Hanford story should have been told a few thousand bombs ago. With each release of new information from the Department of Energy, more stories need to be told. This is just a beginning.

Jimmy Drinkovich was born March 2, 1956, in Hackensack Hospital and was endlessly proud of New Jersey—Frank Sinatra territory. He moved to Los Angeles in 1974 and remained happily ensconced amidst the exotic flora and fauna until his death on October 1, 1992. This adorable young man, sweet and gentle, sarcastic and mischievous, cherished by all who knew him, was a gifted writer, actor, singer, cable talk-show host, caterer, butler, lover, son, brother, uncle—a candle in the darkness for the many who turned to him and were never turned away. In this lifetime, his many friends describe him as a true "mirror," a teacher, a visionary. Jimmy was a spiritual guide who often understood

our thoughts before we thought them. His garden was a magical place.
His home held treasures from all eras: art, furniture, pottery, JFK salt
and pepper shakers, high-heel shoes, books, music. How he loved to
dance barefoot across his hardwood floors to the music of Tina Marie,
Joni Mitchell, and of course, Frank. And how he loved to entertain his
friends and family in the warm, comfortable ambience he so lovingly
created. Possessed with a biting sense of humor and boisterous laugh
that still rings in our ears, Jimmy also had a dark side. He was hospitalized only once—a painful and terrifying experience. A short time later,
he wrote "Westbound Train." [Peter Sykes]

Alan Erenberg was the middle of three sons of a mattress manufacturer from Beverly Hills. He inherited great style and good looks from
his flamboyant father and his beautiful Latin mother. He loved to tell
humorous stories about his family and friends, and there was always a
twinkle in his eye when he did. Alan was one of the last true gentlemen,
and he lived with great style appreciating life to the fullest. He was
known as a connoisseur of good food, wine, design, and the arts, and
he was the envy of anyone who ever dreamed of looking elegant in
designer clothes. Alan was a family man who had two sons whom he
loved very much. In 1994 he died at the age of forty-four. [Deborah
Irmas]

William M. Franklin [Editor's note: On February 1, 1995, Bill dic-
tated this to me from his hospital bed two weeks before he died. He
had requested and been given some morphine that morning: "a little
vacation," I remember he said. While he switched back and forth between first and third person and past and present, he was completely
lucid and loved telling the tale. This is the last story I heard Bill tell,
and I haven't changed a thing. I made the notes in brackets for friends
of his. When he was partway into it, I laughed and told him, "Bill, your
note is going to be longer than your story," and he said, "You'll have to
edit." I've chosen not to. In those last two weeks of his life, he continued to tell stories, shorter stories, until finally silence outweighed the
words.]

    William M. Franklin grew up in Southern California amidst the
promise of turquoise-green swimming pools, undulating palm trees,
and martinis. Instead, what he got was a middle-management, defense-

industry father, a mother who wore flip-flops and muumuus, and a brother who would tell him how Jewish he looked every chance he got.

Other highlights of my adolescence were the two years I spent at the Carlsbad Military Academy, where I learned how to hold a nickel in my anus and to make a bed that will flip a quarter. Luckily for the military academy, they had beachfront property, and a group of "bohemians" took over the surfing part of the school and demanded more "surf time." This is what I have to thank for getting me out of the pressures of doing drugs and dropping acid.

Bill gave up his surfing, his search for his Big Kahuna, and joined the Italian Study Abroad Program at UCSB, where thirty students are sent for a year of scholastic fun in the glamorous capital of Padua, Italy, which seemed an adventure to me.

I loved it and was one of the few people to leave speaking Italian [having met someone named Christiano]. It was only with great reluctance that I left that year and went to Berkeley, where I bolted myself against the Oakland Induction Center against the war in Vietnam—then went on to get straight A's at Berkeley even though I never went to class.

Graduated from Berkeley having met Jean-Jacques Garbarz, a French filmmaker exiled in the U.S. who wanted to show me his Paris [Bill pronounced it "Paree"], and I said, "*Oui*, why not?" On the way to the Oakland airport I had second thoughts. [Later that night] in bed together, while watching "The Black Miss America Contest," there was a knock on the door of the second floor of the hotel we were staying in. There was a guy with a gun who said, "Just turn over in your pillows or you're dead." I lost consciousness. Jean-Jacques was much cooler under the circumstances . . . Jean-Jacques said, "Oh, I am a French student." [Bill did this with a perfect French accent.] We survived that night. . . . It turned out that the guy was a notorious Oakland hotel thief. We do go to Paris via Amsterdam. [Bill was talking faster than I could write and I was running out of paper, so there are numerous phrases missing here.] We stayed with Jean-Jacques's father [this is the Monsieur Garbarz immortalized in the first "Skin" story]. He had specific ways of doing things—such as there was only *one* kind of salad dressing. I started to feel claustrophobic in France and [he shifts into the present tense] I can't go anywhere without his father telling that story. Jean-Jacques desperately wants to go back to the States. I desperately don't. I go to Italy. He goes to Oakland. I looked up Christiano [in '72] living at home on the island of Murano.

We decided to find an apartment in Venice. After about two weeks searching, he got cold feet and I was left on my own. By that time I'd met Francesca and fell head over heels. Her father, a very influential Venetian, helped find me an apartment. Got a lovely apartment on the Grand Canal near Campo Santo Stefano. Got my first publishing deal from Alfieri Books to write a guidebook for young travelers wanting to make a fortnight or so of visiting Venice. Alfieri Books went under. The book was never published.

During the course of the year, Francesca and I became engaged. [Bill was going fast at that point. Bill's dear friend John D'Amico had walked into the room; both he and I were listening. Bill was talking about how Francesca's parents were wearying of him and then started to warm up to him. I wrote down the phrase "The Contessa's Secret Sauce" but have *no idea* what it means. John thinks this might be an indication of the growing intimacy with the family—perhaps Bill was given the recipe for the Contessa's Secret Sauce?] Francesca knew about my checkered, checkered past [which amounted to two people, one of whom was her best friend.]

Then I got a job in a pseudo glass factory. [I stopped writing at this point, and John and I watched as Bill spoke about the glass factory tours he gave and even demonstrated his technique for deceiving American tourists into believing in the durability of the products. He was taught to hold the object and rap the table with his knuckles, proclaiming, "See, it never breaks."]

Francesca, the countess, accompanied Bill back to southern California. My parents allowed us to bunk with them. After a few minutes grace period, they decided they couldn't have their children living in sin like that. They dropped us off in Venice [California]. [Another friend arrived, and again I stopped writing. John remembers that Bill said that the contessa said she was bored in California and went back to Venice. Then he went on.]

The best editorial position I was assigned was to work along with the late David Rivas and Fred Fehlau. David was our money man, Fred, our artistic man, and my job was to come up with creative monthly concepts for a new magazine called *In Style for Men*. [Bill was getting tired and clearly winding down the story.] Over the duration of two and a half to three years we lost about half a million dollars and never had such a good time in our entire lives. And I still run into people today who swear by those issues, which gives me great credit. Nothing else has had quite as much impact since then.

Dedicated to Robert Leal. Robert's piece was written shortly after his death in 1992 in the hot, fevered spirits punctuated by long nights of staring into hot coals of barbecue pits. Out of this experience came a series of experiments focusing specifically on Robert. [The last piece of the quartet "Four Stories about Skin" is one of these.] I first tried to show our life together in a typical not-too-romanticized way, and then I wanted the reader to experience all that we had in terms of the horrors and the indignities and the short reprieves that we were able to knit together from our collective cloth and take home and try to make a life out of it.

Christopher Gorman was born a Catholic and a Sagittarian in Queens, New York, in 1955. In 1968, he chose Blaise for his confirmation name. That year he also played the title role in *Oliver!* at the East Northport Junior High School. He saw his first Broadway show at the Winter Garden Theatre in the spring of 1969. On August 1, 1970, he placed first in the fifty-yard freestyle, boys sixteen and under, at the Larkfield Country Club. After high school, his first job was in the CBS mailroom in New York City. He played the Fool in a production of *King Lear* at Purchase College, graduating from there in 1979. When Christopher left CBS in April 1995, he was Director, Motion Pictures for Television and Mini-Series. He turned forty in November 1995. The rest is unknown.

Tony Gramaglia was born in Cincinnati, Ohio, in 1959. He died in Los Angeles in May of 1995 due to complications from AIDS. During the last years of his life, Tony spoke with dignity, grace, and a surprising sense of humor whenever and wherever possible—in the theater, on national television, and on the streets—sharing the experiences of one person living with AIDS. Upon joining the APLA Writers Workshop in 1991, Tony learned to channel his unique voice onto the page in the hopes that he could leave a permanent record of the victories and defeats inherent in the battle against AIDS. [Sam Avery and Tom Burke]

Donald Robert Hilyard was born in Riverside, California, and was graduated from the University of California with a degree in English in

1976. He worked for B. Dalton (Pickwick) Booksellers until becoming disabled in a work-related accident in 1985. He was an original member of APLA's first creative-writing workshop. He also studied creative writing at UCLA. Robbie's work is featured in the book *Mouth to Mouth,* which was published by the first lesbian and gay writing workshop sponsored by the L.A. Gay and Lesbian Center under the guidance of Malcolm Boyd. Robbie was born on April 1, 1955, and died on March 18, 1992. [Jim Long]

Joe Hogan was in the first APLA writing workshop that Irene started, and he spent two and a half years with the group. "Warts and All" was written during that time. He continues to be involved peripherally with the Workshop as Irene's guy Friday. He has gone on to pursue his heart's desire as an actor and is also writing a second play. He is eternally grateful to Irene for awakening the sleeping artist within and for changing his life. "I saw God's light in her eyes on that first day of class and knew she was very special. She has proved me right."

Ricky Hoyt was taught to play the piano by his grandmother. His life was influenced early toward an artistic direction, attracted especially to the creative aspects of composing, painting, and writing. He received a degree in music composition from California Institute of the Arts and spent four years writing and performing his music with the Lo Cal Composers Ensemble. Meanwhile, he continued writing fiction and gradually the concrete expression of ideas possible in prose became more satisfying than the abstract language of music. He joined AIDS Project Los Angeles first as a volunteer and then, in 1988, as a paid employee, spending Thursday nights in the writing workshop from 1991 until 1994. He left APLA in 1995. Ricky's interest in expression of the spirit through art parallels his interest in religion. Raised a Methodist, he studied other, more mystical expressions of faith on his own. Currently, Ricky pursues his interest in art and the mystery of reality through writing magical realist short stories and by studying for the Unitarian Universalist ministry at the School of Theology at Claremont, California. His short stories have appeared in *Christopher Street* magazine and a journal, *Onthebus.*

"The Vanishing" was written quickly; more than half came out almost in a stream-of-consciousness style during the workshop on the evening of June 11, 1992. The exercise had been to start with a single intriguing sentence and then, without thought as to what story we might like to tell, simply let each sentence influence the next until whatever story lay hidden in that first sentence emerged on its own. I remember considering starting with, "He noticed as he stood in the hallway that his feet no longer touched the floor," but decided I had written too many flying stories and wanted to try something else. The vanishing as a metaphor for Kaposi's sarcoma and AIDS in general was not an idea I had before I started writing, but occurred to me a few paragraphs into it. I finished the story at a second sitting later that same week, staying true to the spirit of the exercise, and with little revision. So much did this story write itself that I hardly feel I can claim it.

Stephen Jerrom is a New Zealand–born photographer who has lived in Los Angeles most of his life. His social and society photographs have been widely published in newspapers and periodicals, and he's had three exhibitions of his photo images and collage art. A more recent emphasis on portraiture has been his attempt to document the faces of those caught in the shadow of AIDS.

Stephen is also an accomplished pianist and composer of music in a contemporary classical style. He has been an active Workshop member for three years; it, too, he says, is his cure. He lives in the hills of Echo Park with his piano, partner Andrew, and cat Kitty.

Droze Kern currently lives in Los Angeles, California. Born forty-one years ago in Breaux Bridge, Louisiana, he grew up in a small French community of five thousand people and enjoys telling stories about "Cajuns," in the true spirit of his Cajun ancestry. He has worked on offshore oil rigs in the Gulf of Mexico, and as a male hustler in New York City, spent five years in a Catholic monastery where he studied for the Catholic priesthood, came to his senses, and returned to New York City where he completed his graduate studies in clinical social work at Columbia University. Droze currently is in private practice as a psychotherapist, but God only knows what he will do next.

The idea for and first draft of "The Kern Brothers" originated during Writers Workshop in the spring of 1993. It emerged out of two warm-up exercises given at the start of the evening, both to do with "remembering." The warm-up began with a visualization to imagine your body as a museum, holding numerous body memories and experiences. We quickly wrote down every experience seen. One was the first time I saw my brother's body after his death. The second exercise involved a ten-minute "wild-write"; we were asked to write a story about something remembered from the earlier exercise, but to tell it backward. The memory of seeing my brother's body after his death gave way to my recalling the last weekend we spent together in Galveston, Texas, in 1991. That was the story I decided to tell backward. The first line began, "I don't remember what time Michael and I left Galveston Beach, but I remember the sun was setting." I could never have imagined where those two exercises would take me as a storyteller and writer.

Dave Knight has a background in the printing industry, planning the production of books. It is a joy for him to finally be on the writer's side of things. Dave Knight is a pseudonym.

Ezra Litwak was born in Ann Arbor, Michigan, in 1959, attended film school at New York University, and died of AIDS in Los Angeles in 1992. Ezra's lifelong dream was to be a writer, and he achieved part of that dream by cowriting and seeing on-screen his first film, *The Butcher's Wife*, produced by Paramount Pictures in 1991. His association with the APLA Writers Workshop was brief but productive during the last weeks of his life. The contributor of his writings is his loving partner of thirteen years, who dedicates them to Ezra's incredibly supportive family.

Ezra cared about his craft and took great delight in his writing. We could spend hours together just talking about his latest idea—I loved to listen to him "tell stories." He collected inspiration wherever he found it, from the Greek classics to a stoop in Greenwich Village, where we would sit just observing life go by. These short stories were all written in July of 1992 within a three-week span, just one month before he died. "Meeting Barry" was actually the last piece Ezra ever wrote and is something I will cherish for the rest of my life. [Barry H. Schoenfeld]

Steve Maher was born in 1955 and reared in Louisiana, Tennessee, and Texas. After a brief sojourn in Boston and Paris, he migrated to

California in search of fame, freedom, and himself. On a whim in 1983, he began painting on T-shirts at Venice Beach. Mercifully, the business grew beyond his wildest dreams and is known today as On White Design Inc. He lives with his husband, William and their two beautiful (canine) children, Buddy and Darla.

On writing "Laurent": This story of my ten-year transatlantic romance with Laurent Etcheverlepo has been buried under grief and irresolution. Though I'd tried to get at it a couple of times, it wasn't until quite recently that a window opened into the material. It was during a benign Workshop writing assignment that I wrote a description of Laurent's apartment with a clarity of detail that stunned even me. With a little encouragement the rest followed. The experience of writing the *whole* story, as distinct from telling a friend, or reminiscing internally, has been a uniquely satisfying and cathartic experience. Writing is a more generous way to tell a story. One can revel in detail and style that oral communication could never allow. And once written, the story lives again. I write for myself, and only regard myself as a writer because I'm writing now. Sharing it publicly is never the goal, but a confrontive, sometimes rewarding by-product. My deep appreciation to Irene, for teaching me that everyone, including me, has a story worth telling.

I have to go now. I'm leaving for Paris. I just love the way that sounds. And Laurent: *"Je te verrai toujours à Paris."*

⚮

Jeffrey Thomas Benjamin Marcus was born in Vancouver, British Columbia, Canada, on August 21, 1954. My brother was loved for his wonderful ability to make people feel joyful and confident and excited about living. He was demonstrative and compassionate with a highly developed empathy for all living creatures. Yet he had an impish sense of humor and playfulness, expressed sometimes at others' expense, and sometimes at his own. He was courageously introspective. He was devoted to his parents, his sister, and his friends. His passions were fresh flowers, antiques, masks, Buddhas, cafés, dancing, tête-à-têtes, and most recently opera. With a lifelong interest in architecture, a keen aesthetic sense, and great flair, he created wonderfully imaginative and dramatic environments in every place he lived. He surprised us all by painting a beautiful blue sky with sunset-tinged clouds on the ceiling of his dining room. A talented teacher of computer classes and desktop publishing, he wrote the text *Basic in Six Hours*. As he reached his late thirties, his confidence in his creativity increased through creative writing. He also wrote freelance for *Genre* magazine and computer magazines. It is sad that his poem is published posthumously. Nevertheless, we, his family and friends, are happy that his voice will still be heard after his death, and so would he have been. He died on February 21, 1995, at the age of forty. We will miss him forever. [Karen Marcus]

Michael Martin was born in NYC in 1946 and died in Los Angeles in 1994. Michael was a brilliant wit who read insatiably—oftentimes reading two or three or four books at once. He had difficulty walking out of a bookstore without making a purchase. Michael kept voluminous journals, made extensive lists, and was always trying something new. He loved baseball and going to the ballpark. His favorite team was the Cincinnati Reds, whom he rooted for even against the Dodgers. When Michael developed cancer, he did not complain much. Now and then he did gripe about the chemotherapy—mostly about losing his ability to taste. He hated that. But he complained only softly and matter-of-factly about his swollen arm and changing dressings and the pain. The cancer took him slowly and then all of a sudden.

Remembrances—Michael's tongue used to flicker inside his mouth when he was thinking—he had a zillion baseball caps and was a vision in Gap and Eddie Bauer—Michael's eyes were brown—he was funny and fun. His friends miss him terribly. [Richard Hermann]

Leonard Mosqueda, a native Angeleno, was an elementary-school teacher for twelve years. During the past ten years, he was an active volunteer worker for various AIDS organizations in the Los Angeles area. Leonard passionately loved books, music, drama, art, and helping others discover their full potential. In Leo's scale of values the importance of education and the life of the mind were paramount. If life is a celebration, Leonard celebrated his with intelligence, wit, and great conviction. He met his final challenge with equally great courage. Leo died September 30, 1995. [Steve Hanna]

John Mulkeen was formerly an actor and is presently a casting director. John credits the Writers Workshop with jump-starting a third career in short-story writing. He has been lucky enough to have studied under APLA's Irene Borger, poet Eloise Klein-Healy, and Pushcart Prize–winner Lou Mathews.

John was raised in Detroit with his three brothers and eight sisters. His parents are very tired. He lives in L.A. with his lover, Tom Smith (not an alias).

Robert C. Murphy was born and raised in Chicago where he was graduated from the University of Illinois at Chicago Circle. He left for San Francisco to pursue an acting career and after several years there moved to Albuquerque and eventually to Los Angeles, where he spent his last year in Irene Borger's workshop. Never jaded after an entire life in big cities, Robert had the warmth and kindness of a trusted small-town friend.

Robert found serenity in his acting, cooking, and writing. We miss the gaze from his bright blue eyes, which were clear and full of grace. Robert died on July 6, 1995. [Susan Hamilton]

Jan Olof Olsson: I moved from my native Sweden to Los Angeles in 1982. I started writing in the APLA writing workshop and I'm continuing to study and write at LACC and other writing groups. Irene Borger showed me that writing is a wonderful way of communicating, and that my words and thoughts are valid and important.

During my partner's fight with AIDS I found refuge in the writing workshop at APLA. There I found a place where I could write my thoughts, fear, and pain and share them without judgment. I could write fiction or poetry, whatever I chose, and always feel that what I had to say was valid and important. Thanks to the courage I found through the workshop, my words have now been spread through *Citadel* and *Witness* to far more people than I could ever imagine possible. "Coyote" is a collection of impressions and memories from the most painful and vivid time of my life. While writing them down, I could relive those final hours, and claiming them, making them part of my future, and now being able to share them with so many, they will never be forgotten. I hope my story has helped put yet another face and aspect to the fight so many fight every day and to bring further understanding to the tragedy of AIDS.

Rodney Rauch was born in Burbank, California, and spent most of his youth living in and around L.A. Both music and literature played an important role in his growth from adolescence on. He met the love of his life, Roger L. Ross, in 1984, and together they moved to Germany. After five years of working for E. F. Hutton and Merrill Lynch, he and his partner opened a restaurant in Frankfurt in 1990. They both returned to L.A. in February of 1993 with their Bulgarian shepherd, Crimes, and have since adopted a second canine, Kaos, a pit bull terrier. The workshop has helped him live again, after his devastating diagnosis in August 1994.

Scott Riklin grew up in Rye, New York, and is a graduate of Amherst College and the Yale School of Management. After college, he went to San Francisco where he edited an arts biweekly, *Odalisque*.

Scott traveled extensively in the United States, Europe, and Central America, utilizing his language skills. While in Guatemala, at some personal risk, he reported for Radio Pacifica and wrote articles for the *UCLA Studies Report*. Upon returning to the States he produced a film documentary called *Appalachia: No Man's Land*.

After Scott graduated from Yale, he worked for Warner-Amex Cable and Columbia Pictures. He then rejected the corporate world and founded his own investment fund and financial newsletter, called *Rik Pic*.

Jerry Rosenblum was born between the end of World War II and the beginning of America's war in Vietnam. He has survived growing up in Ohio, teaching English, serving in the Israeli Army, working in corporate America, a KGB interrogation, and his mother's cooking. Since moving to Los Angeles in 1985, he has mixed countless drinks at fund-raisers, accumulated T-shirts, and reprimanded inconsiderate drivers. He credits his longevity to getting lots of bed rest and eating lots of bananas.

Jim Rudolph: In 1987, my doctor said I would maybe live another eighteen months. Now that I am forty-nine, I write about being gay,

AIDS, and family secrets; I write about my travels to remote and romantic places; and I keep house with Oznog and our two cats, Meatloaf and Wheatbread. In addition to loving, being loved, and volunteering at AIDS organizations, I live to write, photograph, and go to those places I have yet to visit.

Arthur Shafer: The past forty-two years have brought me to many places, and many people have touched my life. In dealing with my life today, I struggle with trying to put all these events and people in some perspective, one that will make some sense of my journey. Joseph, of my story, is but one of those people, the first of my friends who completed his journey. I remember them all and try to honor them all in the work I do in this workshop.

Philip Justin Smith was a Nebraska-born dancer, actor, playwright, gifted horseman, beloved son and brother, and *compañero* extraordinaire. Philip died just three weeks short of his thirty-third birthday in 1992. His talent as an equestrian was almost mystical, the handsome red-haired, brown-eyed rider on the big sorrel gelding, doing the slow waltz of the western pleasure or the high-stepping cancan of the English tack. He and his beloved Sox communicated in a language not known to humans. Moving to California in 1981, he founded the modern-dance company White Dance and appeared in productions at San Francisco Repertory, Theater Rhinoceros, and Theatre Artaud. In the last two years of his life, as the virus weakened his horseman/dancer's body, his artistic soul found an outlet in the Writers Workshop and sustenance as an agent-in-training at the Judy Schoen and Associates Agency in Los Angeles. Whether Philip was riding horses, waiting tables, dancing, or writing, he lived life with an exuberance that touched more lives in thirty-two years than many people experience in an ordinary lifetime. "He was like a star-burst in our lives. He came and went so fast, sometimes I think I dreamed him." [Virginia Smith]

Steve Smith spent his career in local journalism for CBS radio and television stations in Los Angeles, contributing occasional newspaper and magazine op-ed pieces and features. He lives in West Hollywood and currently devotes his time to political and social activism, making gay music, loving his friends, living with HIV, and developing his skills as a storyteller.

"The Pact" is a fictional account of an actual event that haunted me for months, but which I felt incapable of recounting adequately. I took my initial stab at capturing the "truth" of those events through fiction within weeks of joining the Writers Workshop—a 3 A.M. convulsive spew of stored-up grief and guilt. What followed was six weeks of collaborative editing, reworking, and polishing with Irene—painful, frustrating, and ultimately very satisfying.

"This story is dedicated to the Capris."

Brian Sturtevant is a thirty-four-year-old, transplanted Midwesterner. A graduate of Michigan State University, he recently sold his private-investigations company to focus on his long-neglected early interest in writing. He lives in Los Feliz with his lover, Rummel, two cats, and a dog.

Jeff Sullivan was born in San Fernando, California, in 1959 and has resided in southern California all his life. He has lived with HIV since 1986 and is a member of the Aids Project L.A. Writers Workshop. He also plays the violin and has worked with several local bands since 1985. Jeff attributes the creative process as an important tool in the personal fight against AIDS.

Jerry Terranova is a writer and counselor living in San Francisco. He is also founder of CURENOW, an alternative aids educational network bringing together the scientific questioning of hiv as the cause of aids, holistic-healing approaches, and the exploration of aids as crisis in consciousness.

Marc E. Wagenheim was born in 1957 and spent most of his early childhood traveling around the world with his father and mother, his father being an officer in the Foreign Service. He attended Georgetown Prep in Washington, D.C. for his high school years and was a graduate of Tufts University. Upon college graduation, he moved to Los Angeles and worked as an executive writer for an advertising firm before finding out he had AIDS at the age of twenty-nine. His illness prompted him to "get involved," and he spent the last four years of his life as a volunteer for APLA lecturing to the public about HIV. He received the APLA Volunteer of the Year Award in 1991 just months before his death. Marc's most treasured moments during his five-and-a-half-year illness were spent in Irene Borger's Writers Workshop at APLA. He is remembered most by his mother, Margaret, and his lover of ten years, Mark Winsten. His determination and insights about living through a terminal illness live on in the hearts and memories of those who cared deeply for him, as do the incredible stories he wrote during the time spent in the Workshop. [Mark Winsten]

Darian Walker: When Darian was born, the world received a gift, a gift of internal life that surpassed the meaning of friendship and love. When we first met, it was as if I had known him all my life. Through his wisdom and courage one found strength and tranquillity. When the days were long due to times of trouble, when the sun just did not shine and difficulties continued to invade your life, Darian was able to subdue the agony by reminding you of the important thing of life, LOVE. The only thing left to say: "He lived a fabulous life and made others better." In loving memory of Darian Walker. [John Sacco] [Ed.: Darian had been a hairdresser. He loved beauty. When I visited him in the hospital a few weeks before he died, I asked him if he'd like to dictate a short biography to me. Instead, he urged me to look out the window at how glorious the June day was and launched into a story of the first time he saw the Notre Dame Cathedral.]

Frank Wang: I was born in wartime China. I was moved to the United States at the age of eight. Five years in Christ's Home helped me to sharpen my sensitivity to the world. I have lived my life balanced on the brink. I earned my living as a dancer, a Tour Director, a choreographer, a teacher, and whatever else was necessary to sustain life. AIDS is mine. I own it completely. I live to write.

"My Boy Bill" came to life in the workshop. The assignment was to choose a significant moment in my life and try to recall as many details as possible. The events depicted were heart-held for thirty years. The story fought for release when the president of the United States propagated the "don't ask, don't tell" agenda. I found it surprising that the man who keeps a bust of Harry Truman on his desk in the Oval Office could so deny his history. Integration of blacks into the military was by Executive Order of the Commander in Chief. Why not gays? Are WE GAYS to be the niggers of the nineties?

I began writing "My Boy Bill" in the workshop on 13 May 1993. Its first public appearance was at MOCA in June of the same year.

APPENDIX

ON STARTING A WRITERS WORKSHOP

Irene Borger

Artist in Residence
AIDS Project Los Angeles

Praise Allah, but tether your camel to its post.
— SUFI SAYING

How-to manuals may be useful for learning to poach a salmon, put on a condom, or wrap a sarong in fifty fetching ways. But, as with writing, creating a workshop isn't a matter of following someone else's recipe. The workshop that *you* organize (or organize *and* lead) will be a reflection of your particular constellation of beliefs, goals, education, worldview, passions, quirks, limitations, aesthetics, teaching and learning style (as well, of course, as the needs, desires, aesthetics, limitations, etc., of the people with whom you work). No magazine, book, or appendix can offer you a ready-made solution. (That's part of the creative pleasure of it.) Still, there are many things to consider and sources on which to draw.

I began developing a list, "Questions to Think About," when I gave an afternoon-long session titled "How to Start a Writing Workshop" at the 1994 *AIDS, Medicine and Miracle* conference in San Francisco. I sent the list to interested parties who contacted me after an article on the Workshop by Louise Steinman appeared in the September/October 1994 issue of *Poets and Writers*. A revised collection of these questions follows.

I am presently (fall 1995) leading a ten-month-long weekly workshop, called "Teaching the Teachers," for a dozen writers who are committed to starting pilot workshops in other AIDS service agencies in Los Angeles County. We touch on these questions organically (rather than as an agenda) as we proceed. There are implications, ramifications, even stories, inside the questions. There's a lot to discuss.

To work with someone who cares to write (or *is* writing) is a gift and a responsibility. To work with someone facing a life-threatening illness demands clear attention, and a willingness to be astonished, disturbed, responsive, in short, to serve as a witness. (Some people assume

343

that such work requires fearlessness, but I know of no such feeling; however, it does propel one to develop the skill—or practice—of working with difficult emotions, one's own and those of others, as they arise.)

The point of all these questions is to enable *you* to shape a workshop that is inspiring, that feels safe *and* challenging, that honors the participants—*and* writing *and* the writing process. These questions are meant to encourage you to create an experience that *matters*. What do you need to do, to develop, so that you can be a skillful teacher, a sensitive group leader, and maybe even a muse?

These questions are meant to whisper in your ear, "*Pssst,* how about thinking about this and *this* or THIS in order to organize, teach, assess, and fund a workshop?" At best the questions will encourage you to articulate your own, perhaps nascent, visions, to draw your attention toward matters you haven't even considered. The questions deal with both issues and logistics. There are no "right" answers. While some of the questions are directed specifically to work with people living with HIV and AIDS, many of these "things to think about" are as useful in setting up a private workshop as they would be in establishing a workshop in other challenged communities (battered women, runaway teenagers, cancer patients, etc.).

When I started the Workshop in 1990, I had taught dance history at the University of California, Riverside, for six years, had been in writing workshops, had been a published writer for seven years, and had been a teaching assistant in graduate school before that, but I'd only taught a handful of day-long writing workshops. If you had asked me then, "How do you keep the focus on the writing and not on AIDS?" or "How do you work simultaneously with people who have varying levels of education and writing experience?" or "What issues may arise in a group in which people are both asymptomatic and close to death?" or "What's the difference between a writing workshop that may be 'therapeutic' and a therapy group?"—I wouldn't have had any answers. So don't be daunted by the mass of questions. They are tools, not an inquisition. They will allow you to take stock of what you already know. Much of what you bring to the table will be intuitive, even instinctive. It might be useful to pull out a notebook, or your computer, and make this an interactive process.

While planning is essential, so is being open and fully present to the moments that arise (Anne Lamott says we're allowed to use these words in California), drawing on things you've developed for years, and *not holding anything back.* (It's as Annie Dillard wrote about writing: "Spend it all, shoot it, play it, lose it, all, right away, every time. . . . Anything you do not give freely and abundantly becomes lost to you. You open your safe and find ashes.") If you are called to do this work—I'm not sure how one could do it conscientiously or for long otherwise—and you're patient, and you don't need to become rich, you will find a way to do it well.

BEFORE

- What is your motivation in wanting to start a workshop?
- Do you have an "agenda"? Political, spiritual, emotional, literary, other? Will that guide you? Focus you? Limit you?
- Have you worked with, lived with, cared for, or lost people living with HIV/AIDS? What emotional issues are you presently dealing with in regard to HIV/AIDS and is this a good time for you to start a writers workshop? How emotionally, creatively, intellectually, physically, spiritually available are you to do this work right now?
- Do you love writing? Do you read a lot? How do you feel about listening to other people's work? To work that isn't polished? Work that may be written by "nonwriters"? Work that may never be revised?
- How good are your listening skills? How can you improve them? What other skill(s) do you think you will need to develop? Can you do them "on the job"?
- Have you taught before? Would you say you have an insider's knowledge of the creative process? Do you like sharing what you know? Have you ever led a group?
- Do you hope to act as the organizer for the workshop and find a skillful teacher or do you want to lead it yourself? If you are looking for someone to lead the workshop, how will you find them? Try them out?
- Are your strengths literary or social? What do you think you'll need to work on to prepare to teach well?
- Are you interested in encouraging the development of both psyche *and* techne (spirit *and* craft)? How will you do this? What practical things might you try to establish an inspiring, private laboratory for work?
- Do you have a writing outlet, a writers community for yourself? Are you presently writing?
- Do you have a support system composed of professionals and/or

peers or tools to enable you to stay clearheaded and openhearted in the face of strong emotions and suffering?

• Do you know other people working with people with HIV/AIDS? Might they be available to speak with and think through issues or problems with you?

• What makes you feel most nervous about starting a writing workshop? About working with people with HIV/AIDS? Are these realistic concerns? How might you address them? Are you familiar with some of the physical and psychosocial problems common to people living with AIDS? Would it be useful for you to take an "AIDS 101" course offered at many clinics and AIDS service agencies?

RESEARCH AND LOGISTICS

• What local AIDS organization, or community group, might be a good sponsor? (With potential clients? Outreach capacity? A newsletter? Ability/willingness to publicize? Convenient location? Available space?)

• Are you interested in working with a special population? Women? Teenagers? People of color? Spanish-speaking people with HIV/AIDS? Gay men? Lesbians? IV-drug users? People in recovery? Or in the hospital? Homeless people with HIV/AIDS? Caregivers or health professionals working with PWAs? Is there an appropriate agency for you to work with?

• If you do not already have a relationship with a local organization, how can you find out more information on the services in your area? How will you research their respective agendas?

• What do you need to do *before* you even propose starting a workshop? (For yourself? In regard to others?) What *information* do you need to acquire and think through to write a solid proposal?

• What will you do if the agency people you contact are overworked, busy with providing health and legal services, counseling, food and meals, home health care, public policy, funding, too many clients, etc.—and don't understand or even have time to think about something to do with "creative writing" or "art"? (How might you prepare a proposal that makes vivid the usefulness of such a workshop, in the context of the agency's mission? And convince them that you are an ideal person to do the work? What practical ways can you make it easy for them to say yes?) How will your workshop support *their* goals?

• Once you have made arrangements with an agency to offer a pilot workshop, would it be useful to ask for an informal letter of agreement detailing your respective obligations and concerns?

- What kind of space is available? Where can you find a room that is quiet, private, comfortable, and accessible to people who may not drive or be able to walk up stairs? Are there tables and chairs? Do they need to be set up? (By whom?) Is there a couch in case someone needs to lie down? Adequate lighting? A nearby bathroom? How's the air circulation and temperature control? Is there a hot plate for boiling water for tea?

- What materials will you need? Pens and notebooks? Boxes of herbal teas and cups? How will you cover the cost of copying handouts and printing initial leaflets? (Could a local merchant supply these things in exchange for publicity somewhere?)

IMAGINING THE WORKSHOP

- Before you go further, imagine the first meeting. If someone was only able to make it to one, and only one, session, what would you want them to get out of it? With that in mind, how will that shape what you do?

- Why do a pilot workshop and not jump into an ongoing project? (You can test out the waters, examine what works and doesn't, see just how much interest there is, how committed you actually are, begin a relationship with a host organization, and gain some experience on which you can draw should you wish to apply for funding.)

- Imagine a pilot project: How many weeks would it be? Six? Eight? Ten? How many hours would each meeting be? (I've found that three hours is a good amount of time for a group of between eight and twelve people; it permits sustained writing and interaction and is not too taxing for most people. Three hours can include a "warm-up" five-minute exercise with a go-around reading, a longer exercise with thirty minutes for writing, a ten-to-fifteen-minute break, and a chance for everyone to read and get feedback.)

- When are you available? How much time for preparation and teaching do you have? If this workshop is to be free for participants, how much time can you spend doing it without getting paid? Or do you need to receive an honorarium or, at the least, coverage for the cost of materials?

- What time of day will sessions take place? How will you balance the needs of people who are sick and may find it difficult to get up early and/or to go out at night with the needs of people who are HIV-positive, healthy, and working a full Monday-to-Friday schedule? Could you offer the class on a weekend?

• What do you propose to do? A workshop that focuses on in-session writing and process? A workshop geared toward poetry? Short stories? Autobiography? A place to bring finished work for guidance and critique?

• Whom is the group for? Anyone living with HIV/AIDS? Caregivers? Practiced writers? Anyone with the desire to write? Any requirements?

• What's the best way for you to learn the creative needs of the people who enroll? An informal conversation? A short form with simple questions?

• Number of people who can join? (Limited enrollment is necessary if everyone is to have the chance to write, read aloud, and get feedback. It seems that in a group of about fifteen people, generally nine to twelve people show up each week. Since people may not be able to attend consistently, it's important that everyone be given the opportunity to read work aloud at each session.)

• Do you want to lead a drop-in group or a workshop with ongoing members? How will this decision affect the group dynamics? The nature and quality of the work and the feedback?

• How will people find out about the workshop? In an agency publication sent to clients? In a flyer posted on a clinic bulletin board? In a neighborhood newspaper? A local bookstore? On the radio?

• Regarding the flyer or advance publicity: How clearly can you state the terms and goals of the workshop? Is there a quote you like that sums up the spirit of what you're intending? Have you listed a telephone number that prospective participants can call for registration and more information?

• Have you made sure that the flyer or article will be published and/or distributed in plenty of time for potential participants to respond and make plans to come?

• Do you want to speak with everyone individually before the first meeting? Are you going to give out your home or office phone number? When will you be available to talk on the phone? How will you make these things clear? How comfortable are you setting these kinds of boundaries?

• Do you have everyone's address and phone number? Are you going to do a phone list? (Does anyone wish to attend meetings anonymously? How will you handle this?)

• As you've proceeded in your planning, has your purpose become clearer? Are you interested in the development of craft? Of expression? Release? Healing? Community? The growth of bold, individual work? Is it possible for you to have high standards without expectations?

EXERCISES, PROGRAM PLANNING, AND FEEDBACK

• How will the material you plan to bring in support your goal and your motives?

• Given that health problems and other commitments may prevent people from attending every week, how will you structure the format so that each meeting is self-contained and not dependent (like a university course) on sequential meetings?

• Do you have a notebook or another system for saving great writing, writing about writing, newspaper clippings, quotes, passages, lists of poems, short short stories, to build exercises around?

• Who are your favorite authors? Who would you enjoy reading aloud to other people? Which books, stories, poems, do you find yourself remembering? Quoting to other people? What sentences, pictures, are tacked up on your refrigerator? Your bulletin board? Is there any writing you are afraid of? Won't read?

• Do you investigate material from various sources? By women *and* men? People of color? By gay, lesbian, and straight writers? Of stylistically varied work?

• What sort of skills are useful in becoming a wilder, more articulate, risk-taking, lucid writer? How can these skills be conveyed or taught?

• How will you model your responses to people so that they can begin to trust their own instincts, so they can feel challenged but not *judged*? How will you allow the *unknown* and the *unconscious* to be alive in the room? How will you make sure that no writing or writer is sabotaged?

• Given your intentions and the goals of the group members, what do you consider useful and appropriate feedback?

• Do you want to be the only person to give feedback? If group response is part of your plan, how will you keep it on track? How might you model feedback to prevent destructive commentary? What studies on the creative process might be of use in communicating this?

Clearly, there are as many styles of response as there are personalities. It seems to me that the best way to decide what feels useful and authentic is to reexamine the function of the workshop and the subliminal, actual, as well as the professed, desires of the writers. New Mexican writer and artist-in-community Joan Logghe responds to in-session writing by repeating the vivid images and phrases. Novelist Jane Smiley, teaching at the university level, critiques manuscripts and eschews the notion of "like" or "dislike." I think there needs to be a difference between the way one responds to a just-written first draft and an almost finished work. One simple technique I use to give feedback developed naturally over time: while someone is reading their work, I jot down particularly strong words, shifts in the text, on one part of the page, as well as my on-the-spot perceptions of underlying issues and the gist of the piece on another. Most of the members of the Teaching the Teachers Workshop have tried this and found that it increased their ability to pay attention and give precise feedback; several other people said it seemed to impair their ability to listen. It takes some practice.

It is essential to figure out how to encourage writers to develop their own—and I use this word in both senses—authority. Choreographer Liz Lerman has developed a feedback process for dance that addresses this; I find her thinking useful in literary matters, too. Her article "Toward a Process for Critical Response" is published in the booklet *Are Miracles Enough* and is available for $15 from Liz Lerman Dance Exchange, 1664 Columbia Road NW, Washington, D.C. 20009. I've just discovered Peter Elbow's book *Writing Without Teachers* (Oxford University Press, 1973) and think it would be of inordinate use in setting up a workshop. The poet Rachel Hadas worked with people at Gay Men's Health Crisis; her book *Unending Dialogue: Voices from an AIDS Poetry Workshop* (Faber and Faber, 1991) is also illuminating.

• How can you see to it that, from the very first meeting, the focus of the workshop is *writing*? How might people introduce themselves, not by doing a lengthy go-around, but actually through their work?

• How will you keep the focus on *writing* when working with people who may be in crisis? (Consider that people have a choice whether to go to a writers workshop or a support group, and some may be attending both.) Do you think there's a difference between "therapy" and "art"?

• When people experience writing as "healing," what do you think is happening?

• Can you imagine creating a "safe space" without being New Age–y or cloying?

• How can you create exercises that heighten awareness of craft while inviting substantive content? That permit a focus or touchstone yet need not be exactingly "followed"? How might you craft an exercise so that it triggers invention or memory (or whatever it is you're trying to elicit), but also make it clear that (a) exercises are simply meant to be like sand in an oyster, (b) that's there's no "right way" to do them, and (c) that the best thing a writer can do is listen for the voices and images that arise in his or her own head?

When I began the Workshop, I asked my friend Deena Metzger (who, by that point, had led workshops for more than twenty-five years) how she thought up exercises. "I don't know," she said, "they just come to me." After a few months of doing the work, transforming exercises I had learned from Deena, from books, and from other workshops I'd taken, I began to notice that ideas for exercises (like ideas for writing) *did* begin to arise out of the air: from a newspaper article, from a remark in a radio interview, from a stack of photographic postcards, or the first line of a poem. It's yet another variant of "build it and they'll come."

There are numerous books with stimulating exercises: Deena Metzger's *Writing for Your Life* (Harper San Francisco, 1992) Robin Behn and Chase Twichell's *The Practice of Poetry* (Harper Perennial, 1992), Anne Lamott's *Bird by Bird* (Pantheon Books, 1994), Natalie Goldberg's *Writing Down the Bones* (Shambala, 1986) and *Wild Mind* (Bantam Books, 1990), and Steve Kowit's *In the Palm of Your Hand: The Poet's Portable Workshop* (Tilbury House Publishers, 1995), as well as the thousands of great books of poetry, short fiction, collections of essays, and interviews with writers. The journals *Poets and Writers, BOMB, Threepenny Review,* and *The American Poetry Review* are rich resources. A member of the Teaching the Teachers Workshop suggested that I list particular books and poems here, but I'm not convinced that would be of use to *you*. I urge you to try out all exercises before you teach them so you can clarify your instructions and see how they might work, and as you proceed, to invent your own exercises so they push boundaries and fit the needs of the people you are working with like a perfect shoe.

Even though I primarily work with the notion of "story" (fiction and nonfiction, autobiography) rather than with the craft of poetry, I find the work of many narrative poets to be ravishing and useful in inspiring attention to language, form, the workings of mind, and intensity. Plus, it's possible to read several poems aloud in one session and still have time to write. (It's not realistic to assume people will read the short stories and essays you may hand out.) The poems of Claribel Alegria, Raymond Carver, Michelle T. Clinton, Mark Doty, Carolyn Forché, Tess Gallagher, Yusef Komunyakaa, Dorianne Laux, Audre Lorde, Susan Mitchell, Paul Monette, Frank O'Hara, Sharon Olds, Michael Ondaatje, Robert Pinsky, Adrienne Rich, Rainer Maria Rilke (as translated by Stephen Mitchell), and many others have lived with us in our rooms. So has the prose of numerous writers including Bernard Cooper, Joan Didion, Gretel Ehrlich, Eduardo Galeano, Susan Griffin, Jamaica Kincaid, Milan Kundera, Carole Maso, Tim O'Brien, Grace Paley, Susan Sontag, Trinh T. Minh-ha, Alice Walker, and David Wojnarowicz.

If you wish to survey AIDS literature, you might view Joseph Cady's essay "AIDS Literature" in *The Gay and Lesbian Literary Heritage,* ed. Claude J. Summers (Henry Holt, 1995) as well as the "Annotated Bibliography of AIDS Literature, 1982–91" by Franklin Brooks and Timothy F. Murphy in *Writing AIDS: Gay Literature, Language and Analysis,* ed. Timothy F. Murphy and Suzanne Poirier (Columbia University Press, 1993).

There are endless sources for writing exercises—visual, auditory, and tactile as well as written; keep your attention tuned and you'll never run dry. I've mentioned several I've used in the introduction.

THE FIRST SESSION

- Imagine yourself in the workshop. (Are you "teaching," "leading," "directing," or "facilitating" it? Does your choice of verb reveal your role and intention?)
- What would be a stimulating, pleasurable first exercise? (Have you tried it out yourself?) What piece of writing will introduce a tone you wish to create? Do you want to inspire? Challenge? Soothe? Fire up? Open consciousness? Astonish with sound and rhythm? With linguistic possibility? Induce wit?
- How will you establish the parameters regarding process, schedule, privacy? How will you introduce yourself? How will you make it safe for people to take personal and creative risks?
- Will you plan on arriving early to make sure that the room has been set up? Do you need keys to enter? Are you giving out notebooks? Copies of material? A roster or a simple questionnaire to fill out?
- How will you proceed if only one or two people, or no one, shows up? What will you do if people arrive late? Or leave early? Fall

asleep? Get sick? Or if it appears that someone is exhibiting the symptoms of dementia?

MONITORING THE PROCESS

- Would it be useful for you to keep a journal to evaluate what did—and didn't seem to—work?
- Can you remember what people said?
- How did you respond to people and their writing?
- What were the social dynamics like?
- What made you uncomfortable? What was difficult? What questions arose that you felt ill-equipped to handle?
- Did you have enough time? Did you try to do too much? Were you rushed?
- If the feedback petered into chat or medical issues, were you able to guide the group back toward writing?
- Were you able to include everyone? What can you do if someone consistently hogs time? If someone doesn't feel comfortable to speak up?
- How did you end the session? Were you able to start and stop at the agreed-upon time?
- Was there something you didn't really want to pay attention to? (What do you remember from the corner of your eye?)
- What writing issues came up? Is there a way you could incorporate them into subsequent sessions?
- Are you allowing everything—content, form, language—to arise in the work? Have you cut off anyone's creative impulses? Is the Censor or the Critic active in the room?
- If someone was blocked or hypercritical of their own work, what methods might you devise to encourage freer writing, experimentation, or playfulness? How can you work with this through writing itself and not veer off into psychological analysis?
- How are you managing to encourage personal expression without having the workshop turn into a therapy group?
- Are there some who didn't come back? Will you call them? Are they ill? Or, did something make them feel this wasn't the group for them? Is there a lesson in this?
- How can you best serve the people who are *actually there* and not your original agenda?
- Given that members of the group may be at very different stages

of health, are you able to acknowledge, support, and incorporate the realities of what's going on with group members—and still keep the focus on writing? (Ask yourself again: What is writing *for?*)

- Are any group members in the hospital? If they'd like to see you, are you available to make visits?

- Would it be useful for you to consult with someone on an ongoing basis (as therapists do with supervisors) in regard to the effectiveness of your teaching and the group process? How can you do this in a professional manner without violating the confidentiality of what goes on in (and who is in) the group?

NEARING THE END OF YOUR PILOT PROJECT

- How can you measure the effectiveness of your workshop?
- What worked? What could work better?
- Has the writing grown? Is it more daring, truthful, inventive, vibrant, lucid?
- Do the group members exhibit or report pleasure in writing? More confidence in their process? In their work?
- What sort of documentation will enable you to demonstrate to others that this was a useful experience for the participants?
- If you are planning to apply for a grant to start an ongoing workshop, what sort of documentation would be useful to have? Your own diary? Examples of the work? (Again, consider the matters of confidentiality, privacy, and anonymity.)
- Will you work with the writers to polish and present their work? Will you self-publish group work? Schedule an informal reading? Do you plan to record it? Does everyone involved agree to that? (For the first nine months of the APLA Writers Workshop we made no attempt to organize a public reading. The first journal, *Witness*, wasn't published until the Workshop had been in formation for two and a half years. This kept the concentration on the writing, on investigation and risk-taking, not performance; it also created a close-knit group. Be aware that if you attempt to document or present the group to others too early, you will interfere with the writing process as well as with the group dynamics. Still, you may want to find a method to celebrate work and, if you are doing a short-term workshop, a way to create closure.)
- Could you plan a small reading at the end of a two-to-three-month session in the space where you meet and limit the invitations to friends of those in the workshop? How would members feel about hav-

ing someone from your host organization in the audience? (If the proposal to do a reading elicits mixed response, what will you do?)

• If you do a second series, or want to start an ongoing workshop, will you open the group to new people? How will you incorporate them into the process?

• Do you wish to organize "sessions"—e.g., eight meetings, a fall series—or do you want to create an ongoing weekly workshop?

ON FUNDING

While the rewards of service or "right livelihood" cannot be measured in economic terms, and while many people enjoy volunteering, if you are highly qualified and there is a need for what you can do, there is no reason that you should not be paid for your work. (For a remarkable book on the function of art and the giving of gifts in a market society, read Lewis Hyde's *The Gift: Imagination and the Erotic Life of Property* [Vintage Books, 1983].)

Given the present state of AIDS funding, the demands on existing services, and the growing population of clients, it is highly unlikely that you will walk into an already-funded arts position in an AIDS service agency. The arts, if they are thought of at all, may be viewed as recreation, entertainment, the icing on the cake. This is not meant to discourage you or to disparage the place or function of art or to indicate that people who work in AIDS care are philistines; it is only to suggest that you may need to initiate research into funding by yourself.

Many city and state arts councils have "artist-in-community" grants with applications reviewed once a year by peer panels. You do not have to hire a grant writer to fill out these forms; most public agencies publish clearly written guidelines and offer free sessions to assist applicants in reviewing the criteria and submission process. (In my experience in California, these grants are given to individuals who are sponsored by a host institution; monies are paid directly to the artist; some grants stipulate that a matching portion must be paid by the agency. In other cases, the agency need only provide a place to work and a strong letter of support.) As you probably know, federal funding for the arts is in disarray; how this will impact the state arts councils that receive a portion of their funding from the NEA is unclear. Take heart: even though these public agencies are, by their very nature, bureaucracies, many of the people who direct residency programs have arts backgrounds and are passionate about their work—and yours.

While thousands of private foundations in the United States fund arts and literary programs, AIDS and other regional services, the bylaws of most foundations prohibit them from giving grants to individuals. In other words, you need either to find those foundations that *can* offer direct grants or to discover sources that the AIDS-service agency you are affiliated with hasn't yet tapped. In the latter instance, you will need a legal relationship with the agency, either as an independent contractor or as a staff member, to receive foundation funding. What is known as "AIDS funding" falls under many categories; it is not just a health issue. Be creative in your search.

A call to the Foundation Center, with branches in a handful of major North American cities, may be your first step (1-800-424-9836, Monday–Friday, 9 A.M.–5:00 P.M. EST). They have up-to-date, cross-referenced foundation directories and many sister libraries at foundations throughout the country; these centers can provide you with funding literature and offer short workshops on how to apply for grants. You might also call the National AIDS Clearing House for information (1-800-458-5231). Lots of luck.

DEATH AND DYING—AND CENTERING

I have the words of a Thai meditation teacher, the Venerable Achaan Chah Subato, on the wall next to my desk:

"One day some people came to the master and asked, 'How can you be happy in a world of such impermanence, where you cannot protect your loved ones from harm, illness, and death?' The master held up a glass and said, 'Someone gave me this glass, and I really like this glass. It holds my water admirably and it glistens in the sunlight. I touch it and it rings! One day the wind may blow it off the shelf, or my elbow may knock it from the table. *I know this glass is already broken, so I enjoy it incredibly.*'"

How will you honor the death of each member who dies while not turning the workshop into a bereavement group or frightening away new members? How will your file of stories and poems, your own emotional and physical health, your view of death and your commitment to writing and to the workshop, enable you to do this?